ONE KINGDOM

ONE KINGDOM

The Practical Theology of John M. Frame

JOHN BARBER

WIPF & STOCK · Eugene, Oregon

Wipf and Stock Publishers
199 W 8th Ave, Suite 3
Eugene, OR 97401

One Kingdom
The Practical Theology of John Frame
By Barber, John

Softcover ISBN-13: 979-8-3852-7207-5
Hardcover ISBN-13: 979-8-3852-7208-2
eBook ISBN-13: 979-8-3852-7209-9
Publication date 12/17/2025
Previously published by Whitefield Media Productions, 2025

This edition is a scanned facsimile of the original edition published in 2025.

“*Whether, then, you eat or drink or whatever you do, do all to the glory of God*” (I Corinthians10:31)

TABLE OF CONTENTS

ACKNOWLEDGMENTS

Without the input and contributions of several important people, this project would not have reached completion. First, I wish to thank my wife, Bonnie, for encouraging the idea for a monograph that would present Frame's practical theology to an expanded audience. During times when I contemplated surrendering the work to other priorities, my wife was a strong encouragement to continue.

Second, the input by Dr. E. A. de Boer of the Theological University, Gereformeerde Kerken into the earliest versions of the manuscript sharpened both the writing and the evolvement of the book in its conceptual framework. He pushed me to produce a well-argued and theologically consistent document.

Third, Drs. Henk Stoker and Sarel van der Walt have kept my central question focused when it was found to be wandering down "rabbit trails." More than anything, I appreciate Dr. Stoker's kindness in allowing me to work through the Thesis version of this book at North West University, Potchefstroom, South Africa.

Fourth, I wish to extend great appreciation to my friend and mentor of many years Dr. John M. Frame who, when I was a seminarian at Westminster Theological Seminary, taught me the gist of Presuppositionalism and that all theology is but philosophical air unless it is *practical*. His availability for interviews, which have added content to my book not found anywhere in his writings, has proved invaluable.

Most of all, I express deepest thanks to my Lord, who quickened my heart and called me to the ministry. His guiding hand is clearly evident in the maturity of this work.

INTRODUCTION

The academic life is not noted for thrills, but there are a few. Finishing a degree program is a major excitement, as is seeing your first article or book in print. Another thrill comes when someone else writes about you, by publishing a response to your article or reviewing your book. But it is a very special experience indeed when someone writes a whole book *about* you. By doing that for the first time,[1] my good friend John Barber has honored me far beyond my deserving.

John was one of my students at Westminster Seminary in the late 1970s. We met again in 2000 when we both attended Covenant Presbyterian Church in the Orlando area. I taught at Reformed Theological Seminary and John wrote for Campus Crusade for Christ. I learned that John had a wide range of interests and abilities. He was a singer and keyboard player, a surfer, had worked as a traveling evangelist, later preached and taught around the world, helped to plant a Christian College in Kenya, guided students through the history of art in Italy, earned two doctorates, all the while serving as pastor to a church in Florida. All of this he undertook in the midst of serious back pains which continue to afflict him.

I wrote a Foreword to John's earlier book *The Road from Eden*,[2] a comprehensive Christian history of culture. I spoke there about John's

> …encyclopedic knowledge of the history of Western culture, with a deep understanding of art, music, sociology, politics, philosophy, theology, and their interactions.

I added,

> Wherever the reader stands philosophically or theologically, he will learn that the issues are more complex than he had before imagined, and that he will have large amounts of new knowledge at his disposal. Further, he will gain much enjoyment from the clear and winsome style of the book, remarkable amid such a torrent of information and technical expertise.

My evaluation of John's work has not changed at all since I made these several comments. So you can well imagine my delight on learning that my renaissance friend had written a whole book about me!

The present book originated as John's dissertation for the Doctor of Philosophy degree in theology at the Potchefstroom Campus of the North-West University, South Africa. Its academic origin ensures that the book is not *entirely* about me (it compares me with a number of other figures) and it does not totally endorse all of my positions. That is fine with me. I've often complained about the tendency in evangelical Christian circles to speak of our prominent thinkers as if they had never said or done anything wrong. My mentor, Cornelius Van Til, was often the beneficiary—I should rather say victim—of this sort of treatment. I resolved when I wrote my book on Van Til[3] that I would not write about him as a plaster saint: the book would contain "constructive critical analysis" of his work. Some disciples of Van Til expressed amazement that a supposed Van Tilian could write about Van Til and actually find something wrong with him. But I maintained then, and still do, that we can make the best use of any thinker's work by careful analysis and critical understanding. To undergo such critical analysis is actually a privilege for a scholar. To deny Van Til that privilege is to show him grave disrespect.

John's differences with me are far less extensive than mine with Van Til. I will mention some of them later in this Introduction. But I do feel privileged that John has given my work the kind of scrutiny worthy of a serious thinker.

As to the book itself, it reproduces my own thought well, and its comparisons are instructive. I have learned much—about myself as well as others—from John's comparisons in Chapter 1 between myself, Van Til, Kuyper, Schilder, and Bavinck. Although I should have expected it from my fascination with Van Til, I was not conscious of being as close as I was to the other thinkers on this list. Yes, I am closer to Schilder and Bavinck than to Kuyper, much as I admire Kuyper. For Schilder and Bavinck do more than Kuyper to integrate God's lordship in human salvation with his lordship over the whole cosmos. The cosmos itself groans (Rom. 8:22), waiting for the fulfillment of human redemption; but the same God who saves human beings from sin motivates the groaning of creation. It is a single process, and Schilder and Bavinck develop its unity cogently. This is the deepest reason for my disagreement with "two kingdom" theology, though I neglected to do justice to it in *The Escondido Theology*,[4] where I present my general case against two kingdoms.

I also learned more about myself in Chapter 2, where John compares me with Abraham Van De Beek, former Professor of Systematic Theology at the Free University of Amsterdam. Van de Beek begins with Luther's "theology of the cross." But, differing from Luther, he argues that since Jesus took our guilt upon himself our whole responsibility in the world is to participate in the suffering of others. This idea is connected to his view that evil is endemic to the world, preceding even the events of Genesis 3. He disavows any suggestion of "optimism," or anything, even in Scripture, that might suggest the advance of God's kingdom in the present age. Even answers to prayer, he thinks, are rare and much overemphasized in evangelical piety. Our knowledge of Jesus is "indirect," "*via* the wretched condition of the world." He does affirm biblical confidence in the return of Christ and the consequent restoration of justice in this world. But he sees no anticipations of such restoration in present salvation history. In present history, the kingdom of God is "not yet," not at all "already."

On the contrary, John rightly describes my view of God as "a loving, personal being who sets blessing and curses before us and who is involved in the day-to-day working out of these twin covenantal aspects for our good." He points out that the radical difference between my view and Van de Beek's comes from our very different views of holy Scripture—its authority, its content, and its proper hermeneutic. On hermeneutics, Van de Beek insists that we should not base our theology on specific passages, but on the overall thrust of Scripture, as interpreted by the tradition of the church. I question, however, whether we can define that overall thrust without a responsible scrutiny of individual passages, and I don't believe that we can properly evaluate different elements in the tradition except by constantly scrutinizing the Scriptures, both their broad structure and their specific passages.

A biblical theology will focus on the principle of the creator-creature distinction: precious to Van Til and to me. John points out that Van de Beek questions the Chalcedon Christology in which divinity and humanity are carefully balanced and distinguished in the person of Christ. This freedom from the church's traditional view of Christ's person enables Van de Beek to modify the Protestant understanding of the saving work of Christ. As John paraphrases Van de Beek: "he is saying that by his person and work Christ did not make payment for sin, but instead assumed the responsibility for humankind's sinfulness—'humankind' understood in distinction from the individual. On the contrary, of course, Frame has no difficulty affirming that Jesus' death was sacrificial and substitutionary."

From here, John is led to many illuminating discussions of universalism, sanctification, the resurrection, suffering and history, and the problem of evil. The latter issue leads to discussion of Van de Beek's affirmation of God's changeability, an idea that I have frequently opposed as it is espoused in open theism. And, while affirming that God changes, he also says that God has made an unchanging choice to be gracious in Christ, a choice that often seems to imply universalism.

In the remaining chapters of his book, John scrutinizes my views on ethics, apologetics, worship, and culture. I will not be able to discuss these in as much detail as I have discussed chapters 1-2. In general I would say that John has accurately presented my positions and has sometimes "filled in the blanks" to respond to questions I have not myself addressed specifically. Let me, however, respond to a few statements here in which John disagrees with my views. Again, I am not disturbed by these areas of disagreement. In academic prose, they are to be expected. Readers may, however, be interested in my responses on these matters.

First, in footnote 81 of Chapter 2, John disagrees with my position that God is the "cause of sin." I understand the reluctance of orthodox theologians to make such a statement, but I do think it reflects the teaching of many Scripture passages, which I have listed extensively both in *DG* and in *NOG*. Ps. 105:24, for example, says that God turned the hearts of Israel's foes "to hate his people, to conspire against his servants." I do not see how one can affirm that type of statement while denying that God ever causes sin. Of course, there are often problems of language in this area of theology. Most all theologians deny that God is the "author" of sin, without defining that term very clearly.[5] Others disown the term "author" but affirm the term "cause." Still others deny that God "causes" sin, thinking perhaps that it is a synonym for "authors." But some of those are willing to say that God "ordains" sin or that sin is "part of God's plan." I have discussed these terminological issues extensively in *Doctrine of God,*[6] 174-82, but I do not claim that my discussion will silence all future discussion of these matters.

Second, John objects to my statement that human beings are a form of revelation.

> [Frame] speaks of "human beings as revelation.[7] That would seem contradictory to the biblical truth that the apostles had authority as *recipients* of revelation (Eph. 3:7-13; Gal. 2:8-9; Rom. 1:1-6) but not as sources of it.

Here, John doesn't consider the larger context of my doctrine of divine revelation. There is a sense in which God himself is revelation, for his word is one with himself (John 1:1). Since God is the creator of all things, all things reflect him (Ps. 19, Rom. 1:18-21). They receive God's revelation, therefore, but they also reveal him to other finite beings. They receive revelation, and on that account they are themselves revelation.

No finite being is an *ultimate* source of revelation; only God is the ultimate source of all revelation. But it is not wrong to say that each of us, having received revelation from God, becomes revelation to others. That is just to say that in an obvious sense we convey truth from God to others. So the apostles have authority because they are recipients of revelation. But in turn their own word becomes authoritative revelation to others. In 1 Cor. 14:37, Paul says that his written words are "a command of the Lord." That is, they describe what Paul has *received* from God and therefore they are themselves a verbal revelation of God's will.

And this revelation extends, not only to the apostle's words, but also to his personal behavior. So mature Christians model God's will to younger ones, 1 Thess. 1:7.[8] Given this fact, I don't think it is wrong to describe the apostles as revelation. Of course, this principle is related to the facts that (1) all human beings are the "image of God" and (2) everything in the world is "general revelation" (Ps. 19:1, Rom. 1:18-21).

Third, John believes that in *The Escondido Theology* I have left the impression that the entire faculty holds to the two-kingdom theory and the extreme separation of law and gospel. Well, I thought I had taken some precautions against that misunderstanding, but evidently those were insufficient. Anyhow, I take John's criticism under advisement. For what it is worth now, I wish to state clearly that Westminster in California is not unanimous in maintaining two kingdom theology. I would reiterate, however, that Westminster is "two-kingdom friendly" to the point where it seems acceptable there for *some* professors not only to teach two kingdoms, but to condemn opponents of this view as being unorthodox. And as I indicate in my book there are other problems at Westminster also, including a radical form of confessionalism that goes far beyond the views and practices of most Reformed churches today.

I do want to thank my good friend John for his careful and comprehensive analysis of my work, and Whitefield Media which has published the book. Whitefield has done many kind things for me over recent years, and I am grateful to God for their role in my life.

John M. Frame Ph.D., D.D.
J. D. Trimble Professor of Systematic Theology and Philosophy
Reformed Theological Seminary
Orlando, Florida

Endnotes

---

1 By "first time" I don't intend to neglect John Hughes, ed., *Speaking the Truth in Love* (Phillipsburg: P&R, 2009), my Festschrift, which consists mostly of articles about me, and which gave me great honor and delight. One of those articles was John Barber's "John Frame's Theology in the Present Cultural Context," 884-907. But Barber's present book is the first systematic analytical exposition of my thought.

2 Palo Alto, CA: Academica Press, 2008; Lakeland: Whitefield Media, 2013. My Foreword is on pp. xiii-xv.

3 *Cornelius Van Til: an Analysis of His Thought* (Phillipsburg: P&R, 1995).

4 Lakeland, FL: Whitefield Media, 2011.

5 I think they understand it to mean that God not only *causes* sin, but in doing so he also *does* sin, so as to be guilty of it.

6 Phillipsburg: P&R, 2002.

7 The chapter title of Chapter 43, *DWG*. Cf., his definition of people *as a "means of divine communication." DWG*, 305.

8 I have discussed this principle in more detail in *Doctrine of the Word of God* (Phillipsburg: P&R, 2010), 316-19.

FOREWORD

John M. Frame is a great gift to the church. He is widely published, and has been thoroughly evaluated, a process that is sure to continue for the foreseeable future. For handy access to his writings, sermons, and web publications one may consult *Speaking the Truth in Love: The Theology of John M. Frame*, the substantial Festschrift in his honor.[1] Rather than go over that ground again, here I will reminisce on some time spent with Dr. Frame, and reflect on what these encounters brought to me.

I first met John in 1968 while I was attending Westminster Theological Seminary. He had just been appointed professor of systematic theology at Westminster, having become M.Phil. at Yale, which, in popular jargon is "ABD" (all but dissertation), a status he would keep throughout his long career. The well-deserved title doctor derives from his D. D. bestowed by Belhaven College. I was once a guest in his home. He showed me box after box of index cards, his notes for the dissertation (that is how most of us organized our material before the computer!). He then told me he didn't think he would ever get around to finishing. There was too much else to do. In effect, however, his life's work has easily made up for this lacuna.[2]

My fellow students and I were marvelously enthusiastic about his courses. However unlikely it may seem, a favorite was called *Aseity*. Unlikely, not because of the subject matter, but the title. From the Latin *a* (from) plus *se* (self), aseity refers to God's self-sufficiency. One of the key texts John scrutinized was God's revelation to Moses, "I am that I am" (Ex. 3:14). Not only is God self-defining but he is unchangeable. And he is self-sufficient, the source of a being. As Paul told the Athenians, "And he is not served by human hands, as if he needed anything. Rather, he himself gives everyone life and breath and everything else" (Acts 17:25). What was riveting about this course was John's use of the Bible. Though his appointment was in the systematic theology department his courses might as well have been on biblical theology. I have rarely met someone with John's breadth of Scriptural knowledge. These were not only proof texts, but they were strung together in the grand Vosian tradition respecting the progressive unfolding of redemptive history.

Those were heady days at Westminster. The professors were committed to working within a dynamic triangle: exegesis - biblical theology - systematic theology. Each informed the other. Typically, we learned as much about exegesis from systematician John Murray as from instructors in the Bible departments. I remember Edmund Clowney, president and professor of practical theology, principally a biblical theologian, explaining systematics to us. He told us how to relate one portion of Scripture to another. His presupposition, so well-expressed in the confessional standard of the school, the *Westminster Confession of Faith*, is that there is a profound unity to the Bible: "the majesty of the style, the consent of all the parts, the scope of the whole..." (1.5). However, if a text from some part of Scripture did not at first appear to fit into the whole, he would say, instead of rushing to smooth it over until everything conveniently fits, "let the text worry you." Clowney believed in the unity of the Bible as much as anyone, but he would not allow us to jam round pegs into square holes. At the same time, if we found a particular passage did not easily support one or another locus of systematic theology, it might be that we are not reading it right. So exegesis can correct doctrine, but the reverse is true as well.

John Frame fit well in this atmosphere. He insisted that we respect not only the different eras in the unfolding mystery, but the different genres of the Bible books and passages. Cornelius Van Til was not yet retired, and so we had the benefit of sitting at the feet of the grand master, but also of his disciple, who would become a leading light in the next generation. Van Til's presuppositional apologetics, which was such a refreshing answer to the prevalent empiricism in the so-called "evidentialist" approach, came out of the Reformed tradition, and was clearly derived from Scripture. Only Van Til himself, upon his own admission, did not quote Scripture as much as he might have. Enter John Frame, who generally shared the same method, but with abundant Bible references.[3]

John's courses modeled his hermeneutics. In addition to the standard methods of exegesis, he added an important dimension to biblical interpretation: the vital imperative of *application*. Indeed, as we got to know his thinking, and then follow his career, it became clear that John's concern for application was central to everything else. He defended this method from several angles. The one I remember from seminary days was his taking issue with Charles Hodge's famous definition of systematic theology. Toward the beginning of his three-volume work, Hodge says theology is a science. Its task is "an exhibition of the facts of Scripture in their proper order and relation, with the principles or general truths involved in the facts themselves, and which pervade and harmonize the whole."[4] John Frame objected that if the Lord had wished to put more order into sacred Scripture he would have done so. As it is, the contents of the Bible are in the "proper order and relation" he intended. Scripture is sufficient.

So then, what is systematic theology? Application. The task of theology is to take the (already organized) biblical revelation and apply it to the needs of the church. It has a broad reach. "Theology," he says, "is the application of the Word of God by persons to all areas of life."[5] Thus, Frame explained, the bishops at Nicaea and Constantinople did not suddenly decide to hold an interesting theological colloquium on the divine Trinity, but rather they had to face a crisis provoked by the Arian heresy in the early 4th century. The bishops needed to take the teachings in the Bible on God's essence and his tri-personal nature and formulate them in such a way as to answer the Arians, who did not believe Christ was fully and eternally God. They applied the Bible to a significant local problem, and in the process blessed the church for centuries to come.

What is apologetics? Apologetics is "the application of the Scripture to unbelief."[6] Frame has been influenced by Ludwig Wittgenstein, learning about him through Paul Holmer, his professor at Yale.[7] John is hardly a Wittgensteinian. What Frame gleaned from both Holmer and Wittgenstein is an understanding of meaning as application. Doubt and certainty, Frame asserts, are practical issues. According to Wittgenstein, when these are removed from a practical context, "it is no longer meaningful, for meaning, to Wittgenstein, is the use of words in their ordinary, practical contexts, in what he calls their language game."[8] Without delving deeply into Wittgenstein's epistemology, especially to its problems, of which Frame is deeply aware, we can say that what attracts various theologians to him is his connection between meaning and ethics.

This applies to his understanding of knowledge, a major concern throughout his career. What are the similarities and what are the differences between what a believer knows and what an unbeliever knows about God and the world? According to Romans 1:18ff. unbelievers know God. They don't just know about him, they actually know the true God. The difference is that their knowledge is unsympathetic, unfriendly, insubordinate. They process that knowledge to wrong ends. Thus, they become foolish. Not because they cease to function mentally, but because they turn their knowledge to selfish, idolatrous ends, which necessarily leads to folly. For John Frame knowledge is so characterized by the moral component one could almost see epistemology as a subset of ethics. In a Frame-ian word, knowledge must reckon with Lordship. If it is unyielding, then knowledge is rebellious. If it yields, it is a servant of the truth (and the truth is a Person).

One of John Frame's constant concerns, then, one that he would develop throughout his career, is the relation of knowledge to moral principles. Frame taught the required Ethics course in my last year at Westminster. He was just beginning to work out his tri-perspectivalism, something he would pursue throughout his life. His intention was to follow Cornelius Van Til's statements at the beginning of his own work on ethics that we ought to study three overlapping concerns: motive, principle and end.[9] While some have worried that the many triads could open the door to relativism, John has been most careful to disavow such a concern. Here is one example of how the ethics triad, standard, goal, motive, can be most helpful. Is deception ever right? If one takes the "standard" (or normative perspective) in isolation from the rest, the answer would appear to be no. The ninth commandment forbids false witness. Passages in the Proverbs such as 14:5 would seem to close the case: "A faithful witness does not lie, but a false witness breathes out lies" (Prov. 14:5). But what about Rahab, whose faith is approved for protecting the spies, partly through deception? (Josh. 2:4-7). Or the Hebrew mothers who lied about their speedy delivery so that their male offspring could survive? (Ex. 1:18-22).

Frame's answer to this is to say there are certain contexts (the goal or "situational" perspective) which may allow for deception. One of them is warfare. How can one conduct a war without some kind of strategy of deception? Please note that this is not "situation ethics" in the manner of Joseph Fletcher. For Fletcher the law can be set aside in the name of love, a love which requires us to respond differently according to the different situations. Situation ethics does lead to relativism. Frame would never say you put aside the law. But the law must be interpreted according to its proper application. Strictly speaking, he is not adjusting the norm to fit the context. He is understanding the norm in a deeper way. The ninth commandment and the Proverb forbid false witness, not any kind of veiling the truth. In a courtroom, when the law requires the truth about an accused person, there is no option. But in warfare, as in games (though the two are vastly different) deception, or the *mendacium officiosum (as opposed to the mendacium perniciosum) is sometimes required.* And motive always enters in. Unless you are doing something from the fear of God you may be following the letter of the law, but it won't be pleasing to God.

One subject which benefits a great deal from his perspectival approach is the nature of Scripture itself. The Bible carries significant content. A good deal of it can be stated in terms of propositions. At the same time, the Bible comes with power and presence. There are commands, illocutionary statements, metaphors of all kinds which cannot, or should not, be reduced to their propositional payoff. And God's law is not only in a book, but in the believer's heart (Ps. 40:8). Coming from a l'Abri background, and strongly influenced by Francis Schaeffer's insistence on the rational, propositional nature of Scripture, I found John Frame's emphasis to be deeper.

John preached at my ordination in 1978. We were headed off to France where I taught at the Reformed Seminary in Aix-en-Provence for over a decade. His text was Philippians 1:3-11. He stressed the need for partnership in ministry. That was prescient of new directions in missions, and it certainly underscored the reason an American was serving in France. We were not there as a "mother church," but to work as partners with the local church for the common goal of training leaders for kingdom work in secular Europe. John is an ecumenist in the best sense of the word. While standing firmly on the bedrock of Reformed theology, he often spoke and wrote about the need for *Evangelical Reunion*.[10] John is considered controversial in this area, ironically. He wrote an article entitled, "Machen's Warrior Children," in which he lists twenty one issues where the spiritual descendents of J. Gresham Machen have engaged in major disputes.[11] At the end he proposes and "unrealistic dream" for working together better than we have. It is at once practical and pastoral.

Perhaps another one of John's unrealistic dreams is his vision for an ideal seminary. I read it when we were trying to shape the curriculum at Aix-en-Provence, and felt strongly Frame was pointing in the right direction. His proposal begins with reducing the traditional academic model to nearly nothing: "I propose first that we dump the academic model once and for all

– degrees, accreditation, tenure, the works."[12] He then pleads that we emulate the model of a smaller group, closely allied to the local church, a setting where character and godliness can be developed, not just academic prowess. Nearly thirty years after, Frame writes that though he is less bold than in his youth, his heart is still in this proposal.

I happen to lead a jazz band. I have spent much of my life studying musicology, concentrating on Bach Cantatas, Stravinsky, Messiaen, with a special place for Brahms' choral music, and black gospel music. John is a kindred spirit. The different connections between music and theology have often been noted. Martin Luther famously said, "I have no pleasure in any man who despises music. It is no invention of ours: it is a gift of God. I place it next to theology. Satan hates music: he knows how it drives the evil spirit out of us." John Frame (who, as is becoming clear, has too many talents!) is an accomplished organist. Just after graduating from seminary I heard him lecture on the biblical theology of music. It was an astonishing expedition through many of the major passages in Scripture relating to music. The take-away for me was the parallel he established between music and language, something I have thought about ever since.

John led the music at the New Life Presbyterian Church in Escondido, California, for a decade. Though his music of preference is classical, he began defending more popular ways to praise God out of a compassion for the unreached. He was influenced by the Rev. C. John ("Jack") Miller whose zeal for evangelism and love for people was unmatched. "I suppose that Jack's greatest influence on me was to make me willing to endure the scorn of traditionalists in the church," John says. "Jack's emphasis on evangelism led him to employ a style of worship at New Life that was far from the Presbyterian tradition." John wrote two smaller books that received considerable criticism as well as praise: *Contemporary Worship Music: A Biblical Defense*, and *Worship in Spirit and Truth.* Without agreeing with all the details, the significance of John's approach is to help us separate "what ought to be" from "what I like." The Presbyterian "regulative principle" in worship is a good one. Boiled-down, it says, only practice it if the Bible commands it. The question then becomes, though, what does the Bible command? Exclusive Psalmody? The Lord's Supper every Sunday? Does it prescribe a particular musical style? The poignant irony in John's contribution to these questions is that left to himself he would really rather listen to Bach and sing the older hymns. But based on the regulative principle rightly understood, he wants to accommodate wider styles, including the much maligned CCM (Christian Contemporary Music) of the time.

John's work on culture has been very helpful to me. He has written about the subject off and on throughout his life. Many of his most important reflections on culture are reproduced in the book, *Doctrine of the Christian Life.*[13] Incidentally, the term "doctrine" is used intentionally for the entire series of four studies, *Doctrine of the Knowledge of God*, *Doctrine of God*,

Doctrine of the Christian Life, and *Doctrine of the Word of God*. John believes that theology and doctrine are synonymous. In keeping with his theme of application, along with his ethical approach to knowledge, he says, "[D]octrine is the application of the Word of God to all areas of human life… I prefer to define *doctrine* therefore, not as theological propositions, but as an active process of teaching that leads to spiritual health: as Paul puts it, 'sound doctrine'."[14] John has expended a good deal of energy defending the Kuyperian view of the Lordship of Christ over every sphere of life. He has a syllabus on film that is most beneficial. One of the best summaries of this traditionally Reformed outlook is the section on "Christ and Culture" toward the end of *Doctrine of the Christian Life*.[15] Among other things, he takes issue with some of the "Two Kingdoms" advocates, faulting them for too great a separation between "cult" and "culture." At the heart of his view, though, is finding a profound unity between the original cultural mandate (Gen. 1:26-30) and its successive iterations, right up to the Great Commission (Matt. 28:18-20).

John and I have taken rather different paths since those early days. But we have stayed in touch, and occasionally have been able to visit. He was celebrated at a special session of the Evangelical Theological Society in November of 2009 in which I was able to participate. Now in his mid-seventies he shows no signs of slowing down. Perhaps one of his greatest contributions, besides his concern for obedient knowledge, is the pastoral tone with which he writes. I believe the reason he writes in an almost conversational manner is because of his respect for his readers. He wants to talk with them, and edify them, not to bark at them.

The book you hold in your hands by one of John's most able students will bring you right to the center of John Frame's views. John Barber has given us a very readable, persuasive defense of John Frame's theology. Indeed, "Lordship" is at the heart of Frame's theology, as it should be of ours as well. You will greatly profit from it.

William Edgar
Professor of Apologetics
John Boyer Chair of Evangelism and Culture
Westminster Theological Seminary, Philadelphia

Endnotes

1 John M. Frame, *Speaking the Truth in Love: The Theology of John M. Frame*, John J. Hughes, editor, Phillipsburg: P & R Publishing, 2009, especially pp. 1029-1070

2 In 2014 John Frame was awarded the Ph.D. from Whitefield Theological Seminary having completed the original dissertation project.

3 There are some differences between the two, some of which Frame himself underscores. This is not the place to explore those. One may consult Frame's presentation of Van Til, *Cornelius Van Til: An Analysis of His Thought*, Phillipsburg: P & R Publishing, 1995.

4 Charles Hodge, *Systematic Theology*, vol. 1, Grand Rapids: Eerdmans, 1968, 18.

5 John M. Frame, *Doctrine of the Knowledge of God*, Phillipsburg: P & R Publishing, 1987, 81.

6 Ibid., 87.

7 See:[http://www.rts.edu/Site/Resources/FacultyArticles/Backgrounds_to_My_ Thought_JFrame.pdf], 11.

8 See [http://www.frame-poythress.org/certainty/].

9 Cornelius Van Til, *In Defense of the Faith*, vol. 3, *Christian Theistic Ethics*, Phillipsburg: P & R Publishing, 1980, 1-3.

10 His book on the subject is subtitled: *Denominations and the One Body of Christ*, Grand Rapids: Baker, 1991.

11 See [http://www.frame-poythress.org/machens-warrior-children/].

12 I first read the essay, "Proposal For a New Seminary," in the *Journal of Pastoral Practice* 2:1, Winter, 1978, 10-17, though it was written earlier. See [http://www.frame-poythress.org/proposal-for-a-new-seminary/].

13 John Frame, *Doctrine of the Christian Life*, Phillipsburg: P & R Publishing, 2008. This is Part Three in his Lordship series.

14 Ibid., 9.

15 Ibid., 853-908.

AUTHOR'S PREFACE

I recall the day I drove onto the campus of Westminster Theological Seminary in my 1974 Ford Pinto (In the late 70s the Philadelphia campus was the only one). I got out of my car, looked around, and to my surprise, I could see only one person. An elderly man wearing what appeared to be a polo shirt and jeans was standing at the top of the stairs leading into Machen Hall. But what seemed odd to me is that he wasn't moving. He was just standing there. As I walked a little closer to him, I thought to myself, "This old fellow must be the groundskeeper."

Looking for the admission's office, but without a clue as to where it was, I walked past the old gentleman and down a driveway that exited onto another road. As I glanced over my shoulder, sure enough, there he was, as if fastened to the top stair, just staring at me. Not wanting to appear foolish, I instantly turned around and headed back in the old fellow's direction with one of those *Jacques Clouseau* looks on my face—the one which says, "I knew all along that this driveway leads to the exit."

Suddenly he spoke. "May I help you?" "No, that's OK", I replied. But I had no idea what I was doing and the old man knew it. So once again, he said, and sternly this time, "May I help you? My name is Cornelius Van Til." I thought that to be a rather impressive name for the custodian. Finally I swallowed my pride, and said, "I'm looking for admissions." With his thumb pointing over his shoulder, he briskly retorted, "It's in there." With that, he walked down the stairs and headed off.

Just before classes began, students were gathered and placed in little circular groups so we could talk and get to know one another. At one point, a student brought up Van Til. I thought, "Did the old man die?" Well, it took but a few minutes for me to realize that Van Til was not the school custodian. Then sometime later during my first semester I had an insight. It was that Van Til was in fact the school custodian. But a custodian of a different type! He was a custodian of Truth. A guardian of Scripture. And one of its ablest defenders.

Now back to the group of students sitting in that circle. As we were talking, a youngish John Frame walked up, and said, "So what are you guys talking about?" One student said, "Van Til." Without hesitation John gave us students a very quick and effective lesson on Van Til. He said, "All of Van Til can be boiled down to two points: all men know God but suppress the truth in unrighteousness, and the only way to approach them is to pull the rug right out from under them."

That brief encounter with John changed my life. Not only did he provide the "lens" through which a relatively new Christian, and former College music student, was able to understand all the coursework at Westminster, but since then, my entire ministry has been nothing more or less than application of John's brilliant summation of Van Til.

It should come as no surprise, then, that I became an avid reader of John's writings, and of the man himself. He was a follower of Van Til, and yet in some ways he had more to say. Of greatest interest to me were his twin ideas that all theology is practical, and that in God's world everything is a perspective on the whole. Both ideas reverberated with my call to evangelism and with my academic interest in worldview studies relative to theology of culture.

A few years ago, I was invited to write for John's *Festschrift*. That led to an idea: a book about John's theology. Why? Beyond my preoccupation with the theologian, presently the literature on John is virtually non-existent. The *Festschrift* is quite excellent, but it presents a compendium of assorted articles, rather than sustained research by a single author. That, I thought, leaves room for new and meaningful development.

What is my main research question? It is, "*What does the concept of 'lordship' mean in the theology of John M. Frame?*" Following this question, the book demonstrates how Frame's lordship principle creates original outcomes in the area of dogmatics, most particularly his *perspectivalism*. Even more precisely, we will see how the Framian theology of lordship shapes his view of ethics, apologetics, and culture. It is my hope that this first thrust into Frame's theology will generate many more such studies, all of which will prove fruitful to the growth of dogmatics as both a spiritual and an academic discipline.

In case the reader might benefit from a similar distilled explanation of John Frame, just like the one John gave us of Cornelius Van Til, I will state here what I have also written in the body of this work. All of Frame can be boiled down to one thought.

> There is one kingdom, ruled over by one Lord, who governs the affairs of all people by a single rule of faith and practice, and everything is related perspectivally.

My great hope is that God will use this book to encourage us all to love and good deeds and to be a practical resource for reaching a world in need of Christ.

John Barber
Tequesta, Florida
Soli Deo Gloria!

List of Figures

Abbreviations

In the footnotes, I will refer to John Frame's titles by abbreviation, as he does himself and is commonly done by his main publisher, Presbyterian and Reformed Publishing Company.

ACT	*The Academic Captivity of Theology*
AGG	*Apologetics to the Glory of God*
CVT	*Cornelius Van Til: An Analysis of His Thought*
DCL	*The Doctrine of the Christian Life*
DG	*The Doctrine of God*
DKG	*The Doctrine of the Knowledge of God*
DWG	*The Doctrine of the Word of God*
NOG	*No Other God: A Response to Open Theism*
ST	*Systematic Theology*
TET	*The Escondido Theology*

Additional abbreviations:

LW	*Luther's Works*, American Edition
WA	The Weimar edition of *Luther's Works*, also known as the *Weimarer Ausgabe* (WA)

Chapter 1

The Significance of Lordship in Frame's Theology

Distinguished Calvinist theologian and philosopher John M. Frame (b.1939) is especially noted for his work in presuppositional apologetics and a broad range of disciplines within the field of systematic theology. Within his opera of works, his Theology of Lordship series, which includes *The Doctrine of the Knowledge of God*, *The Doctrine of God*, *The Doctrine of the Christian Life*, and *The Doctrine of the Word of God*, develops a synthetic system of enormous strength and importance. Added to this is his *Systematic Theology*, which develops many of the themes found in his Lordship series.

The Priority of Lordship

The *sine qua non* of Frame's theological statement is God's lordship. This is due to the fact that Frame holds to a very high view of Scripture, and, as far as he can see, it is Scripture that reveals lordship as maintaining a locus of first importance. As the theologian so decisively puts it, "The first thing, and in one sense the only thing, we need to know about God is that he is Lord. Surely no name, no description of God, is more central to Scripture than this."[1] Even more emphatically, he states, "The central message of Scripture is that God is Lord."[2] Frame justifies his claim that lordship is Scripture's central message by locating its prominent position in the self-disclosure of God. "When God met Moses in the burning bush and announced that he would deliver his people from slavery in Egypt, Moses asked his name.[3] Then God replied, 'I am who I am. This is what you are to say to the Israelites: 'I am has sent me to you' (Ex. 3:14) . . . So the name of God, the name by which he wants his people especially to remember him forever, is Yahweh or Lord."[4]

The Lord of the Covenant

Frame consistently approaches lordship within the bounds of the biblical framework of covenant. "First of all, lordship is a covenantal concept. 'Lord' is the name God gives to himself as head of the Mosaic Covenant and the name given to Jesus Christ as head of the New Covenant." By way of definition, "We may, therefore, define divine lordship as covenant headship."[5] Though primary, covenant lordship does not prohibit additional necessary biblical data such as faith, community, and deliverance, but in fact lordship "provides a key for us to understand how the other themes fit into the overall biblical history. And it often liberates us from the temptation to set one theme against another, or to affirm one and to deny the other, for in the covenant these apparently diverse concepts and themes display a wonderful unity."[6] Indeed, considering the vast array of central motifs that theologies are frequently built around, such as reconciliation, history, hope, liberation, and justification, says Frame, "we find it a bit surprising that so few of them focus on the concept of divine lordship. In view of the centrality of lordship in Scripture's own doctrine of God, and specifically in its Christology, it would seem to be an obvious choice as a central motif for a theological discussion."[7]

A further axial and consequential point is that that Frame believes that the exigent demands of covenant bind *all* nations and peoples of the earth, not just the faithful. Lordship is universal in its scope. Now to say that the aggregate peoples of the earth are covenantally responsible to Yahweh presents a theological acclimatization that might fairly be viewed as cryptic. However, there are two central reasons why Frame believes that each and every person is duty-bound before the divine covenants of Scripture.

First, the global jurisdiction of the covenants is found in their language.

> In a broad sense, all of God's dealings with creation are covenantal in character. . . . During the creation week, all things, plants, animals, and persons are appointed to be covenant servants, to obey God's law, and to be instruments (positively or negatively) of his gracious purpose. Thus everything and everybody is in covenant with God (cf. Isa. 24:5: all the 'inhabitants of the earth' have broken the 'everlasting covenant'). The Creator-creature relation is a covenant relation, a Lord-servant relation. When the Lord singled out Israel as his special people to be Lord over them in a peculiar way, he was not giving them an absolutely unique status; rather, he was calling them essentially into the status that all men occupy yet fail to acknowledge."[8]

By the same token, "all human beings, not just Israelites and Christians, are related to God covenantally. . . . The covenant between God and Adam includes the whole human race (Rom. 5:12–21). . . . And we are also members of God's covenant with Noah's family (Gen. 8:20–9:17), in which God pledges his presence to maintain the seasons and to delay the final judgment. The Noachic covenant is made not only with Noah's family, but also with 'every living creature on earth (9:10)."[9] The covenants are therefore no discriminator of persons.

Second, all people of the world are subject to the divine covenants of Scripture because God intends both the Old Testament Israelite community and the Christian Church to be a blessing to the surrounding nations via common grace.

> In the new covenant, God reaches out to all nations, not only to Israel (Matt. 28:18–20). Indeed, that has been his purpose in all the covenants, throughout the history of redemption. God's covenant with Israel is specifically with them, but they are to be his witnesses to all nations, for in Abraham all the nations of the earth are to be blessed (Gen. 12:3). . . . It is therefore God's covenant that provides the blessings of common grace, the kindness of God to all his creatures. So then, "God's covenant lordship is not limited to Israel. His kingship is over all the nations, over all the earth" (Ps. 47:7–9).[10]

A seminal aspect of Frame's arrangement of theology is that he reverses many traditional theological categories that have featured significantly in the history of dogmatics for centuries. "Thus, I shall discuss God's acts before his attributes. . . . I will proceed from history to eternity, from the ethical to the metaphysical, from the communicable to the incommunicable."[11]

Though he justifies this reversal on the grounds that it serves a "pedagogical difference" that can make theology more comprehensible to people who lack training in philosophy, and for purposes of edification, I cannot also help but see this reversal as the natural outcome of Frame's stress on covenantal lordship.[12] For to begin theological reflection from the vantage point of the Lord of the covenant is to begin in the concrete, not in the abstract.

Perspectivalism

Emerging from Frame's compendious view of God's covenantal lordship is a particular theological structure called perspectivalism. Throughout his works, Frame may also refer to triperspectivalism, multiperspectivalism, the lordship triad, the lordship attributes, or the lordship principle. The exact lordship attributes Frame prefers to sum God's relationship to the creation are control, authority, and presence (hereafter referred to as CAP).[13] Functionally, the three attributes work together in mutual connection. So "The three lordship attributes are 'perspectivally related,' that is, each one is involved in the other two. None of them can be rightly understood, except as inseparably related to the others. Redemption necessarily involves God's control and authority, as well as his presence."[14] Frame is committed to seeing everything about God, to his acts, to the way in which creatures have knowledge of God, according to this fully integrated formulaic structure.[15]

It can hardly be overstressed that Frame writes theology perspectivally, not because he thinks it is an intriguing approach that he wishes to explore in a recondite way. He is prompted along this path of research because, to repeat the earlier point, he understands lordship in an intensely covenantal context. God is always the Lord *in relationship to* the creation, especially to his people. This idea is of leading importance, in that the covenant represents the redemptive and geo-political constitutionalism that binds God with ancient Israel and later with his Church. But the question Frame came to ponder in his early years as a theologian is which comes first: God or his creation? In other words, where do we begin theology? Prompted by John Calvin's early statement in the *Institutes*, in which Calvin observes the inseparability between the knowledge of God and self-knowledge, stating that he did not know which came first, Frame set out to develop the implications of Calvin's point into a fully shaped perspectival theology.[16] A basic premise of triperspectivalism is thus that one cannot understand Scripture without understanding the world and the self to which it applies.

An abridged formula of what has been stated about Frame's theology up to now can read as follows. *There is one kingdom, ruled over by one Lord, who governs the affairs of all people by a single rule of faith and practice, and everything is related perspectivally.*

There is a very important point that must be clarified in order to advance understanding of Frame on lordship. Augustine denied that lordship is an eternal attribute of God.[17] Frame agrees with the Bishop of Hippo, but only in a rather nuanced way. Like Augustine, Frame believes that lordship presupposes servanthood, and servanthood presupposes creation. So Frame is not willing to speak of lordship *in abstractio*.[18] However, he still insists that lordship is a necessary and defining attribute of God. Is Frame conflicted here?[19] The remedy to the apparent paradox might be posed in a question: "How shall we define the attribute of lordship?" The answer is that God is such a being that whatever he does create in time and space will necessarily be a servant to him. In other words, the nature of God is such that from eternity, he is *poised*, for lack of a better word, to be Lord and to demonstrate his lordship once he does create something. We might call lordship *an attribute in waiting*. Frame admits, "Maybe I shouldn't call that lordship. But it is certainly the root of lordship. I think it's important that Lordship be seen as rooted in such an attribute."[20]

Frame also wonders if much theology, in manifestation of the *mysterium tremendum et fascinans*, has not made God's attributes *a se* higher, or in some sense more important, than his communicable attributes. Yet Frame muses, "Why should we assume that the most central theological characterizations of God must be necessary attributes? The fact is that we don't look down on God; we look up. So we should think about God in terms appropriate to our servanthood. We should think of him as Lord."[21]

How can Frame know that there is an eternal attribute of God called "lordship" awaiting creation in order to actuate? The subjective idealism of George Berkeley denied the possibility of unperceived existence, when he said, "*Esse est percipi*" ("to be is to be perceived"). From that axiom has come the familiar question: "If a tree falls in a forest and no one is around to hear it, does it make a sound?" Perhaps the most important topic the riddle offers is the division between perception of an object and how an object really is. If a tree exists outside of perception, then there is no way for us to know that the tree exists. So, then, what do we mean by "existence" with respect to lordship? Frame would reply that we can know the existence of lordship because Scripture refers to God as "Lord" more than 7,000 times and acclaims his lordship to us in multitudinous contexts. Based on the biblical witness, lordship is a necessary attribute of God, which means that everything he creates *will be* his servant.

Frame's grounding of the existence of lordship on canonical grounds portends broader differentiations with like thinkers who share his basic commitment to the universal implications of Christian theism. He believes that thinkers continuing the legacy of Kuyper, such as Herman Dooyeweerd, D. H. Th. Vollenhoven, and, later, James Olthuis and H. L. Hebden Taylor, were drawn far too deeply into speculative thought, while his approach seeks to be unapologetically biblical. Cosmic time, supratemporal heart, modalities, sphere sovereignty, Subject-Object relation, ground-idea, Gegenstand relation, intentional inexistence, and much more are, according to Frame, all truth-seeking insights but imprecise formulations, nonetheless, by which the self-sufficiency and cogency of Scripture seem lost.[22] As will be shown, Frame believes that even Kuyper's theory of common grace, once weighed in the scales of Scripture, is wanting on some levels.

The Practicable Nature of Theology

Given everything that can be said with respect to Frame's basic theological commitments, that *theology is application* may be his most pressing concern. Frame frequently makes reference to this point.[23] "And remember that theology itself is the application of Scripture to all of human life."[24] In a different place, he says, "So I offer my definition of theology: theology is *the application of Scripture, by persons, to every area of life*."[25] He does not merely mean that the discoveries of theology are to be practiced, but that the very nature of doing theology is in itself an interaction with the Lord and is therefore to be done in submission to him. Theology is not the possession of the educated elite. On the contrary, theology must set out clearly, correctly, and precisely the moral obligations of all people before God.[26] He says quite clearly, "Remember that ethics, considered broadly, embraces all of theology."[27] Clarifying his point, he adds, "Ethics is not a part of theology, or a branch of theology. It is theology, viewed from a certain perspective."[28] In a sense, then, it is an oxymoron to discuss the "practical theology" of John M. Frame when in fact he intends the whole of his theology to be practical.

Why does a polemical discourse on medieval scholasticism appear in the "Introduction" to Frame's *Doctrine of God*?[29] It is there as a foil against the very philosophical imperialism and traditionalism that Frame contends has made theology into an exercise of mind without concern for the practical needs of the masses. In this regard, "the Protestant scholastics differed from Luther and Calvin mainly in that the former were seeking to develop academically rigorous systems, while Luther and Calvin saw the main task of theology as pastoral and polemical."[30] So, then, any doctrine of God ought not to be a "nitpicking venture" or a dialectical study in historical theology that never seeks to arrive at the truth. Rather, in keeping with the intent of the Magisterial Reformers, theology ought always to be relevant to practical Christian life.[31]

Frame traces his emphasis on the practical nature of theology to a personal dilemma he experienced in his formative years. Although as a young man he yearned to be active in ministry, his first choice being that of a missionary and, second, that of a pastor, he eventually faced the fact that he would not make a good missionary or pastor. His true gifting was in academics, so he opted for a teaching profession. "But my passion (and I do not boast of this) was different: to help people to know Jesus. . . . Although I had entered an academic calling, my real passion was elsewhere, in the practical ministry of the church. There was, then, a deep tension between my interests and my abilities. My abilities were exclusively academic, but my interests were almost as exclusively practical."[32] The outlet Frame found for his passion was to make theology as practical as possible. It is from this fervor that the perspectival system of theology was birthed.

The model began by teaching "students a definition of theology that bridged study with the Christian life." Frame defined theology as "the application of the word of God, by persons, to every area of life."[33] From that definition, Frame worked out a triperspectival scheme of ontology, epistemology, and ethics that sought to correlate norms, situations, and persons, respectively, for the general purpose of implementing his unique definition of theology. From there, the lordship scheme developed into its present and more mature form. The salient point is that the heartbeat of perspectivalism is to boot theology from its bookish cloister and transform it into a forum where we encounter the living God who brings together rigorous academics, personal spirituality, and a disciplining vision for the setting in which we live.[34]

Frame the "Radical"

Frame's perspectivalism indicates that he is not without interest in constructive theology. One thinks of Stephen W. Brown's endearing but accurate description of Frame as "the closet radical."[35] What is the basis of Brown's account of Frame's radicalism? Those who know Frame on a personal level have often characterized him as "irenic."[36] Not only is his personality calm and nonbelligerent, but his polemical interaction with other writers is always even-handed. For example, although his Christian ethics can classify non-Christian ethics as "bankrupt," his perspectivalism still allows him to find some semblance of truth in secular systems of thought. This is not the sort of writing ardent traditionalists are apt to applaud. So Brown's observation is really a reflection of how others perceive Frame.

The origin of Frame's radicalism is in his commitment to place Scripture above all else in the working out of his theology. On his triperspectival view of revelation, he says, "But we must remember the primacy of Scripture, which governs our understanding and interpretation of general and existential revelation. Our interpretation of general and existential revelation must be tested by Scripture . . . then the ultimate norm is Scripture, not general or existential revelation by itself."[37] And, "A fully

Christian ethic accepts only God's word as final."[38] These statements do not appear radical to conservative-minded theologians. But when, for example, he rejects the idea that Scripture limits corporate worship to traditional Protestant forms, arguing instead that Scripture specifically prescribes very little for post-Resurrection, New Testament worship, strict confessionalists think that Frame is prepared to abandon parts of a distinct Reformed identity for the sake of pragmatic gains in collaboration with broad evangelicals.[39] In actual fact, it is Frame who thinks that his opponents have gone beyond the Bible by elevating tradition to the word of God.[40] It is ironic how a man who walks so softly can create so many tremors.

I must therefore be quite clear what I mean by "constructive" theology. The use of that term is not meant to convey the re-definition of systematic theology. As some see it, the potential problem underlying systematics is that in constructing a system of theology, certain elements may be overlooked, while others are made primary in order to maintain the logic of the system taken as a whole. From the various creedal formulations of PaleoChristianity to the Westminster Confession of Faith, to Lindbeck's cultural-linguistic approach, Pannenberg's theology of hope, Reuther's feminist liberation theology, and Tillich's method of correlation, all have emphasized certain aspects of theology based on the historical and cultural pressure points of the day. Against this, constructive theology presents a case for doing theology according to the present need of each generation and of the church, which means that constructive theology will always remain unfinished, extending as far as to cardinal beliefs classical orthodoxy deems essential.

What is meant here by Frame's interest in "constructive" theology is that he has always valued original work in theology but in such a way that it remain true to the classic Protestant doctrine of Scripture; its meaning is not open to revision, depending on the *sitz im leben* ("setting in life"). He is not curious to reconstruct theology from the ground floor up but wants to re-conceptualize the *task* of theology along practical and pastoral lines. Perspectivalism achieves this end. The term *constructive* may also refer to the ever-growing need for fresh applications of Scripture to changing needs and questions. But differently from the present constructivist trend, Scripture is never the earliest point of the confessional life of God's people. It is God's words to us, the standard for the confessional life of the church.[41]

The early Meredith G. Kline is an example of one who stimulated a young John Frame to think constructively. Even though Frame came to disagree with Kline's later view of the relationship between cult and culture, in his student years "Kline was one of my heroes. He stood for the Bible against Reformed traditionalism and taught me how theology could be wonderfully creative within the bounds of orthodoxy."[42] Frame is thinking mainly of Kline's *The Structure of Biblical Authority*. Upon reading it, Frame saw it was quite different from other defenses of biblical authority. The book drew on ancient Near Eastern scholarship and was very carefully and cogently stated. What motivated Frame most was the thought that a scholar could remain squarely within the bounds of classical orthodoxy, while being innovative and not kowtowing to traditional positions.

A surprising stimulus in connection with Frame's commitment to applicative theology is Ludwig Wittgenstein. Although Frame works from a very different theological context and arrives at vastly different conclusions, "Wittgenstein . . . is a thinker I often turn back to. His view that meaning is, in most cases, its *use* in the language certainly influenced my own view that "theology is application."[43]

The Important Link to Bavinck[44]

The influences on the constructivist model of perspectivalism must also consider historical precedents. For a time, orthodox Calvinist theologian and churchman Herman Bavinck was a professor of dogmatics at the Theological Seminary in Kampen. One of Bavinck's most notable disciples was Louis Berkhof, even though Vos was also instrumental in Berkhof's early training. Berkhof would later become professor of systematic theology and president of Calvin Theological Seminary. It has been documented that Berkhof relied heavily on Bavinck's *Reformed Dogmatics* in his well-known *Systematic Theology*.[45] The relevance of this history is in the fact that Van Til, who did the most to crystallize Frame's thought, studied under Berkhof at Calvin Theological Seminary. Not only was Van Til exposed to Bavinck's ideas in Berkhof's classroom, but also he spent many hours in careful study of Bavinck's *Gereformeerde Dogmatiek*. That contact, I think, was a critical period in the formation of Van Til's interpretation of Christianity, which would later influence Frame.[46] Evidence in support of this line of influence is appreciable.

First, a central thread of Van Til's epistemology is that human knowledge is analogical, not univocal. Bavinck affirms this particular structure of thought by limiting human knowledge of God, both quantitatively and qualitatively. "But though God is thus beyond our full comprehension and description, we do confess to having the knowledge of God. This knowledge is analogical and the gift of revelation."[47] Although a reading of *The Doctrine of the Knowledge of God*, for example, shows how Frame uses various gradations of analysis to nuance, and in some cases counter, Van Til on analogical knowledge, ultimately, he affirms Bavinck's and Van Til's epistemological premise that knowledge is essentially analogical in character.[48] Paraphrasing John Murray, he writes, "We know God by means of analogy, but what we know is not a mere analogy, but the true God."[49]

Second, it has been noted that the first page of Calvin's *Institutes*, in which he states the inseparability of knowledge of God and knowledge of self, was of major influence on Frame's perspectival theology. But Van Til is a more proximate influence. In *An Introduction to Systematic Theology*, Van Til develops a perspectival schema that takes into account nine categories of revelation.[50] Frame freely admits, "These insights of Van Til's are one major source (together with others) of the 'perspectivalism' expounded in my *DKG*."[51] But who inspired Van Til? The answer seems obvious when we read Bavinck. On the topic of providence, he states,

> Preservation, concurrence, and government, accordingly, are not parts or segments in which the work of providence is divided and which, being materially and temporally separate, succeed one another. Nor do they differ from one another in the sense that preservation relates only to the existence of creatures, concurrence only to their activities and government exclusively to guidance toward the final goal of these creatures. But they are always integrally connected: they intermesh at all times. From the very beginning preservation is also government, and government is concurrence, and concurrence is preservation.[52]

Third, on theology of culture, Van Til affirmed Kuyper's idea that common grace has made culture a good and necessary condition for God's redemptive purposes in the earth. One *loci* in which he differed with Kuyper was over the issue of dual mediatorships. Kuyper believed that both individuals and the non-rational creation were predestined for redemption, but that the history of civilization met that goal incentivized by the means of common grace according to its own *nebenzweck* ("secondary aim"). Van Til joined Douma's critique of Kuyper by looking to Paul's condensation of God's single rule. "Let us rather be satisfied with the words of Paul when, speaking of Christ, he says that 'from him and through him and to him are all things.' When we do this then we recognize and honor the mystery of God's revelation to man in Christ for the salvation of the world."[53] Although Van Til looks to Douma, and also to Schilder, to counter Kuyper on this point, I cannot help but note that the most prodigious thinker among the Dutch theologians on "grace restores nature" was Bavinck. In response to the mechanical determinism of his Leiden professors, he said, "Grace does not remain outside or above or beside nature but rather permeates and wholly renews it. And thus, nature, reborn by grace, will be brought to its highest revelation." This means that "Christianity does not introduce a single substantial foreign element into the creation. It creates no new cosmos but rather makes the cosmos new. It restores what was corrupted by sin. It atones the guilty and cures what is sick; the wounded it heals."[54] In critiquing Thomistic dualism, Frame echoes Bavinck and Van Til's concern that "Scripture does not warrant the Roman Catholic distinctions between nature and grace, natural reason and revelation, or the doctrine of the twofold end of man."[55]

Fourth, balanced evenly with the creation/recreation motif is Bavinck's antipathy toward any sort of sacred/secular dualism. "In Christ all things are gathered into one (Eph. 1:10; Col. 1:20). The world, which was created by the Son, is also predestined for the Son as its heir (Col. 1:16; 2 Pet. 3:13; Rev.11:15). So it is not a random aggregate of things but an organic whole that is known by God in election and saved by Christ's redemption."[56] This is a theme of immense import to Frame, as we will see in the chapter on culture. In rejecting Kuyper's *nebenzweck*, Van Til also said, "We join

Schilder in rejecting Kuyper's distinction between Christ as the mediator of creation and as the mediator of redemption. We must unite the idea of creation in Christ with that of His redemption of all things."[57]

Finally, on presuppositionalism, so central in the apologetics of both Van Til and Frame, Bavinck says, "Scripture, one must remember, never makes any attempt to prove the existence of God, but simply presupposes it."[58]

Divine Lordship in Relationship to Ethics, Apologetics, & Culture

The foregoing thoughts pave the way for some preparatory remarks on the three areas of Frame's theology that, in upcoming chapters, will be the subjects of extended research. Although Frame has written on virtually every area of dogmatics, along with numerous philosophical issues, always bearing in mind the practical import of his study, the next chapters will focus on his work in the related fields of ethics, apologetics, and culture. These areas are chosen for the reason that in Frame's theology, they represent the clearest integration between his theology and practice.

Relationship of Lordship and Ethics

A unique aspect of Frame's thought is his belief that all things, thoughts, and acts reduce ultimately to ethics. The primacy of ethics is established in the fact that the holy nature of the Lord is the antecedent qualification to all human thought and behavior. Now to say that all things can be reduced to ethics should not be taken in a restrictive sense: that the juncture linking abstract ideas with concrete instances precipitates ethical consideration. The idea is far more nuanced. He means that all things are literally of the nature of ethics. Nothing, neither abstract thought nor the objects of ideas, can exist autonomously, but all things find meaning and definition in God. Even propositional truths are to be interpreted ethically because "propositional knowledge is based on knowledge of a person. He supplies the norms, the justifications that are missing in secular accounts of knowledge, as well as the truths that we are to believe and the mental capacity for us to come to knowledge. . . . He is the ultimate *truth*: the truth is what he is and what he has decreed to be."[59]

Absolutely different from Frame's Christian ethic are varied secular ethical systems. Frame's chief criticism with these approaches is that they are not built on a belief *in* something but are the product of non-belief. Frame contends that this unbelief is inherently utopian. Pithily, he remarks, "But we cannot exist without ultimate values, so we become gods ourselves."[60] This accounts for the secularist tendency toward relativism and dogmatism. Because secular liberalism discards God, almost anything in the area of ethics is acceptable. But since such an idea can only lead to bedlam, the secularist exchanges God with a new moral absolute: autonomous moral judgment, whether individual or collective. Seeing as this judgment is of the nature of a false god, it seeks to inflict itself on others—hence its assertively utopian temperament.[61] In Frame's view, unbelief is thus a force to be reckoned with. In *The Doctrine of the Christian Life*, especially, he thus expends a great deal of energy critiquing secular presuppositions and answers.

A question that continues to beleaguer secular thinkers is, "Is it possible to speak theologically of a coherent moral vision?" In search of a solution, such ethicists have, according to Frame, probed the teleological, the deontological, or the existential fields of inquiry. The increasing specialization of academic interpretations of these three specializations in autonomy from divine lordship has produced what Frame calls a "rational/irrational" tension, which is close in conception to the relativism/dogmatism motif clarified above. As we shall see in more detail in the chapter on lordship and ethics, this inherent tension in thought results in a plethora of ethical theories that are unable to unite absoluteness and relevance, objectivity and inwardness, and abstract theory and content. The sophists, Hume and Rousseau, Marx and Nietzsche, Wittgenstein, Heidegger, and Sartre, and the postmodern thinkers Lyotard, Derrida, Foucalt, and Rorty and more, have spoken for the existential tradition. Epicurus, Aristotle, Bentam and Mill, and Dewey worked to advance the teleological tradition. And Plato, Immanuel Kant, Hegel, Bradley, Bosanquet, Moore, and Pritchard committed themselves to the deontological tradition.

In Frame, all of these traditions find ample and balanced expression. How so? Frame turns a complex presentation of biblical ethics, represented in the teleological, deontological, or existential traditions, into a unified system. He does so by carefully distinguishing, but also coalescing, three different perspectives: the situational perspective, the normative perspective, and the existential perspective—all of which draw currency from the fundamental lordship attributes of CAP.[62] In my opinion, until Frame, no one had successfully brought together the three major schools of thought in ethics.

Relationship of Lordship and Presuppositional Apologetics[63]

The quintessence of Frame's apologetics is to take no prisoners. As a student of Dr. Frame, I recall quite vividly a day when he remarked to a group of us students, "Everything Van Til ever said can be reduced to two ideas: that all men undeniably know God, and that the only way to approach them is to pull the rug right out from under them." Frame's Van Tilian reduction takes as its cue that withstanding principle of presuppositional apologetics: "no neutrality." This principle is grounded in Divine lordship, as well as the inspiration, infallibility, and authority of Scripture. In Frame, all apologetics must demonstrate pistil reliance on Scripture, and any proofs of the faith must be in service to that final authority.

As we might expect by now, Frame's apologetics is also perspectivally related. He speaks of apologetics as proof, defense, and offense—all of which correlate with CAP.[64] Securing a win in the internecine battles over which specific apologetic strategy best honors the Lord is not Frame's concern. I will discuss this penchant under the chapter on apologetics. What is far more important to Frame is that every Christian—from the halls of academe to the farms of Cameroon—recognizes his mandate to practice apologetics as a response to the lordship of Christ. "Our theme verse, 1 Peter 3:15, begins by telling us, 'In your hearts set apart Christ as Lord.' The apologist must be a believer in Christ, committed to the lordship of Christ (cf. Rom. 10:9; 1 Cor. 12:3; Phil. 2:11)."[65] Frame is not saying that "if" we choose to practice apologetics, then we must be committed to Christ's lordship. Lordship is its own justification for apologetics and thus a non-exceptional duty. He in fact criticizes that "Some theologians present apologetics as if it were almost an exception to this commitment."[66]

An important aspect of Frame's apologetic is seen in relationship to the open struggle of postmodern thought to make available a unified elucidation of the universe. For example, in recent times a postmodern apologetic has emerged that claims inspiration from the New Light emphasis of Jonathan Edwards and which professes to bring together the Enlightenment rationale in scientific method and rational empiricism with natural and revealed religion.

In this case, Quantum Spirituality is a hybrid. The “new” New Light emphasis is designed to function as an apologetic, demonstrating to modern people that the church is biblically reformed, yet scientifically, culturally, and philosophically informed in the right ways.[67] In contradistinction to postmodern apologetic solutions (the Quantum system representing one), Frame’s triperspectival apologetics presents us with an organic interpretation of the universe and thus a coherent presentation of the world in which we live.[68] It does so by fully avoiding cross-pollination between Scripture and art nouveau forms of philosophy, theology, and science, while maintaining a close dialogue between Scripture and new developments in philosophy, theology, and science.

Relationship of Lordship and Culture

According to H. Richard Niebuhr’s now famous five-tier breakdown of the historic Christian positions on Christ and culture, Frame supports the “Christ, the Transformer of Culture” model. Having researched the other four models Niebuhr covers, Frame claims to have arrived at the fifth position “by process of elimination.”[69] That should not be taken to suggest that Frame is a transformationist because he cannot find a better position among the other four of Niebuhr’s categories. There are positive reasons for his affirmation of the fifth position, all of which are the natural outcome of the larger imperative of lordship.[70] Mainly, he notes a clear corollary between the universal claims of God and our comprehensive response of obedience, such that “[T]he Christian should seek to bring biblical standards to bear in all areas of society and culture.” To be clear, Frame is not advocating for theonomic militancy. His response is missional in nature. As he says, "Our motive is not to try to make non-Christians live the Christian life, but simply to work out the implications of our faith in all areas of life."[71]

While the theologian speaks on culture adjacent to more centralized topics in theology, by accenting God's covenantal lordship in and over the whole world in everything he writes, the matter of culture inexorably comes to light as a prima facie obligation in theology. As a result, readers of his works cannot help but to reflect culturally and to see their own cultural participation as an "ought."

Significance of Lordship Theology as a Whole

American evangelicalism is demonstrating a growing antipathy toward the practice of lordship.[72] The different cultural and religious constituencies that make up our pluralistic culture have worked to create disparity between the public affirmation of Christ as Lord and the lack of empirical proof regarding its evidentiary value in American evangelical life. The challenge has always been to live out in practice what one confesses doxologically. Yet the inherent conflict between belief and its embodiment in action has intensified with the demands and temptations of different cultural and religious pressures that compose our pluralistic American culture, resulting in a deepening of competing loyalties. No doubt, the inclusion of business, psychological, and social theories in the related areas of church growth, evangelism, and missions, beginning in the 1970s, did little to reverse this trend but only hastened the modernization of American evangelical life and the devaluation of lordship values.

Then there is the European scene. There is little question that in the increasingly postmodern—indeed, post-rational—European context, the very thought of a magisterial, personal Lord who evaluates our every move is becoming more and more passé. Certainly, European societies, to one degree or another, continue to demonstrate religious belief. But assent to the claims of a personal Lord is being progressively overshadowed by collective religious interest in the experiential aspects of spirituality, and often without clear definition. James A Reimer addressed this very phenomenon in the form of the rise of non-foundationalism in theology. "What distinguishes the postmodern period from the modern, Enlightenment period (e.g., Kant) is that we have come to recognize that there are numerous rationalities (each one intratextually coherent), and consequently numerous understandings of ethics (virtue, goodness, justice, etc.)."[73] It is no wonder, then, that by the 1970s, M. F. Wiles could speak of the problem of trying to isolate "the beginning" of religious authority."[74]

Gradually more pluralistic, the new cathedrals of Europe are no longer found in massive edifices of theology in art, but in the private world of sibylline mysticism. One thus searches for verification of a point of contact in European social and religious life for the authentication that "Jesus is Lord."

If God's lordship generates deep questions, and even visceral reactions, it also invites theologians to grapple with its import. If taken seriously, it forces one to think through the fundamental questions of life, which include meaning, existence, and salvation. How one comprehends the nature of God, and the world in which one lives, is fundamentally affected by one's response to God's lordship. Frame has dedicated his life's work to grappling with, deciphering, and applying the all-importance of God's lordship to the various forms of human existence. This integration is most evident in Frame's work in the aforementioned areas of ethics, apologetics, and culture.

An introduction of Frame's lordship theology could very well provide a fresh assessment of theology, one in which even competing interests in Western theology can find renewed inspiration. On one hand, Frame reaffirms the archetypal structure of theology, which enabled medieval thought to create a basis for Christendom and for the Reformers to speak of Christianity as embracing the whole of life. Yet similar to Kant, his lordship criterion limits reason, reminding us that all knowledge of God is "creaturely." But *contra* Kant, Frame presents us with a unified worldview that is able to dialogue with science and culture, without leaving the realm of faith to enter the phenomenal—thus demonstrating the applicability of faith to the concrete processes of our living environment. Like the Neo-Orthodox theologians, he affirms the high role of Scripture, but unlike them he is not burdened by a philosophical view of God's transcendence that is sometimes at odds with Scripture and with God's immanence. So Frame's theology shows us the linkage between God's transcendence and our need to live culturally.

Further still, Frame's historical position is like Pannenberg and Moltmann on one level only: it is proleptical. Yet whereas these men sacrificed God's transcendence and his acts in history for the vindication of faith at the end of history, Frame maintains both emphases, creating much needed balance between the two.[75] Frame's consistent obsequiousness to God's lordship in the processes of history provides us with a proleptical view of history, in which history is not a mere hopeful event but a descriptive event that anticipates a coming reality. In all, I believe that to the extent people are exposed to Frame's theology, they will find in it a treatment of Christianity that is rigorous in theory, yet consistent and practical. It may be an important step toward furthering the return of Christian theology from the edges of marginalization to a central and high role.

The remaining chapters of this book develop more thoroughly the subthemes of Frame's ethics, apologetics, and theology of culture outlined in this introductory compendium. However, looking into these topics requires more than further explication; it also requires interrogative interaction. So the next chapter will provide a biblical-theological evaluation of the Framian idea of lordship. This will be accomplished in dialogue with the eminent Dutch theologian Abraham van de Beek. Here the specific question to be addressed is, "How do Framian perspectivalism and his concept of lordship connect and contrast with the Western European, systematic-theological concepts of Abraham van de Beek and his particular theology of the cross?"

Endnotes

1 *DG*, 21.

2 Ibid., 25.

3 Ibid., 21.

4 Frame provides a deeper word study into the translated name 'Lord' (JHWH, *Adonai, kurios*) in *ST*, p. 25.

5 *DKG*, 12.

6 Ibid. See also John M. Frame, "Covenant and the Unity of Scripture," IIIM Magazine Online 1, no. 6 (April 5 to April 11, 1999); available at the Third Millennium website, http://www.frame-poythress.org/covenant-and-the-unity-of-scripture/; date of access: Aug. 12, 2012. In *ST*, 66–92, Frame offers a perspectival analysis of the covenants of Scripture.

7 *DKG*, 22.

8 *DKG*, 13.

9 *DKG*, 102. Here Frame is dependent on Kline, who notes the parallel import of the creation narrative recorded in Genesis 1 and 2 with the establishment of subsequent covenants. See Meredith G. Kline, *Images of the Spirit* (Grand Rapids, IL: Baker Book House, 1980). However, as will be discussed further in Chapter 5, Frame came to disagree with Kline, largely when Kline changed his views on the meaning of the fourth commandment. The early Kline stressed the call to "rest," thus making worship a subordinate aspect of that rest. Because rest is something one does mainly from cultural activities, the early Kline saw an essential continuity from creation narrative to culture(s) under the other covenants in Scripture. The latter Kline stressed worship as the primary meaning of the fourth commandment, whereby we have no obligation to cease from cultural labors. He thus saw the Sabbath administration in discontinuity from the New Covenant, whereby God does not reinstate the Cultural Mandate of Genesis 1 and 2 to us. So the latter Kline made the general culture, or "non-sacred sphere," free from God's law and lordship. For this difference, cf., Kline, *Images of the Spirit*, with his later *Kingdom Prologue* (1991, privately published), 21–26 especially.

10 *DG*, 34. Further considerations of this idea will be explored in successive chapters, especially as the focus shifts to culture.

11 *DG*, 14.

12 He explains in *DG*, 14.

13 More forthrightly, "Control, authority, personal presence—remember the triad. It will appear often in [*The Doctrine of the Knowledge of God*], for I know of no better way to summarize the biblical concept of divine lordship." *DKG*, 17.

14 *DG*, 41.

15 In the chapter titled, "Images of God," in *DG*, Frame comments that even God's "Names, images, and attributes, then, are perspectivally related: they tell us the same truths about God in different ways." For this reference, see *DG*, 362f.

16 Cf., *DG*, 30, with *Institutes* 1.1.1–3.

17 *De Trinitate*, 5.17.

18 "Yet I would not want to say that lordship is metaphysically central to God's nature in a way that holiness, love, eternity, and righteousness are not." *NOG*, 51.

19 E.g., "God's lordship is grounded in his eternal nature, and therefore in his attributes. God's covenant lordship, as we've seen, is a relationship between God and creatures in history. But his lordship in history should help us understand his lordship in eternity." *DG*, 388. Observe that in the same breath Frame speaks both of lordship as a covenantal attribute in relation to creation and of lordship in eternity (*esse*). So there is a lordship in eternity. If lordship does not exist "in itself," then how can Frame distinguish between covenantal and eternal lordship? The answer, as we continue to read above, seems to be in the revelatory character of Scripture.

20 In an email to the author, dated January 9, 2013.

21 Email to the author, dated January 9, 2013.

22 Frame locates many examples of said imprecise formulations. For example, he claims that "Dooyeweerd says much about God as creator and lawgiver, and as that 'origin' which must be presupposed by all thought . . . Dooyeweerd thinks it is impossible to have any concept of God, since in his view there can be no theoretical knowledge of God and since he regards all concepts as theoretical. The whole idea of 'knowing' God is rather obscure in the Amsterdam philosophy." Frame, *The Amsterdam Philosophy*, 20,http://www.frame-poythress.org/wp-content/uploads/2012/08/FrameJohn AmsterdamPhilosophy1972.pdf; date of access: Nov. 29, 2013. Furthermore, "Dooyeweerd sees the 'central message' of Scripture as having no 'conceptual' content." *CVT*, 375–376. As well, he says that "Dooyeweerd admits that there are 'genuine *conceptual* contents' of God and the human ego, but he insists that these conceptual contents 'do not transcend the modal dimension of our temporal horizon of experience.'" Frame concludes, "What Dooyeweerd seems to be saying is that if anything in Scripture is 'conceptual,' then it describes only the world, not God." *CVT*, 385. More will be stated on the Amsterdam Philosophy in the upcoming chapter on culture.

23 For similar statements of Frame's that theology is the application of Scripture, see *DG*, 7; *DCL*, 9, 33; *DKG*, 81–85; ACT, 23; and *DWG*, 230, 276. I will revisit Frame's point that all theology is application in greater detail in the chapter on ethics.

24 *DWG*, 230.

25 *ACT*, 18.

26 Or, as he says elsewhere, "Remember that ethics, considered broadly, embraces all of theology." *DWG*, 230. The connection of all theology to moral responsibility is enlarged in the chapter on ethics.

27 Ibid., 230.

28 *DWG*, n. 13.

29 For this exposition, see *DG*, 9–11.

30 Ibid., 9.

31 Warfield states, "It is probable that Calvin's greatest contribution to theological science lies in the rich development . . . which he was the first to give—to the doctrine of the work of the Holy Spirit. . . . The *Institutes* is . . . just a treatise on the work of God the Holy Spirit in making God savingly known to sinful man, and bringing sinful man into holy communion with God." Benjamin B. Warfield, "John Calvin the Theologian," in *Calvin and Augustine,* ed. Samuel G. Craig (Phillipsburg, NJ: P&R Publishing Company, 1971), 485–486. For a full treatment of Luther on this point, see Timothy J. Wengert, *The Pastoral Luther: Essays on Martin Luther's Practical Theology* (Grand Rapids, MI: Eerdmans, 2009).

32 *ACT*, 7.

33 Ibid., 8.

34 That provides some insight into why Frame left the Philadelphia campus of Westminster Theological Seminary in 1980 to move to California to help implement his ideas for a new seminary that would provide much more opportunity for integration between academics and church life. His early vision is stated in "Proposal for a New Seminary," at http://www.frame-poythress.org/proposal-for-a-new-seminary/. Frame's ardor for the assimilation of theology with embodied living also explains the motivation behind his writing of *The Academic Captivity of Theology*.

35 This phrase can be found in Steve Brown, "John Frame: The Closet Radical," in *Speaking the Truth in Love: The Theology of John M. Frame*, ed. John J. Hughes (Phillipsburg, NJ: P&R Publishing, 2009), 137. The book is a festschrift in honor of John Frame on his seventieth birthday.

36 That makes Frame's tersely worded book *The Escondido Theology*, which I will engage more fully later, all the more astounding and highlights the extent to which he thinks that most of the faculty at the school have veered from Scripture.

37 *DCL*, 166.

38 *DG,* 195. That does not mean that a triperspectival view of revelation equates the normative perspective with Scripture. "The normative perspective (like the other two perspectives) includes everything, because everything reveals God in one way or another. Scripture is not the same thing as the normative perspective, but it is one object within the normative perspective (and indeed within the other two perspectives as well)." However, "It is the norm that norms other norms, the *norma normans*, the covenant document, etc." Email message to the author, April 2, 2009.

39 For example, R. Scott Clark "Peace (with Evangelicalism) in Our Time," Oct. 7, 2009,http://heidelblog.net/2009/10/subjectivism-and-peace-with-evangelicalism-tim-keller/; date of access: March 4, 2011.

40 An example is Frame's rejoinder to Darryl Hart in "The Regulative Principle: Scripture, Tradition, and Culture: An Email Debate between Darryl Hart and John Frame" (February 1998), http://www.frame-poythress.org/frame_articles/1998HartDebate.htm; date of access: March 4, 2011.

41 Another excellent example of how theology can marry analytical and practical interests, according to a tripartite perspectival model, is offered by Frame's close associate and friend Vern Poythress, *Symphonic Theology: The Validity of Multiple Perspectives in Theology* (Philipsburg, NJ: P&R Publishing, 2001). A more concise formulation of a three-fold perspective on leadership for pastors is offered by Jim Fitzgerald in *Triplex: The Three Faces of Leadership* (Chattanooga, TN: Sunny, 2010).

42 J. Hughes, ed., *Speaking the Truth in Love: The Theology of John M. Frame* (Phillipsburg, NJ: P&R Publishing, 2009), 27.

43 Ibid., 22.

44 The section involving Bavinck is the product of original research and is not found in Frame's "Backgrounds to My Thought."

45 "In the Preface to his *Introductory Volume* published in 1932, Berkhof acknowledged that the general plan was based on the first volume of Bavinck's *Gereformeerde Dogmatiek* and in a few chapters he followed Bavinck's argumentation as well. . . . In his Systematic Theology, Berkhof was only slightly less dependent on Bavinck." Henry Zwaanstra, "Louis Berkhof," in *Reformed Theology in America: A History of Its Modern Development*, ed. David F. Wells (Grand Rapids, MI: Eerdmans, 1985), 166–167.

46 Of course, much has been stated of Van Til's attraction to Idealism. J. Oliver Buswell went so far as to charge Van Til with being "deeply mired in Hegelian idealistic pantheism." J. Oliver Buswell, "The Fountainhead of Presuppositionalism." *The Bible Today* 42, no. 2 (1948): 48. Van Til did read Hegel and was in correspondence with idealistic Francis Herbert Bradley, Bernard Bosanquet, and Andrew Seth Pringle-Pattison. However, that connection to Idealism is unfairly overstated with respect to the intellectual context out of which Van Til worked. A representative exposition critical of Van Til's adherence to Idealism is Timothy I. McConnell, "The Influence of Idealism on the Apologetics of Cornelius Van Til," *JETS* 48, no. 3 (September 2005): 557–588.

47 H. Bavinck, *Reformed Dogmatics*, vol. 2, ed. J. Bolt (Grand Rapids, MI: Baker Academic, 2004), 28. Frame is right to point out, however, that Bavinck was somewhat unclear on the nature of analogical knowledge. "[Bavinck] says, 'There is no knowledge of God as he is in himself,' but on page 337 of *Doctrine of God* he announces, 'Thus far we have dealt with God's being as it exists in itself.'" *DKG*, 32.

48 The heart of this discussion is in *DKG*, 18–40, esp. 36–37.

49 Ibid., 37. The paraphrase is of a statement in Murray's unpublished "Lectures on the Doctrine of God." Just one of Frame's central concerns with Van Til's teaching on analogical knowledge hinges on the nature of Van Til's philosophical language to describe what he means by "analogical." Frame typically characterizes that language as "ambiguous." *DKG*, n. 34.

50 The whole schematic can be found in Van Til's *Introduction to Systematic Theology*, 64–65.

51 *CVT*, n. 21.

52 H. Bavinck, *Reformed Dogmatics*, vol. 2, ed. J. Bolt (Grand Rapids, MI: Baker Academic, 2004), 605.

53 C. Van Til, *Common Grace and the Gospel* (Phillipsburg: NJ: P&R Publishing, 1972). Citing Jochem Douma, *Algemene Genade* (Goes: Oosterbaan & Le Cointre, 1966), 305.

54 In Bavinck's address on common grace given in 1888 at the Kampen Theological School. Op. cit., Herman Bavinck, "Common Grace," trans. Raymond Van Leeuwen, *Calvin Theological Journal* 24 (1989): 59–60, 61. One writer is convinced that the "grace restores nature" motif in Bavinck has been overstated and misinterpreted. See Jon Stanley, "Restoration and Renewal: The Nature of Grace in the Theology of Herman Bavinck," in *the Kuyper Center Review*, vol. 2 (Grand Rapids, MI: Eerdmans, 2011), 81–104.

55 *DCL*, 606.

56 H. Bavinck, *Reformed Dogmatics*, vol. 2, ed. J. Bolt (Grand Rapids, MI: Baker Academic, 2004), 404.

57 Cornelius Van Til, *Common Grace and the Gospel* (Phillipsburg, NJ: P&R Publishing, 1972). http://presupp101.files.wordpress.com/2011/08/van-til-common-grace-and-the-gospel.pdf; date of access: Jan. 17, 2013. By *nebenzweck*, we are not to infer from Kuyper that the state is to function according to natural law only. He believed that the state, like the Church, is subservient to the word of God. This point will be documented in the area on culture.

58 H. Bavinck, *Reformed Dogmatics*, vol. 2, ed. J. Bolt (Grand Rapids, MI: Baker Academic, 2004), 30.

59 *DG*, 480–481.

60 Ibid., 114.

61 For Frame's fuller discussion on this topic, see *DCL*, 899. On page 858 of *DCL*, he makes a very helpful and similar point regarding the totalitarian nature of world religions.

62 A full treatment of the three perspectives is found in *DCL*, 131–360.

63 Some explanation of apologetics is needed with regard to historical theology. In older theology, it was common to speak of the discipline of elenctics as a subdivision of practical theology. In J. H. Bavinck, apologetics has more to do with addressing problems (what today we commonly call the *classical* defense of the faith), while elenctics engages the person directly. In the latter case, the twin ideas of *convicting* of sin and *convincing* a person of his need for relief from its guilt, shame, and dominion are dominant. The process seeks not only to make the skeptic the defendant but also to bring to him to the awareness that he has been his own prosecutor all along. It is in this way that Paul accentuates the accusatory work of the human conscience before the Law: ". . . in that they show the work of the Law written in their hearts, their conscience bearing witness and their thoughts alternately accusing or else defending them" (Romans 2:15). Following John 16:8, Bavinck readily admits that only the Holy Spirit can convict and convince men. See Johan Herman Bavinck, *An Introduction to the Science of Missions*, trans. David, H. Freeman (Phillipsburg: NJ: P&R Publishing Company, 1960), 221. In

contemporary theology, *apologetics* has become a global term that now takes in the older division between apologetics and elenctics. What used to be called apologetics is now considered the realm of classical evidentialism, while elenctics has been subsumed under an enlarged understanding of apologetics with its schools of thought.

64 The perspectival nature of apologetics is addressed in *AGG*, 3.

65 Ibid., 3–4.

66 Ibid., 4.

67 The case for this new form of apologetic is made by Leonard I. Sweet, *Quantum Spirituality: A Postmodern Apologetic* (Trotwood, OH: United Theological Seminary, 1991).

68 For a detailed examination of Frame's thinking on worldview, or metaphysics, as he calls it, see *AGG*, 34f.

69 *DCL*, 874.

70 A succinct presentation of these reasons is found in "In Defense of Christian Activism," ibid., 943–950.

71 Ibid., 973.

72 John MacArthur made this point well when he said that the effects of modernist theologies "have introduced into the churches a theology of pragmatism and a spirit of worldliness that left unchecked will eventually reap the same bitter harvest as the modernism of a hundred years ago." John MacArthur, *Ashamed of the Gospel: When the Church Becomes Like the World* (Wheaton, IL: Crossway Books, 1993), 37. See also this author's book on the dissolution of American evangelicalism, *My Almost for His Highest* (Eugene, OR: Wipf and Stock Publishers, 2010).

73 J. Reimer, *Paul Tillich: Theologian of Nature, Culture and Politics* (Munster, Germany: Lit Verlag, 2004), 168. For an excellent discussion on new experiential directions in theology, one stemming from Tillich, the other from Barth, see Terry D. Cooper, *Paul Tillich and Psychology: Historic and Contemporary Explorations in Theology, Psychotherapy, and Ethics* (Macon, GA: Mercer University Press, 1996), especially 195–197.

74 See M. F. Wiles, "Religious Authority and Divine Action," *Religious Studies* 7 (1971): 1–12.

75 Pannenberg sees history as a gradual process of revelation of divine reality. See Wolfhart Pannenberg, *Revelation as History* (London: Sheed and Ward, 1969), especially 16. A factor that motivates him to think this way is to argue for a definitive *kerygma* does not permit questioning of that reality. Idem., 66. In Moltmann, God and history exist in a dialectical relationship. That relationship, Moltmann thinks, rids Christianity of all prejudice about God that has plagued the churches. See Jürgen Moltmann, *Theology of Hope: On the Ground and Implications of a Christian Eschatology* (New York: Harper, 1967), especially 107.

Chapter 2

Lordship Theology: A Study in Contrasts

In its philosophical and mundane manifestations, the West is home to an overall culture of melancholy, despair, and self-criticism. So Robert B. Pippen, singling out present-day Western culture—Europe, in particular—can observe that "Everywhere the images have been and are the images of death and loss and failure, and the language is the language of anxiety, unease, and mourning."[1] In theology, Jürgen Moltmann attempted a complete repositioning of the answer to human alienation. His *Theology of Hope* admits no hope for the present, only discontentment. "A proper theology would therefore have to be constructed in the light of its future goal. Eschatology should not be its end, but its beginning."[2] Following theologians such as Moltmann, the post-structuralist Christian philosopher Paul Ricoeur sees in the biblical witness the promise of the restoration of present evil and gloom. But it is only a promise. Despair over evil portends a promise of the reconciliation that is "not yet." In this light, the only viable alternative is to await the promise of freedom from evil.[3]

Wrestling with the conditions leading to the possibility of hope remains a dominant force in Western theology. There are two sides to this observation. Not only is despair an important point of entry into theology, but also the inability to reconcile despair with the *kerygma* continues to configure theology. This is problematic, for it makes much modern theology rife with the very problem it seeks to alleviate. If Protestant theology still sees its mission as exploring and elucidating the conditions for hope realized, and Westerners are interested in that explanation, then we must do better than tell people to muster "the courage to be." The need of the hour is to call people to "a living hope through the resurrection of Jesus Christ from the dead" (1 Peter 1:3).

It is with these thoughts in mind that a model of theology and of ministry that can help achieve this end will be further explored. As has been verified, a major point of emphasis in the theology of John Frame is that his work is thoroughly "practical." However, a principle feature of that practicality has not received appropriate attention by other scholars. It is hope. That is unfortunate, in light of a world that is struggling in various ways to set itself free from the bonds of despair. Thus, as a first step toward answering the main question of this book, "What does 'lordship' mean in the theology of John M. Frame?" this chapter will present an evaluation of key areas of Frame's theology, in order to show its relevance for "a living hope."

The chosen interlocutor for this evaluation is Abraham van de Beek, former professor of Systematic theology at the Free University of Amsterdam. He is the choice for the reason that his Christology, especially, is shaped by *immedicabile vulnus* ("an irreparable injury")—that dark, wounded presence, which in his view will be remedied only at the *eschaton*.[4] The comparison is also important for the more general reason that it provides the opportunity to *test* Frame's view of lordship in the context of careful theological analysis.

To clarify the foregoing, the question this specific chapter raises and that will serve to elucidate the main research question of this book is, "How do Framian perspectivalism and his concept of lordship connect to and contrast with the Western European, systematic/theological concept of Abraham van de Beek and his particular theology of the cross?"

General Observations

There is an important area of continuity between the two men. Van de Beek is much like Frame, inasmuch as the two share a similar starting point. Both approach theology by reversing traditionally held theological categories. As established beforehand, by stressing God as Lord of the covenant, Frame begins theological reflection, not in the abstract, but in the concrete realm.[5] Van de Beek takes as his point of origin the concrete realm as well, but differently. His approach to dogmatics begins with Christology, the incarnate Lord, not the doctrine of God or the doctrine of Holy Scripture. This is because "Jesus is the revelation of God. He is God's son, God's representative, he makes God's will known to us, he is the human being God intended us to be."[6] Thus, according to Van de Beek, we cannot write about God until we have first addressed Christology.

There are also important areas of discontinuity between the two thinkers. These disassociations accentuate Van de Beek's contribution to the enduring theological crisis rooted in despair. It can first be seen in the structure of Van de Beek's *theologia crucis* (theology of the cross).[7] The distilled essence of Van de Beek's position is this: We are sinners. Sin has created guilt and forlornness. This is our state. Sin is not principally against God but mainly everything evil that we do to one another. God's response is to reveal Godself in Jesus.[8] Jesus comes to participate, or to partake in, our grave existence. The cross is God's primary way of participating in our suffering. There, Christ did not so much remove our guilt before God as he took on himself our guilt for the evil we have perpetrated against others. His taking of our guilt is central to the state of his suffering. Because Jesus' participation is for all humankind, his cross has universal import: it is non-exclusionary. Our response to Jesus is faith in him and to participate or partake in the suffering of others.

Prompted by the writing of Irenaeus, he notes that the total human race is lost.[9] We are thus suffering a "forlorn existence."[10] Therefore, "In order to heed the liberating message of the incarnate Word of God, we must first become aware of our forlornness and disorientation."[11] Once we are aware of "our forlornness and disorientation," the question can be asked, what then is the essential import of the "liberating message" of the Son of God? In effect, we are liberated to share in the sufferings of Christ, to walk the long, hard road to Jerusalem each day.

Theology from Below

By way of critique, however, the problem of evil comes into view, seemingly hindering Van de Beek from embracing Easter Day as vigorously as he embraces Good Friday. Perhaps the most gloomy and dispirited section of *Jesus Kyrios* is found in his response to evangelicals who believe that God answers prayer in "factual salvation history."[12]

> However, [evangelicals] think that God's intervention can be positively identified as factual salvation history. This I do not believe . . . Prayers are rarely answered and Christians rarely become active and selfless servants of humanity. And God did not save the very people who cried out for the Lord God to intervene or offer a helping hand. Just as I say to Bultmann: "God can indeed intervene," I have to say to the evangelicals, "but he doesn't" (or maybe especially to the

> latter less specifically: "but all we can do is to keep asking the question in the margins of our existence)."[13]

Wanting to avoid gross characterization of this select quote, I cannot refrain from noting that Gericault's *The Raft of the Medusa* could not portray better the continuing wonted mood of estrangement in Western society. The call to live as Christians "in the margins of our existence" might well be typified as a "theology from below." This is not to be confused with the "Christology from below," as developed by Wolfhart Pannenberg, in which he derives his dogmatic claims from a critical examination of the life and particularly the resurrection of Jesus of Nazareth, and his programmatic statement of the notion of "History as Revelation."[14] By "theology from below," I mean a relatively *indirect* knowledge of Jesus and his cross via the wretched condition of the world.

Van de Beek balances his dispirited Christology with the eschatological promise of the future when Christ returns and restores justice. But until then, God is *not* at work in history. Similar to Moltmann and Ricoeur, there is no "semi" eschatological age moving toward fulfillment, only the silent waiting for the dawn in the darkness of affliction and oppression. His pietism is also quite adverse to Frame's transformational view of culture (which will figure prominently in the chapters on culture). Although Van de Beek can enlist the language of "kingship," it is only as a prophetic marker of the Day. Frame's "lordship" is a surmounting power in the present age.

Theology from Above

Balanced against Van de Beek's *theologia crucis*, Frame's starting point is a broader program by which the lordship of God is the overarching theme for all theological discussion, including the person of Jesus. Within this expansive syllabus, Frame is especially concerned to begin his lordship theology with the *actio Dei* ("acts of God") in covenant relationship with people. For Frame, the Lord is always *Lord of the covenant.* Since God is the One who initiates the covenants as revealed in Scripture, Frame's theological point of departure can be called a "theology from above." The question that comes to mind is how can this description of Frame's theology be warranted? Three answers can be given, which interconnect with the lordship principle of control, authority, and presence (CAP).

First, the description finds warrant in Frame's own writings. Although he recognizes that Reformed theologians typically begin their discussion of God with subjects focusing on his transcendence, such as the incommunicable attributes, Frame begins with God's *presence.* More specifically, the covenantal acts of God in history. He does so anticipating the charge that his is a theology from below. Some of this is repeated from Chapter 1, however: (1) He notes the biblical pattern that reveals God's nature in his acts via his covenants. (2) As a teacher, Frame is intently concerned that theology is not merely for seminarians and those with philosophical training and interests, but for the general public. He also believes that the initiation of theology from the concrete acts of God is more comprehensible and appealing to the general audience.[15] (3) Frame believes that God's ethical qualities, such as his love, mercy, and justice, are no less important than his immensity eternity, and simplicity, but also that the texts of Scripture that do the most to describe God do so in concrete, ethical terms. (4) Following Calvin, he believes that one cannot even understand Scripture without understanding the world and the self to which it applies.[16]

Second, Frame's is a theology from above, insofar as the central motif of lordship theology, *Lord*, is a personal name that connotes a tangible person. If by Frame's covenantal context we can speak of a form of biblical subjectivism, Christ is not a projection of emotion, only proximate. It is through the media of revelation that we learn that Jesus is a person who desires intimacy with us. Again, God's *presence* is paramount here. The Lord in fact lays before us the urgency to enter into a redemptive bond with him. "The Bible, then, is the story of how God seeks these people (John 4:23), to make then his Son's prized possession."[17]

Herein is hope. God of the covenant is a loving, personal being who sets blessings and curses before us and who is involved in the day-to-day working out of these twin covenantal aspects for our good. As a loving father, God leads his children through the wilderness with a pillar of fire by night and a cloud by day and causes water to flow from a rock because he sees their thirst. It is Jesus who looks with compassion at thirsty people who have been following Him for many miles. He is the God who cries over Lazarus. Nonetheless, his love for us is not to be tested. He is a jealous God. Thus, according to his *control*, He floods the world, opens the earth to swallow the disobedient, and removes Ananias and Saphira for lying to the Holy Spirit. But this is no different than any person with whom we experience a dynamic relationship. The difference is that Jesus is Lord. And he is not one from among us.

Third, the structure of the Framian lordship theology discloses a theology from above as it is dependent first and foremost on *revealed* truth. God speaks with all *authority*. Thus, all that the theologian intimates about the *actio Dei* is based in the objective revelation of God in nature and in Scripture. For "Anyone who seeks to validate a theological idea must be willing to show where his idea comes from in Scripture."[18] When Frame says he makes no "pretense of religious neutrality," he is affirming the Bible as his authoritative *inceptum* for all of his theological deliberation. Interacting with Meredith Kline's explication of the literary form in the Decalogue (Exod. 20:1–17), in which he identifies the Book of Deuteronomy as a whole as a suzerainty treaty between Yahweh and Israel, Frame remarks, "The covenant document stands as a witness: not man's fallible witness concerning God, but God's infallible witness *against* his disobedient people (Duet. 31:26). The emphasis is on the divine authority of the document."[19] As well, there is an *existential* perspective to revealed truth in Frame. The covenantal God loves us so that "Another expression in Scripture that shows the deep penetrations of God's revelation into our being is the writing of God's word on our hearts."[20] That God wills to reside in our hearts inspires the type of hope so lacking in Van de Beek's theology of the cross.

Scripture's Role in the Debate

Were our hypothetical conversation to continue, Van de Beek would undoubtedly note to Frame that the New Testament authors are not God's spokesmen, but "stand between Jesus and us."[21] Although he rejects the authority of individual Bible passages, Van de Beek does manage to find a basis for a common Christian confession. He locates this common confession in the unity of affirmation on the part of the apostles and the most important creedal documents of the first-century Church. By placing the locus of authority in the creeds and confessions of historic Christendom, he attempts to secure a "middle way" between fundamentalist hermeneutics, resulting in what some have despairingly called "biblicism," on one hand, and liberal, textual criticism, on the other, much like that attempted by George A. Lindbeck.[22] The basis for dogmatics, then, is "the whole of the tradition" or what Van de Beek calls the "mosaic" of the Bible.[23] Were Luther present in this discussion, he would most certainly contest the view that individual texts lack authoritative and interpretive power. He said, *"Sui ipsius interpres"* ("Scripture is its own expositor").

How might Frame reply to Van de Beek? Frame also rejects "biblicism" but *only* if its representatives insist on certain *limiting criteria.*[24] However, like Luther, Frame would defend the divine inspiration of the Bible and the essentiality of *individual* Bible passages and verses in the work of theology, not just the "mosaic of the New Testament." The coordination in lordship of *authority* and Scripture is again present in Frame, as he, in fact, exploits Luther's jargon to say,

> Hence *Scriptura ipsius interpres.* This demands attention to contexts, narrow and remote. For an interpretation falsified by a relevant context is not an interpretation of *Scriptura.* Interpretations must also be consistent with what we know about the literary genres and historical backgrounds of the texts under consideration. . . . But for all this attention to contexts both scriptural and extrascriptural, *sola Scriptura* also demands that theological proposals be accountable to Scripture in a specific way. It is not enough for theologians to claim that an idea is biblical; they must be prepared to show in Scripture where that idea can be found.[25]

How might the question of Scripture's authority be settled? The self-authentication of Scripture as God's word ought to have a revered place in any discussion of this nature. On this subject, John is clear that the seven letters to the churches are written by Jesus Christ (Revelation 2–3). And Paul is protective that his transmittal of the gospel is fully Scripture. "For I would have you know, brethren, that the gospel which was preached by me is not according to man. For I neither received it from man, nor was I taught it, but I received it through a revelation of Jesus Christ" (Gal. 1:11–12). Elsewhere, Paul indicates, "All scripture is given by inspiration of God" (2 Timothy 3:16; Gk., *theopneustos*, "God-breathed"). The Pauline definition of Scripture as *theopneustos* strongly affirms that we hardly need to "make do," as Van de Beek suggests, with the New Testament accounts but are to receive them as God's word. Frame would thus reflect that the question is not as Van de Beek states it, that "we must ask ourselves whether the writers of the New Testament agree with us or not," but whether we agree with them or not.[26]

The Person of Jesus Christ

Who is Jesus to Van de Beek? The answer is endemic to how many other theologians throughout the West articulate the meaning of, and search for, the historical Jesus.

First, he makes clear pronouncements that Jesus is God and also other statements that come very close to this assertion. In defending his reason for not drafting a lengthy prolegomena to *Jesus Kyrios*, he states, "What should be said first, is that God *in Christ* is in our midst."[27] More clearly, he says, "Christ is truly God."[28] "Whether high or low, all christologies say that we know God, in the deepest sense of the word, in Jesus."[29] And, "Christ is truly God. It is the confession of the orthodox faith."[30]

The question is, of course, "On what basis is Jesus God to the scholar?" The basis is the church's confessional documents, that is, *extra scriptura*. With expertise in Patristics, he affirms that "The earliest creedal statements of the church begin, therefore with Christ. They find their center in the phrase 'Jesus is Lord.'"[31] Frame would certainly join the Dutch thinker in the commonly held Christian confession that Jesus is God. He sums up the whole message of redemptive history affirming that "God is Lord'—that is the message of the Old Testament; 'Jesus Christ is Lord'—that is the message of the New."[32] While in agreement on this important point, Van de Beek is not prepared to make substantial claims on Christology from the pages of the Old Testament. For he sees "little purpose in traditional reconstructions of the life of Jesus. We cannot go back to realities prior to the New Testament."[33]

Frame's conviction is that of a Christocentric theologian who finds Christ in the Old Testament. The lordship orientation of *control* is obvious in his thought. "He is the Creator, the one in whom all things hold together, supreme over all (Col. 1:15–20). . . . He is the Holy One of Psalms 16:10, who cannot see corruption (Acts 2:27; 13:35). . . . *The Alpha and the Omega, the First and the Last*, and *the Beginning and the End* are also divine titles. . . . But the book of Revelation often applies these phrase to Jesus, even putting them on the lips of the risen Christ himself (see Rev. 1:17–18; 22:13)."[34] So, in Frame, Jesus is more than the *anticipated* God in human form. He *is* God from all eternity.[35]

The division between the two theologians is important for arriving at a demonstrable conclusion on their identification of Jesus of Nazareth. In the case of Van de Beek, the beginnings of Jesus coincide with his birth, and his exaltation occurs as a human being, while Frame's descriptions of Jesus amplify that God became a man in Jesus, who was exalted as the God/man, and who proved his authentic Divinity in his rising from the dead.

Chalcedon

Van de Beek's interaction with Athanasius of Alexandria gives us every reason to believe that he finds the historic position on the dual natures of Christ problematic.[36] That conclusion is reinforced by Van de Beek, "For nature has to do with a concrete person. Besides the notion that there are two natures (for there is truly a God and there are truly human beings) one must at the same time speak about the one nature of Christ, or else Christ is not truly a person. For each person has his or her own character, and thus a particular nature."[37] Van de Beek thus takes from Acts 17:31 that Jesus was a "human being" whom God raised from the dead.[38] Although he intends his interpretation of the verse to underscore Christ's sympathetic oneness with us in his work, I wonder if it does not hint at an underlying "apotheosis of Jesus" in his Christology. I could counter that Lazarus was a human being whom God raised from the dead. Is he God? The scholar indeed appears to deny the full divinity of Jesus. "[Jesus] was born human and not as God. Nonetheless, he was God's presence in our midst. Yet not because of his birth, but because God was completely bound to this human."[39]

To help clarify matters, the original Greek word for "man" in Acts 17:31 is not *anthropos* but *aner*. It is a word used often in Acts to refer to a generic group of men. *Aner* is used a total of ninety-three times in Acts. In this particular case, Paul exploits the word as a means of identification of God in Christ with the men of Athens, in order to say that just as Jesus was raised from the dead, so also will all men be raised and judged in righteousness (Acts 19:30–31). The argument is important for Paul, insofar as the Stoics and the Epicureans denied the resurrection from the dead. Epicurean philosophy, founded by Epicurus, taught that reality is made up of imperishable "atoms," which, when they disintegrate, yield death. Deities were real but were physical like humans, and they had no part in shared human existence and therefore could not liberate people from death. The Stoic philosophy founded by Zeno taught a form of pantheistic monism: God infuses all things as a dynamic principle in nature that is empowered by the cosmic Logos. Man shares in deity for the reason that he is part of the Logos. Moral living is in harmony with nature, and death is simply the end of life, over which neither god nor man has any say.

The Creator-Creature Distinction

Returning to our two dialogists, Frame may possibly augment the conversation by looking to lordship to build on the Creator motif a referent that Christ and man exist on different levels of metaphysical reality. This reply would be especially pertinent to Van de Beek's hesitancy on Chalcedon. For Frame to say that Christ exists on a different plane of reality is to uphold what he, and Van Til before him, calls the "Creator-creature distinction."[40] The distinction emphasizes that reality is not a great "chain of being," as taught by Aristotle, by Plotinus's Neoplatonism, or by Gnosticism (the unknowable One brings about lesser beings by "emanations" as light from a lamp")—all of which assume a continuum of being between the Creator at the top and the material universe below. Frame is defiantly against these and all systems in the whole history of philosophy and theology, for, in his view, they inevitably connect to an unbiblical view of God's transcendence and immanence.[41]

The Van Till-Frame metaphysic, conversely, makes no pretense to degrees of divinity. God is God, and we are not. That the cosmos consists of different levels of metaphysical reality is to say that God is the Lord and the universe serves him. As for the extent of his lordship, "His lordship extends to everything that he has made."[42] With reference to metaphysics, Van Til used to draw his "two circle" analogy on a blackboard before his students at Westminster Theological Seminary (Philadelphia). The upper circle represented God; the lower circle represented the creation, including man. Van Til elicited the circles to stress that the two realms are distinct, not a continuum.

The problem, as Van Til saw it, is that nonbiblical thought is "one-circle" thinking: it places the Creator and the creature on the same level. So, though it is true that man is a being, and God is a being, one is not an extension of the other. Instead, creation is derivative. God is the standard, the prototype of being, not just the top of the ladder of being. God is good, and man, even in his fallen state, exemplifies the qualities of goodness. But man's goodness is that of a creature: never perfect, but always dependent. So we are not *less good* than God. God's goodness is of a *different type* of goodness. God's wisdom, grace, mercy, patience, and so forth, are not just more extensive and deeper than ours, but also different in nature. That we are created in the *imago Dei* does nothing to minimize the metaphysical division. We are made to be like him and to grow in holiness. Indeed, God calls us to love one another as Christ loves us. "But even here the difference is evident: his love is the model and ours is the image. Or, as Abraham Kuyper and Herman Bavinck used to say, God's love is the archetype, and ours is the ectype."[43]

As previously mentioned, the import of the explication of the Creator-creature discussion is vital, as it intersects with Van de Beek's caution on Chalcedon. Both Frame and Van Til believe that the real message of the confession is that even in the person of Christ, where we find the most remarkable level of personal communion between God and man, the Creator-creature distinction remains. For even here, there is no "confusion or change." Contrary to Van de Beek, who believes that the "dual natures" formula is unhelpful to establishing the person of Jesus, Van Til and Frame point out that the genius of Chalcedon is not in its defense of the two natures of Christ, but in that it defends God from being a more advanced man. It stands as a bulwark against any diminution of the Creator-creature distinction. It is in this way that Chalcedon accentuates who Jesus is to Frame.

To the previous discussion can be added precisely why it is that concurrence with the dual natures of Jesus is important. If, as Athanasius rightly insisted, Jesus is the same *homoousios* with the Father and is God, this must be reconciled with Jesus' humanity, as recorded in the New Testament. Chalcedon was aimed at the Nestorian and Eutychean heresies. Nestorianism's error was the failure to unite the two natures in one person.[44] Each nature was thought to represent separate persons in some way possessed by the man, Jesus. Eutycheanism fell on the opposite end of the spectrum. The human nature of Jesus was believed to be subsumed by the divine nature creating a fusion. The solution at Chalcedon was to affirm the unity of Jesus' person and the duality of his natures, and thus his identity with the divine substance. Chalcedon provides a correct conception of Jesus' deity, humanity, the unity of one person, and the distinction of the two natures, in accord with what is being taught in the Bible. Shedd gives emphasis to the magnitude of Chalcedon. "It substantially completes the orthodox Christology of the ancient Church."[45] Van de Beek's aversion to Chalcedon solidifies his problem with Jesus' identity with the divine substance.[46]

Redemption[47]

What has Jesus done for us? This practical question is pivotal in soteriology and, again I think, has immense meaning for the state of forlornness that is the mark of the present-day Western world. Christ and his redemption are the main themes of Scripture, so if I were writing a complete systematic theology, it would necessarily need to deal in a thorough manner with the Incarnation, the Atonement, the Resurrection, and the *ordo salutis*. Since this is not the purpose of the present volume, I will proceed no further than to connect and contrast only a few areas in the doctrine of redemption via our imaginary tête-à-tête.

The Substitutionary Atonement

First of all, both men agree that all people are sinners.[48] Sin has created guilt and forlornness. This is our state. But second, and dissimilar from Frame, Van de Beek sounds rather guarded about the substitutionary atonement of Jesus. There are two words that stand out in his view of redemption. They are "partakes" and "participates." In a series of quotes, he says that "God partakes of our life and thereby saves us."[49] And that "Human existence is perverted. It is that very existence that God wants to partake in."[50] "In Christ, God took our place in order that we may partake of God's glory."[51] "Because God now participates in our life our life participates in God. Immortality participates in mortal existence and this grants immortality to mortality."[52]

It is surely legitimate to confess that God in Christ does "participate" in our fallen lot. The writer to the Hebrews declares, "Therefore, since the children share in flesh and blood, He Himself likewise also partook [Gk., *metecho*] of the same, that through death He might render powerless him who had the power of death, that is, the devil and might free those who through fear of death were subject to slavery all their lives" (Hebrews 2:14–15). However, even as the scholar is right to discern the activity of God by this biblical metaphor, his redemptive orientation vetoes the express biblical context of atonement for individual sins and the satisfaction of God's justice. Beginning with a call for us "to carefully analyze the motives of the physical doctrine of redemption championed by the Alexandrians (and their spiritual ancestors)," he embarks on a description of the work of Christ that uses familiar language of the atonement but in the end denies it.[53] "The crux of the issue is that Jesus does not ransom individuals from the consequences of their sins but takes upon himself responsibility for that sinfulness."[54] He is saying that by his person and work, Christ did not make payment for sin, but instead assumed the responsibility for humankind's sinfulness—"humankind"—understood in distinction from the individual. He supports his refutation of Christ's intercessory payment for the actual sins of individual people, claiming that the Satisfaction Atonement theology of Anselm must "be read against the backdrop of Roman law."[55]

Since *metecho* is part of the biblical language, Frame would concur with Van de Beek that Christ "partakes" or "participates" in our sorrow and forlornness. Frame, all the same, would most certainly be firm before Van de Beek that this participation is of the nature of sacrificial atonement for individuals.[56] Frame has no reticence about the substitutionary atonement of Christ; that his cross was the singular point in history when God interceded on the behalf of his people, the sum of which is God's glorious Church.[57]

Moreover, per Frame, the intercessory work of Christ, like all things, finds its place in the larger context of lordship theology. Even Good Friday is shaped by the Creator-creature distinction (two realities). God did not need to redeem us any more than he needed to create the world. We have no right to claim redemption; we have no claim on God. God's essential attributes are necessary, but his eternal decrees and saving acts of creation, providence, and redemption are not; they are *free*. But free, not in the compatibilist sense or in a libertine sense, "but in the sense that we know nothing in God's nature that constrains these acts of perverts their opposites."[58] The Creator-creature distinction is at one with Frame's lordship triad of CAP. By God's *control*, he determines if he will love creatures and to whom he will show his saving love and blessings. By his *authority* he defines what love is and also what redemption means. By that same authority, he supernaturally and providentially arranges the situations leading to each person's regeneration and conversion. And by his *presence*, he enters our lives, changes our dead spiritual hearts, and gives us hearts of flesh, and he begins to conform us to his Image.

By way of additional interpolation, Van de Beek's idea that Christ assumed our responsibility for our treachery against the throne of God is true in part, as would be the case for anyone who intercedes on behalf of another to take his or her punishment. But is it fair to speak so narrowly of Jesus assuming our responsibility minus any recourse to his propitiatory payment without undercutting the requisite value of his assuming our responsibility? I could argue that assumed responsibility is all that God requires of man, but what value does this place on God's justice in the light of sin? For one to take responsibility for the acts of another places one in the precarious position of having to make good before the offended party. If God sees no need for sinners to provide some form of remedy for the offenses they have committed against him, then on what basis does he hold them responsible, other than the standard of justice?[59] Therefore, it can be concluded that assumed responsibility must involve atonement as a precondition for salvation and reconciliation with God.

The "Satisfaction" Theory in Historical Theology

Van de Beek is quite right, however, to point out that the soteriological concept of satisfaction, though traced to the writings of Tertullian, Cyprian, and Augustine, received its true refinement by the theological prowess of Anselm. The effect of this has carried over to our day, whereby the perspective of redemption as satisfaction is now a central motif in the mainstream discussion on atonement. Trevor Hart has added to the discussion important background information.[60] He points out that Anselm's development of the metaphor of satisfaction takes from the Old Testament language of sin and estrangement, which is the result of the breakage of covenantal life, and fine-tunes it with the feudal medieval social structure. Hart goes on to explain the natural outcome of the failure to comply: some form of reparation must be enacted by the overlord, and if this is not forthcoming, then punitive action is soon to follow.

It ought nonetheless to be observed that although the word *satisfaction* is not noticeably expressed in the Bible as an action performed by Christ, and although it is true that Anselm looked to extra-biblical ideas in expressing his views on it, the doctrine is still fully present in the Bible. In other words, that Anselm advanced the discussion on satisfaction does not mean he invented it. It is found in Scripture.[61] What Christ has suffered in the stead of sinners is what we call satisfaction, and this is amply declared in the Bible, where we are reminded of the demands of the Law, and that the sacrifice of Christ, being of the nature of a sweet-smelling savor to God, did what the sacrifices under the Law could not do, but only bring to remembrance our sins year after year (Hebrews 10:1–3). But by the perfect, once-for-all sacrifice of Christ, sin is put away forever (10:10). Numerous other texts use terms and phrases that capture the idea of satisfaction, such as *reconciliation* (Roman 5:10), *atonement* (Numbers 35:50, Romans 5:11), *propitiation* (Romans 3:25, 1 John 4:10), and *expiation* (Numbers 35:33).

The Question of the "Dominion" of Sin

Associated with the words *partake* and *participate*, Van de Beek employs the word *bear* and its derivatives. What exactly did the person of the Logos bear? He bore humanity's *guilt*. However, it is also right to say that he released people from the *dominion of sin*, not merely from their guilt. This aspect is not completely missing from Van de Beek's Christology. He observes, "When Paul speaks about the power of sin and the body of the death to which we are subjected, there is deliverance by Jesus Christ, our Lord (Rom. 7:25)."[62] But the deliverance of which he speaks is mainly situated in, and has meaning for, the horizontal plane of social justice. This narrower, social conception is contrasted with the broader lordship paradigm of Frame that holds out promise for individual redemption first and social transformation second. In Frame, then, Jesus died not only to free a corporate body of individuals from the *guilt* of sin, but also from its *dominion*. Far from understanding this later concept as a late ecumenical contribution to Christology, Frame says that "Sin does remain in the believers, not to be wholly eradicated until the return of Christ. But the dominion of sin is gone forever (Rom. 6:14)."[63]

How does all of this connect us with hope? Unless God destroys the dominion of sin in the human heart that holds people in captivity, sanctification is impossible. During the early nineteenth-century, Robert Haldane (1764–1842) began teaching at Geneva. He introduced the idea that said, Yes, Christ died for sins, but the effect of it in our lives is that we have died only to the guilt of sin.[64] It is a beautiful aspect that Christ died so we can be free from guilt. But if that is all his work means, then let us join with Paul's facetious statement, "Let us eat and drink, for tomorrow we die." If all a child knows is that his guilt is removed, then what sense does it make to discipline him?

In John Bunyan's *Pilgrims' Progress*, Prudence asks Christian,

> "Do you not think sometimes of the Country from whence you came?"

Christian responds,

> "Yes, but with much shame and detestation: Truly if I had been mindful of that country from whence I came out, I might have had opportunity to have returned; but now I desire a better Country, that is, an Heavenly."

Prudence is always a lure to the former life, but Christ has delivered us from its power and dominion. We struggle with sin, as Paul notes in Romans 6–8, for there remains an "indwelling sin." But this is radically different from the dominion of sin under which we were held captive. In sin, the disposition of the *old man* with his lusts and appetites is directed away from God. He can do nothing less. Romans 1–3 describes this disposition in great detail.

Who can kill the power of sin? We should love the idea that Jesus takes our guilt. But being united with Christ in his death and resurrection, we also know that he killed our old heart. We now have a new citizenship. If I change my citizenship from the United States to Great Britain and later I receive a tax bill from the American Internal Revenue Service, I can write back and say, "I am no longer under your control. Now I am subservient to the British Crown." The forlorn Westerner can thus say to depression, anxiety, and anguish, "I am no longer under your control. I have a new Master—one who provides me hope, truth, and a yoke that is light." Furthermore, just as the old master dominated my appetites for sin, so now my new Master, Christ, has given me new appetites for holiness (Romans 6:1–7). Because we are united with Christ in his death (and resurrection), the dominion of sin is destroyed whereby we receive his power and thus a new desire, a new propensity to live a new life of hope and victory over despair and forlornness, and the promise of everlasting life, rather than a future in an eternal hell.

Suffering and History

Significant areas in redemption have been examined. Redemptive history is a subset of history. So the present discussion is asking the reader to consider a broader set of criteria, in addition to God's work in redemptive history. The concern here is not a chronology of a particular people, country, period, or person, but with a *theological interpretation* of history. Though far too concise to do full justice to the subject, the following will seek to decipher the theological point of departure and major conclusions Frame and Van de Beek arrive at in their theological interpretations of history. Moreover, the focus will be on a specific issue within the theological interpretation of history: God's relationship to suffering. One might wonder why, then, this section is not titled "Suffering." It is titled "Suffering and History" for the reason that suffering does not happen in a vacuum but in real time: real history. Suffering raises serious questions about God's sovereignty over the processes of history. The two ideas are inseparable.

The Problem of Evil

In his work *Why? Suffering, Guilt, and God*, Van de Beek sets the stage for his own answer to the existence of suffering or, more generally, the problem of evil, by first adducing his perception of the theological tension between God's omnipotence and God's goodness. If God is fully omnipotent, then does this not suggest that he is the cause of all evil and suffering? And what are the implications of this view? Alternatively, if God is good, is suffering not against his will? And what are the implications of this view?

Change in God

Van de Beek's fundamental position respective of the problem of evil is that God is changeable. He assents to the proposition that unless we pose God's omnipotence and goodness in a "timeless juxtaposition," we are left with abstract concepts relative to the problem of suffering and no real way to rectify the two. But once we introduce the idea of *progressive history*, an ingenerate solution exposes itself. For then God can change in his being. He elaborates,

> Like all other attributes, "omnipotence" and "goodness" belong essentially to the way in which God relates to the world. In thinking about change in God we are thinking about change in the attributes. . . . Then, "omnipotence" will not always mean the same thing. Today's goodness will be different from that of yesterday. If one drops the third premise, that of the immutability of God, one can no longer speak in such an absolute sense about "*the* omnipotence" or "*th*e goodness" of God, but only about the omnipotence as it was at a given moment or the goodness as it was manifested at a certain time. In other words, one can only read the omnipotence and goodness of God from the revelation of God's omnipotence and goodness in history.[65]

In essence, then, Van de Beek's answer to the problem of suffering is that God's being, his attributes, "change" moment by moment, depending on the historical event or a person's thought, or what he also calls a "zigzag" pattern.[66] What omnipotence or goodness or any of the other attributes of God, for that matter, will look like at a specific moment is determined by the deeds of God *at that moment*.[67] Thus, the *only constant in God is change*. Regulating the consistency of God's deeds is his faithfulness. In the semi-eschatological age, because God is always presented with a set of "possibilities" that would either deter or enhance his faithfulness, he continually "opts" for his people. Even so, at no time during the Old Testament period was the way to Christ an "established road."[68] Then came the moment of supreme choice. Jesus is taken, brutalized, and killed. Will God choose according to his faithfulness yet again? Three days pass. All of heaven is silent. But God, who could not put up with darkness and who said, "Let there be light," is the same who could not put up with the darkness of death in Jesus. So God repents yet again, raising Jesus from the dead, and thus "proves to be the God with a heart, the God who can change his mind."[69] Jesus Christ is God's ultimate choice.[70]

Although Van de Beek claims that God made his ultimate "choice" for the world and for our salvation in Jesus, still the ultimate outcome of history is not assured. History remains "open." History is open because "as long as God continues to act, all sorts of things can happen."[71] If anything, the future history is bleak. Not only can we not escape the fact that most people refuse belief in God, but also "the realization of God's own choices fail to occur and does not even exhibit unambiguous signs on the horizon."[72] Yet again, it is an answer to the problem of evil that only returns us to the bounds of estrangement.

The Perspectival Answer

There are troubling aspects to this dialectical answer for Frame. In a broad sense, Framian perspectivalism is similar to Van de Beek's theological model, in that it seeks to provide equilibrium between God's omnipotence and goodness. Perspectivalism always insists on a view of God's attributes as consistently equalized. That is really to say that triperspectivalism lays before us the idea that God's defining attributes, jointly and severally, unfailingly describe his simple essence. So God *is* love, but God *is* also justice, as well as God *is* wisdom, and so forth. Simultaneously, God is also *all* of his attributes *at once*. Dissimilarly, the IS of "God *is* omnipotent" and "God *is* good," and so on, means that God's essential nature, his characteristics, never change. The perspectival scenario is especially important for the discussion underway, because it is in this fashion that we can speak of God's attributes as *static*. The Lord is the same yesterday, today, and forever. Thus, as shall be demonstrated shortly, Frame can answer the questions raised by suffering without appeal to a third way.

Yet beyond this point, Frame demurs. The proportionality of God's attributes does not permit us to situate one attribute of God—for example, faithfulness—above his other attributes, and from that fundamental attribute deduce the nature of the minor ones. Stated somewhat differently, we cannot set one attribute against another or diminish attributes in order to achieve the higher end of a special attribute. Triperspectivalism is of the nature of theologoumenon, but within the framework of established dogma. The static quality of God's nature, and thus of the equality of all of his attributes, presents a major challenge to the idea that the only thing consistent about God is change, save for the fact that he always remains faithful to his paramount choices.

Indeed, it is not beyond reasonable limits to ask, "What is it about God's faithfulness that demands that it be higher than his grace or omniscience?" Are we on dangerous ground here? For the sake of argument, let us assume that God's faithfulness is the constant that keeps the rest of his attributes in movement. How do we keep God from becoming a servant to his own attribute of faithfulness under the structure of this theology? The Dutch thinker answers that the *potentia absoluta* is limited by *the potentia ordinata*. Who made this choice? God. But when did God make this choice? Was there ever a time when the power of God was total? It had to be for God to be in a position to choose to make his absolute power limited by his ordinate power. But if at some unknown time God did so freely choose to limit his absolute power to his ordinate power, and if Van de Beek is right that *potentia ordinata* represents what we mean by saying, "God can manage all things," then who or what manages the management?[73]

There are serious points here. Has God, in order to make certain that he remains faithful to his choices, purposefully handcuffed himself to the armchair of his ordinate power? And why did God believe this necessary? Does he not trust himself? If not, then what does this say about his faithfulness, even under the constraint of his ordinate power? Moreover, were we to assume that God acts only from the limitations set by his ordinate power, are we at last willing to say that nothing God does appears contradictory to us? And most important, what is a self-limited God? How do we call this God "Lord" in the purest sense? Based on the lordship principle, Frame treats God's attributes as *normative* "for they provide the most literal and detailed descriptions, which necessarily therefore tend to govern our thinking about other kinds of descriptions."[74] He thus asserts that the free reign of God's absolute power, for "Scripture teaches that God's power is not exhausted in history, that God is able to do many things that he does not choose to do."[75] One example of Scripture's teaching Frame uses is Mark 14:36: "Abba, Father," he said, "everything is possible for you. Take this cup from me. Yet not what I will, but what you will."

The Specter of Open Theism

I am dealing with two thoughts: God's being and God's plan relative to the flow of history, with special concentration on the problem of evil. Further discussion on the potentiality of the changeableness of God's being and plan proportionate to history might best be carried out in the context of the contemporary polemic over open theism.

Although the name of Van de Beek is *not* associated within the known circle of proponents of open theism, the contexture of his third way evinces so closely to the modernistic doctrine that the obvious correlations cannot be overlooked. And since Frame is a known as an antagonist of open theism, the potential conversation is far too tempting to pass up. What is open theism? According to Frame, "Open theists teach that God is not above time, that he does not control all of nature and history, that he does not know the future exhaustively, that he sometimes makes mistakes and changes his plans, and therefore that he is in some ways dependent on the world."[76]

Comparison with Clark Pinnock

An important figure in the launch of this idea is Clark Pinnock. Pinnock clarifies what he means by open theism in a way reminiscent of Van de Beek's differentiation between God's omnipotence and goodness.

> Two models of God in particular are the most influential that people commonly carry around in their minds. We may think of God primarily as an aloof monarch, removed from the contingencies of the world, unchangeable in every aspect of being, as an all-determining and irresistible power, aware of everything that will ever happen and never taking risks. Or we may understand God as a caring parent with qualities of love and responsiveness, generosity and sensitivity, openness and vulnerability, a person (rather than a metaphysical principle) who experiences the world, responds to what happens, relates to us and interacts dynamically with humans.[77]

Pinnock advocates the second model, singling it out as open theism. Van de Beek's third way is Pinnock's second way. The difference is that Pinnock is not willing to say that God's being changes to accommodate change in the world; only his decisions change. Van de Beek, as we have seen, is willing to go as far as to say that even God's attributes adjust to historical change.

Frame's response to open theism is based on his view on Lordship and is basically this: God does not change or suffer loss in his essential nature.[78] The divine being is not in any way contingent on changing circumstances in tangible history. God does not depend in any way on the world; the world is wholly dependent on God. There are significant implications of this idea for God's eternal plan. It cannot suffer any defeat. God's plan is rooted in the a priori decision of the eternal Godhead; thus, the plan's validity, maturation through time, and assured objective remain independent of God's observation of history or of human experience. History exists in the mind of God prior to, and independent of, experience. God moves deductively from general law to specific outcome and situations. Open theists and Van de Beek, conversely, ask for a posteriori deciphering of God's being—one that minimizes his Lordship. The principle moves inductively from the changing specifics of historical experience and human thought to construct a general theory of God's being.

Frame on God's Will(s)

In support of the Lord's sovereign dominion, Frame makes many fine distinctions, among which only the more outstanding ones will be covered.

First, Frame distinguishes the Lord's sovereign dominion, according to the decretive will of God and the prescriptive will of God. The decretive, or secret, will of God refers to all of those things God planned to do before the foundations of the world but that he does not reveal to people by way of declaration. The revealed will of God is what God has given us, namely, in the Law and the gospel. In *The Doctrine of God*, Frame discusses the decretive will of God under the lordship principle of God's *control* (the "C" of CAP). God's eternal decrees apply to redemption—that is, to the number of those who are saved (Rom. 9:18)—as well as to his dictates regarding the movements of the kings of the world (Daniel 4:34–35) and to suffering.

God's control furnishes even finer distinctions within his decretive will. His control is over both *general* and *specific* historical events. Generally speaking, Frame is one with the biblical writers who ascribe events in the natural environment directly to God (Ps. 65:9–11; 135:6–7; 147:15–18). Not a microbe of the creation exists in natural autonomy from the Lord. Even events that appear most random and even vicious are under his sovereign control. "What we call 'accidents' come from the Lord (Ex. 21:13; Judg. 9:53; 1 Kings 22:23)."[79] Even so, "God brings about our free decisions."[80] Not a nanosecond of our lives is independent from the Lord God. To introduce even a speck of *interderminancy* into the universe is to topple the sovereignty and immutability of God.[81]

God's *prescriptive* will "involves his valuations, particularly as revealed to us in his Word (his 'precepts'). God's decretive will cannot be successfully opposed; what God has decreed will certainly take place. It is possible; however, for creatures to disobey God's preceptive will and they often do so."[82] Evidently, much suffering is the result of direct disobedience to God's precepts. Summing these thoughts perspectivally, in general, God's decretive will represents his *control*, and his preceptive will denotes his *authority*.

Second, not only does God's preceptive will involve his valuations, the Lord's sovereign dominion over history *prioritizes* what he values. I may speak here of God's *presence*, thus rounding out the lordship attributes.[83] In other words, there are states of affairs that God genuinely values (and therefore desires) but does not bring about. God values/desires a thing but is willing to defer it, due to the higher priority of something else. So, God desires event A to happen but is willing to suspend his desire for the greater good of achieving event B. The suspension of event A is not due to weakness in God; that is, he is unable to achieve event A before reaching event B. Nor does it suggest that he is changing before the ebb and flow of history. Rather, the suspension of event A is a sovereign choice. The goal of this choice assures the prioritization of what God values.

God's prioritization of his values takes into consideration two things. (1) Time. "God also has many desires, variously valued and prioritized. Some he achieves immediately. But since he has created a world in time and has given to that world a history and a goal, some of his desires, by virtue of his own eternal plan, must await the passage of time."[84] (2) God's respect of people's integrity. That is not to say that he respects their libertarian free will and thus must change, as Van de Beek or the open theists suggest. Rather, according to his decretive will, God respects the integrity of each event, person, and thing, as it fits into *his purpose*. For example, God has said that we are to be fruitful and multiply. This is a divine value: what God desires. But God will not permit Joe to have five children if five interferes with God's long-range plan. There are implications here for suffering, insofar as God's broad intentions for history apparently prohibit the blessing of a world existing without any history of evil.[85]

Frame on God Changing

Frame can speak of God changing, however. God's immanence insists that he joins us in looking at his creation *from within*. For example, Frame points to Amos 7:1–6, in which we see God interacting with his people in a way that is analogous to human behavior. In effect, "God with us," the author of history, has written himself into the redemptive drama as the lead, dialoging with other characters as if he were one of us.[86] In contrast, God's atemporal existence never changes. God is open to forgiving Israel through his use of Amos's intercession, but his readiness to forgive is the result of his sovereign and eternal decree, which cannot but bring all things to pass. Frame also discusses divine change as is consistent with *sovereign vulnerability*. He is vulnerable in his personal interactions with his people. Here, he suffers grief (Eph. 4:30). He made himself susceptible unto death (Phil. 2:5–8). And he was distressed (Isa. 63:9).[87] So, then, God is unchanging in his nature and eternal plan, but his relationships with creatures are dynamic—a point of accord between classical theology and open theism.

Frame is unsatisfied with nouveau postulations that submit God's being to the changing currents of history. But he is equally unsatisfied with queries that center on *why* suffering exists in God's world. To ask "why" is never to arrive at a resolution, for we can never fathom the mind of God. And if we think we have, then we have followed the path of least resistance by crafting a god after our own image. The legitimate question for Frame is *how* can God ordain evil and remain true to himself? His solution amounts to two points: one *philosophically analogous* in nature; the other, biblical. Reconsidering a point made earlier that God is the author who has written himself into the play of life, the American thinker finds a way of correlation that provide us with a handle on evil and suffering. God is to evil what Shakespeare is to the death of Duncan.

> . . . as I analyze the language that we typically use in such contexts it seems clear to me that we would not normally say that Shakespeare killed Duncan. Shakespeare writes the murder into the play. But the murder took place in the world

> of the play, not the real world of the author. Macbeth did it, not Shakespeare. We sense the rightness of Macbeth paying for his crimes. But we would certainly consider it very unjust if Shakespeare were tried and put to death for killing Duncan. . . . Thus, "To author evil is to do it. But in saying that God is related to the world as an author to a story, we actually provide a way of seeing that God is not to be blamed for the sin of his creatures."[88]

Like any analogy, once taken to its logical extreme, this one falls short. So Frame finally relies on Scripture's own answer that turns on God's sovereign activity. Taking from Paul, God is not required to offer a defense against charges of injustice and evil, even though he sovereignly causes all things to happen. God is the potter, and we are the clay. God does not feel he needs to provide us with an intellectually satisfying answer to this dilemma, but he has solved the problem of evil *in us* by giving us new *hearts* through the power of his Word.[89]

This chapter began with the notion that Protestant theology must see the present forlornness that circumscribes the West as the "need of the hour." Since it is Frame's belief that all theology is practical, a point to be carefully analyzed when I discuss Framian ethics is what *hope* does God's sovereignty over all of creation, including suffering, offer the forlorn? In Frame, the singular lordship of Christ over all things is the assurance of the final outcome of history. Nothing is left "open." The present and the future are assured. All is an established road. The promise of final consummation is guaranteed by God's decretive will. We hear from Frame.

> Simply put, God's power always accomplishes his purpose. God does not intend to bring about everything he values, but he never fails to bring about what he intends. Creatures may

> oppose him, to be sure, but they cannot prevail. Now we should remember that God decrees, not only the end of history, but also the events of every moment of time. For his own reasons, he has chosen to delay the fulfillment of his intentions for the end of history, and to bring about those intentions through a complicated historical sequence of events. In that sequence, his purposes appear sometimes to suffer defeat, sometimes to achieve victory. But each apparent defeat actually makes his eventual victory all the more glorious. The cross of Jesus is, of course, the chief example of this principle. So God intends not only his ultimate triumph, but also his apparent defeats in history. He intends that history be exactly as it is. Therefore, all his decrees, both those for history and for the consummation of history, always come to pass.[90]

Frame's "complicated historical sequence of events" is much like Van de Beek's "zigzag" path of history. But for Frame, God makes the zigzag happen. God even "intends" his defeats, which include evil in every form. He does so to force history along a preconceived path toward its final outcome. Accordingly, though God's children may suffer persecution and loss in this life, God is in control, causing all things to work together to serve his eternal ends. That the divine scheme appoints even suffering to mediate the flow of history toward its designated end is therefore a powerful antidote to hopelessness and despair, such that "Scripture speaks over and over of God's purpose to glorify himself, to defeat evil, and to redeem a people to give him eternal praise. It presents to us again and again the promise of final consummation."[91] God's sovereign Lordship gives men hope and certainty.

The Coming Pages

We have covered some basic features of Frame's lordship theology in colloquia with the *theologia crucis* of Van de Beek. This hypothetical conversation has been placed in the broader context of the culture of alienation and despair that continues to be eminently noticeable not only in Western cultures, but also in much academic theology that only seems to mimic the crisis. This is evident in the displacement of God's magisterial sovereignty in and over his creation to make room for autonomous freedom, whereby it is said that God has changed or is ever-changing. Frame wants us to see that the gospel is a *chimera* minus God's sovereign being and purpose. Building on that fact, the next chapters focus on what else lordship means in Frame's theology as in the discipline of ethics and, after that, apologetics and culture.

But before we move on, the insight of Frame into the meaning of lordship for a world lost in sin must be internalized to make the connection to the goodness of days the Lord has in store for those who love Him. "A gospel of grace is a gospel of divine sovereignty. That message may be distasteful to modern people, but it is the word of God, and without it we have no hope. Free will leaves us in despair. Only sovereign grace can bring salvation, faith, and hope."[92]

Endnotes

1 R. Pippin, *Modernism as a Philosophical Problem: On the Dissatisfaction of European High Culture* (Hoboken, NJ: Wiley-Blackwell, 1999), xii.

2 J. Moltmann, *Theology of Hope: On the Ground and Implications of a Christian Eschatology* (New York: Harper, 1967), 16.

3 This idea is developed in Paul Ricoeur, *Oneself As Another*, trans. Kathleen Blamey (Chicago: University of Chicago Press, 1992), 24.

4 He also makes a good conversation partner with Frame for Americans doing theology in America because he is published in English and has thus made himself accessible to the English-speaking world. See A. van de Beek, *Jesus Kyrios: Christology as the Heart of Theology*, Studies in Reformed Theology, Supplement 1 (Zoetermeer: Meinema, 2002), and *Why? On Suffering, Guilt, and God* (Grand Rapids, MI: Eerdmans, 1990). Both titles also provide the point of interaction with Van de Beek in this work. A Festschrift written in his honor is also available in English, and several noted American theologians now communicate with him from America. The Festschrift is titled *Stanger and Pilgrims on Earth: Essays in Honour of Abraham van de Beek*, ed. E. van der Borght and P. van Geest (Leiden: Brill, 2011).

5 Frame says that one rationale for beginning theology at the level of God's covenantal relationship with us, rather than with God *in himself*, is because "All of our thought about God, even about his aseity or eternity, should be qualified by our status as covenant servants of God. We never escape the status of servants, even when we studying theology." *DG*, 30.

6 A. Van de Beek, *Jesus Kyrios: Christology as the Heart of Theology*, Studies in Reformed Theology, Supplement 1 (Zoetermeer: Meinema, 2002), 13.

7 *Theologia Crucis* ("theology of the cross") is a term coined by Martin Luther to refer to theology that points to the cross as the only source of knowledge concerning who God is and how God redeems. It is distinguished from the *theologia gloriae* ("theology of glory"), which places greater stress on human abilities and natural reason. Walther von Lowenich has shown that Luther's *theologia crucis* is not a special chapter of his theology but defines his whole theology. See Walter von Loewenich, *Luther's Theologia Crucis* (Belfast, 1976). Also, Alister McGrath, *Luther's Theology of the Cross* (Oxford: Blackwell Publishing, 1990).

8 "Godself" is perhaps better translated from Dutch as "himself."

9 A. Van de Beek, *Jesus Kyrios: Christology as the Heart of Theology*, Studies in Reformed Theology, Supplement 1 (Zoetermeer: Meinema, 2002), 31.

10 Ibid.

11 Ibid., 35.

12 Ibid., 259.

13 Ibid.

14 For more on the general contours of this idea, see Wolfhart Pannenberg, "Christology from Below," in his *Jesus: God and Man* (Philadelphia: Westminster Press, 1968), 34–35.

15 See *DG*, 14.

16 Summarizing why he does not accept the charge of a theology from below, Frame writes, "My intention here is not to develop a 'theology from below' as some contemporary writers understand the phrase. That language indicates a plan of starting with a religiously neutral analysis of the history of Israel and Jesus, in the hope that from that analysis we can derive our Christian theological convictions about God and Christ. On the contrary, my methodology will be governed by God's revelation in Scripture and will thus be 'theology from above,' in the understanding of that phrase. . . . Accordingly, [*The Doctrine of God*] will be a theology from above that sometimes, with biblical precedent, and without any pretense of religious neutrality, begins pedagogically with what is from below." *DG*, 14–15.

17 *ST*, 59.

18 Ibid., 59.

19 J. M. Frame, "Covenant and the Unity of Scripture,' *IIIM Magazine Online* 1, no. 6 (April 5 to April 11, 1999), http://www.frame-poythress.org/covenant-and-the-unity-of-scripture/; date of access: Aug. 12, 2012. Kline's most outstanding work in this area is *The Structure of Biblical Authority*, 2nd ed. (Grand Rapids, MI: Eerdmans, 1972; rev. 1975, 1989). Kline's complete works are at http://meredithkline.com/?page_id=55.

20 *DWG*, 324.

21 A. Van de Beek, *Jesus Kyrios: Christology as the Heart of Theology*, Studies in Reformed Theology, Supplement 1 (Zoetermeer: Meinema, 2002), 115. Van de Beek contextualizes the authority of Scripture in a way reminiscent of Karl Barth. See A. van de Beek, "Scriptural Authority and the Incomprehensibility of God," in *Verbum et Ecclesia* 24: 205. For an excellent treatment of the autopisty of the Bible, see J. Van Genderen and W. H. Velema, *Concise Reformed Dogmatics* (Phillipsburg, NJ: P&R Publishing, 2008), 95.

22 Lindbeck's work is far more nuanced in this regard. With his 1984 work, *The Nature of Doctrine: Religion and Theology in a Postliberal Age*, Lindbeck lays the foundation for a "postliberal theology," in which he attempts to strike a balance between three historic approaches to theology. (1) The *cognitive* or *propositional* aspects of religion that sees religion as a series of propositions and truth claims about objective realities using a cultural-linguistic approach to Christian doctrine. (2) The *experiential-expressive* view that interprets doctrines as non-informative and non-discursive symbols of inner feelings, attitudes, or existential orientations. (3) The view held ecumenically by Roman Catholics, who are inclined to combine the first two emphases. His aim is to forge doctrinal reconciliation among different faith communities through the evolution of doctrine, which he locates in the historic confessions of the Church. He calls his way of conceptualizing religion, and the change he envisions, the "cultural-linguistic" approach, and his view of confessional church doctrine as "regulative" of such change toward the goal of constructive ecumenical discussions.

23 *DG*, 117.

24 For Frame's "limiting criteria" see J. M. Frame, "In Defense of Something Close to Biblicism: Reflections on Sola Scriptura and History in Theological Method," *Westminster Theological Journal* 59 (1997): 269–318; http://www.frame-poythress.org/in-defense-of-something-close-to-biblicism-reflections-on-sola-scriptura-and-history-in-theological-method/; date of access: February 16, 2010.

25 Frame, "Covenant and the Unity of Scripture." Date of access: Aug. 12, 2012.

26 A. Van de Beek, *Jesus Kyrios: Christology as the Heart of Theology*, Studies in Reformed Theology, Supplement 1 (Zoetermeer: Meinema, 2002), 115. Van de Beek gives indication that he holds a low view of Scripture. The best treatment on the inspiration of Scripture remains Loraine Boettner, *The Inspiration of Scripture*, at http://www.reformed.org/bible/boettner/index.html. See also Philip Edgcumbe Hughes, "The Inspiration of Scripture in the English Reformers Illuminated by John Calvin," *Westminster Theological Journal* 23, no. 2 (May 1961): 129–151. For a general overview of all the points that make up a high view of Scripture, see Keith Matison, *The Shape of Sola Scriptura* (Moscow, ID: Canon Press, 2001). An excellent discussion from a "low" view of Scripture position is in Leander Keck, *Taking the Bible Seriously* (Nashville: Abington Press, 1962).

27 A. Van de Beek, *Jesus Kyrios: Christology as the Heart of Theology*, Studies in Reformed Theology, Supplement 1 (Zoetermeer: Meinema, 2002), 10.

28 Ibid., 36. See also 43, 98, and 122, for similar pronouncements that Jesus is God.

29 Ibid., 10.

30 Ibid., 36.

31 Ibid., 10.

32 *DKG*, 12.

33 A. Van de Beek, *Jesus Kyrios: Christology as the Heart of Theology*, Studies in Reformed Theology, Supplement 1 (Zoetermeer: Meinema, 2002), 198.

34 *DG*, 674–675.

35 For a fuller treatment on the divinity of Jesus in Frame, see *DG*, 644–684, esp., 663–672.

36 Athanasius is, of course, important as a stubborn defender of Christ being of the same substance as that of the Father. See R. E. Olson, *The Story of Christian Theology* (Downers Grove, IL: Intervarsity Press, 1999), 652. Also see J. L. Gonzalez, *A History of Christian Thought*, vol. 1 (Nashville: Abingdon Press, 1987, 400. And T. F. Torrance, *The Trinitarian Faith: The Evangelical Theology of the Ancient Catholic Church* (London: T & T Clark, 1995), 345.

37 A. Van de Beek, *Jesus Kyrios: Christology as the Heart of Theology*, Studies in Reformed Theology, Supplement 1 (Zoetermeer: Meinema, 2002), 91. On pages 77–82 of *Jesus Kyrios*, Van de Beek justifies his critique of Chalcedonian formula, pointing to the backdrop of Roman law that, according to him, gave rise to its preoccupation with practical clarity, e.g., the two natures of Christ.

38 For this idea, see Van de Beek, *Jesus Kyrios*, 14.

39 Ibid., 19.

40 The distinction is replete through Cornelius Van Til, *Christian Apologetics* (Phillipsburg, NJ: P&R Publishing, 1975). It is noteworthy that the distinction was made prior to Van Til by Herman Bavinck, who, as stated in Chapter 1, I believe provided much early inspiration to the shape of Van Til's thought.

41 The choice of phrases "different levels of metaphysical reality" and "a different plane of reality" requires some clarity. At the center of Thomas's metaphysics is his distinction between *esse* ("being") and *esentia* ("essence"). The former describes *that* something is, while the latter describes *what* something is. Thomas understands "*esse*" as giving universal meaning to "*essentia.*" "The term 'quiddity,' is derived from what is signified by the definition, while essence is used because through it and in it, that which is has being." Thomas Aquinas, *On Being and Essence*, trans. Armand Maurer (Toronto: Pontifical Institute of Medieval Studies, 1968), 32. Although Frame does not revise dramatically the medieval metaphysic, especially the idea that concrete reality finds meaning in God, the main difference is that Thomas is burdened by an Aristotelian cosmology that assumes a continuum of being. As stated, Frame's cosmology is without degrees of being or divinity, hence the choice of language I am here clarifying. Frame critiques the Scholastic cosmology in *DG*, 214–225. Those with greater interest in the Thomistic distinction are referred to G. Klima, "The Semantic Principles Underlying Saint Thomas Aquinas's Metaphysics of Being," *Medieval Philosophy and Theology* 5 (1996): 87–141; "Aquinas' Theory of the Copula and the Analogy of Being," *Logical Analysis and History of Philosophy* 5 (2002): 159–176.

42 *DG*, 217.

43 Ibid., 219.

44 Source: Walter A. Elwell, *Evangelical Dictionary of Theology* (Grand Rapids, MI: Baker Book House, 1984), 758.

45 P. Schaff, *The Creeds of Christendom*, vol. 1 (Grand Rapids, MI: Baker Book House, 1998), 30. For Calvin's explicit support of Chalcedonian orthodoxy, see *Institutes*, 2.14.

46 See Van de Beek, *Jesus Kyrios*, 28, paragraph one especially.

47 For Frame, "Redemption is, of course, the main theme of Scripture." *DG*, 244.

48 Problematically, Van de Beek maintains a non-historic approach to Adam's fall. See *Why?* 138.

49 A. Van de Beek, *Jesus Kyrios: Christology as the Heart of Theology*, Studies in Reformed Theology, Supplement 1 (Zoetermeer: Meinema, 2002), 28.

50 Ibid., 29.

51 Ibid., 35.

52 Ibid., 31–32.

53 Ibid., 26.

54 Ibid., 273.

55 Ibid., 206. St. Anselm of Canterbury first articulated the satisfaction view in his *Cur Deus Homo.*

56 Frame speaks of the personal meaning of redemption in relation to Abraham, Sarah, and Isaac, for example. See *DG*, 526.

57 In his discussion on how believers are to imitate the Lord, he upholds the idea of atonement as paramount. "My present, point, however, is simply that the Atonement is a profound representation of God's very nature." Ibid., 422.

58 Ibid., 235–236. See also pages 152–153 of the same book, in which Frame discusses "Divine and Human Causality" and the question of God's choices among possible alternatives.

59 The Socinians vigorously opposed any notion of Christ's death providing any sense of satisfaction to God. See Alister E. McGrath, *The Christian Theology Reader*, 3rd ed. (Oxford: Blackwell Publishing, 2007), 365–367.

60 Trevor Hart, "Redemption and Fall," in Colin E. Gunton, ed., *The Cambridge Companion to Christian Doctrine* (Cambridge: Cambridge University Press, 1997).

61 Per the notion that Christ died for individual people, see the Parable of the Talents, in which a single person is responsible (Matt. 25:14–30), the encounter between Jesus and Nicodemus (John 3:1–12), and the encounter with the rich, young ruler (Luke 18:18–23), just to mention a very few examples.

62 A. Van de Beek, *Why? On Suffering, Guilt, and God* (Grand Rapids, MI: Eerdmans, 1990), 176.

63 *DWG*, 31. Cf., *DG*, 135.

64 His views are best expressed in R. Haldane, *An Exposition on the Epistle to the Romans*, vol.2 (London, 1842), 24.

65 A. Van de Beek, *Why? On Suffering, Guilt, and God* (Grand Rapids, MI: Eerdmans, 1990), 263.

66 Ibid., 261.

67 Established before now is the fact that Frame's covenantal framework reverses long-held conceptions of a theological starting point. Van de Beek, however, reverses categories *within* the Godhead. In the older language of theology, the *economic* Trinity is the interpretive key to knowing the *ontological* Trinity. In other words, we do not know God's deeds by his attributes; we know his attributes by his deeds.

68 A. Van de Beek, *Why? On Suffering, Guilt, and God* (Grand Rapids, MI: Eerdmans, 1990), 300.

69 Ibid., 285.

70 This expostulation of God's deeds in history, especially the point that after Jesus, God's liberty is limited by the manner of grace, draws currency from the nominalistic tradition of William of Occam. According to Van de Beek, *potentia absoluta* is delimited by *potentia ordinata.* The distinction between *potentia absoluta* and *potentia ordinata* is complex. Simply put, the former suggests that God can do whatever he wants, even what he has not willed, even what he does not choose to do. In its extreme form, this idea has given rise to the old question in theology, "Can God make a stone he himself cannot lift?" By the latter term, we refer to God's power to do things he chooses to do. For Van de Beek's explanation of the twin ideas, see *Why? On Suffering, Guilt, and God* (Grand Rapids, MI: Eerdmans, 1990), 12.

71 Ibid., 315.

72 Ibid., 305.

73 Ibid., 12.

74 *DG*, 344.

75 Ibid., 523. It is hard to discern where Frame stands on the nominalist question, unless one understands that as in all areas of his theology, the subject is treated with evenness. For example, in addition to his view that Scripture teaches that "God's power is not exhausted in history," in another place he says, "We have seen that, according to Scripture, there are some things that God cannot do." *DG*, 524. So, which is it? Does Frame hold to *potentia absoluta* or *potentia ordinata*? Frame sees little use for the terminology, as Scripture says very little about the distinction. He sees the playoff between the two categories as a classic case of nominalistic (overall medieval) preoccupation with philosophical minutia. As a result, he does not feel it important to use these terms at all. Still, they represent a question of the scope of God's power, a question that does not go away. His observation is that "If we do choose to give these terms some positive meaning in accord with Scripture, we may define God's ordinate power as the power exerted in the things he chooses to do. Absolute power, then, would be God's power to do things other than those he actually chooses to do." *DG*, 525. Thus, whereas Van de Beek exploits the nominalist distinction to substantiate his idea that God changes, Frame consents to God's ordinate power only insofar as it is taken to mean that for God to be consistent within himself, he must be consistent with his creatures and with his plan. In other words, if all of nature were a jigsaw puzzle, God is always putting it together. Yet the pieces of the puzzle are not contingent on the fact that they are made by the events and thoughts of others, but the pieces of the puzzle are manufactured by him. So God freely *limits* himself by what he knows about Bill's thoughts, but God foreordained Bill's thoughts and therefore God's own response in time to his thoughts. So if Frame were to use the nominalistic language, it would not be in accord with Van de Beek's view of divine restraint (and, I might add, the general theory of open theism) that makes God's actions consequent to contingency. Rather, he would keep the language within the structure of God's immutability and abiding plan. Frame handles this issue in *DG*, 518–521, and *ST*, 339–341.

76 *NOG*, 10.

77 C. Pinnock, *The Openness of God: A Biblical Challenge to the Traditional Understanding of God* (Downers Grove, IL: Intervarsity Press Academic, 1994), 103.

78 For an exposition of this thought, see *NOG*, 172.

79 *DG*, 52.

80 Ibid., 62.

81 On page 68 of *NOG*, Frame lists five areas over which God's will is paramount: the natural world, human history, individual human lives, human decisions, and sin. His position on this last area is controversial, and one I disagree with, in that he ultimately makes God the cause of sin. As he says, "[I]t is important to see that God does in fact bring about the sinful behavior of human beings, whatever problems that may create in our understanding." He qualifies this, saying, "It is more helpful to point out that Scripture itself regards this problem as a mystery (Job 38–42), and that God has a supremely good purpose for ordaining evil that one day will silence all his critics and

evoke praise (Rom. 8:28–39; 9:17–24; Rev. 15:3–4)." Against this is James 1:13, "Let no one say when he is tempted, 'I am being tempted by God'; for God cannot be tempted by evil, and He Himself does not tempt anyone."

82 *NOG*, 109.

83 See *DG,* 531.

84 *NOG*, 531.

85 For more on Frame's reasoning on the decretive and preceptive wills of God, see *NOG*, 110.

86 See Ibid., 164. He fleshes out this idea according to the processes of temporality in *NOG*, 176.

87 See *NOG*, 19.

88 *DG*, 181–182.

89 Chapter 7 of *AGG* covers this issue in full.

90 *NOG*, 197. Frame denies the possibility of autonomous freedom as a cause of the problem of evil. See *NOG*, 125.

91 *DG*, 277.

92 *NOG*, 212.

Chapter 3

Lordship and Ethics

As the previous chapters have shown, God's lordship provides us with immeasurably important points of reference for all of life. The lordship orientation thus allows us to view human life as a whole and, from there, to make the critical distinctions necessary in order for us to discern how we are to live as covenant children of God. That all-important orientation positions the ethical dimension of life front and center to Frame's entire opera of works. None of his works is as specific on the discipline of ethics as *The Doctrine of the Christian Life* (hereafter *DCL*). This chapter will draw heavily from that work, although attention will be paid to cognate writings of Frame's where appropriate.

The aim of this chapter is to show how Frame's multiperspectival approach to ethics provides a lucid and God-honoring moral vision and does so by bringing together the various emphases of secular ethics.[1] As will be documented, Frame indicts all secular ethics for emphasizing only parts of God's world at the expense of other parts, and doing so without reference to the God of Scripture. Frame's triperspectivalism challenges the *piecemeal* approach of secular ethics through the lordship principle. The research design will begin with a description of Frame's fundamental contributions to the field of ethics vis-à-vis lordship. This will be followed by a descriptive analysis of Frame's Christian ethical methodology. In that the heart of Frame's ethics is the Ten Commandments, general and specific considerations of perspectivalism relative to the Decalogue will bring this chapter to a close. It is in the account of Frame's ethical methodology, but especially in the final sections on the Decalogue, that this chapter's aim is mainly substantiated.

Ultimately, the goal is to use this contexture to expand on the initial question that prompted this exploratory work: "What does the concept of lordship mean to John M. Frame?" As a mode of reasoning in ethics, Frame envisions the lordship principle, most essentially expressed by the perspectival method, as a tool to help us arrive at choices that demonstrate intrinsic moral value before God and neighbor.

Frame's Distinctive Voice in Ethics

Though *DCL* appears with a later publication date than *The Doctrine of God* and *The Doctrine of the Knowledge of God*, it contains thought that informs Frame's earlier works. This point is not merely taxonomic but serves as prolegomena to his unique contribution to the discipline of ethics. That contribution is most conspicuous in the following ways.

First, the lordship principle makes ethics foundational to the whole of Frame's other theological postures. In Frame, "ethics is not merely a branch of theology, but is in fact the whole of theology, viewed a certain way."[2] So "All theology, then, has to do with ethics."[3] That affects the relationship of ethics to epistemology. In terms of the old "chicken or the egg" question, we can ask, "Which comes first: human behavior before God, or specific and generic ideas of God gained through rational means?" Frame makes ethics first, and epistemology its outcome. That is holding to the fact that knowledge of God is always a heart-knowledge. In other words, "obedience is the criterion of knowledge."[4] Or we can say that because all thought is essentially an *activity* before God, epistemology is overtly ethical. Here Frame follows Cornelius Van Til, who said that "the intellectual itself is ethical."[5] We can sum up Frame as he has summed up himself. "Everything can be boiled down to a matter of ethics."[6]

There is a reciprocal idea. If all theology is ethics, then all ethics is theology. In other words, unlike ethicists who give separate consideration to metaethics, Frame does not believe that metaethics, normally considered the underlying structure of moral problems, can be contrived apart from ethics proper. Instead, "like Christian ethics, a Christian metaethic must be subject to Scripture and thus must be theological."[7] Theory is thus an aspect of practice. The effect is that Frame reduces metaethics to normative ethics. As will be interpreted more expansively, Frame takes a typical reductionist approach to the variegated history of secular ethics, classifying the nature and method of ethics under existential, teleological, and deontological categories. The existential focuses the ethical question on *self*, the teleological on the *goal*, and the deontological on *duty*. Frame believes his multiperspectival system of ethics (a systemization of his own metaethic) includes these emphases. The difference with these systems is that his perspectival methodology is not an abstracted vision of human nature but, like any specific ethical command of Scripture, derives from that same source.[8]

Second, Frame's unique effort in ethics is seen in the degree to which he applies lordship to the whole of the theological task and to life generally. Like Martin Bucer, who defined theology as the "art of living a virtuous and orderly life," John Frame sees the supremacy of lordship extending compendiously to all areas of life.[9] Because *all* choices are ethical in nature—although some are different in kind and therefore induce lesser or greater effects on human lives—the polemical responsibility of theology is to help people walk with God in all of the varied striations of life. Or, as he says, "[T]he work of theology is not to reproduce the emphasis of Scripture . . . but to apply Scripture to the needs of people."[10] In short, "Theology is application."[11]

These two preliminaries ground Frame's strict definition of ethics. "Ethics is theology viewed as a means of determining which person, acts, and attributes receive God's blessings and which do not."[12]

The Square of Opposition

This last point leads naturally to his third distinctive input into the field of ethics: his intense critique of non-Christian ethical systems. His principal disparagement of non-Christian ethical systems is that they are not built on a belief *in* something, but are the product of non-belief. The non-Christian point of origination is, in Frame's mind, inherently utopian in nature and therefore threatening to the Christian witness and mission. It also can be said that materialistic and profane ethical systems are nihilistic in orientation, but such is true only in so far as they reject biblical norms. The revolutionary can never reject all laws and institutions, in that he is a law unto himself. Frame's system of ethics is therefore closely allied with his apologetic interest to undercut error.

The considerable amount of space Frame gives to sharply critiquing non-Christian ethics, especially in *DCL*, acquires a philosophical archetype that serves his analytical interests. He calls this model "The Square of

Opposition" (hereafter called "the Square").[13] The core of Frame's strategic attack against non-Christian ethics takes two forms: (1) transcendence and immanence, and (2) irrationalism and rationalism.

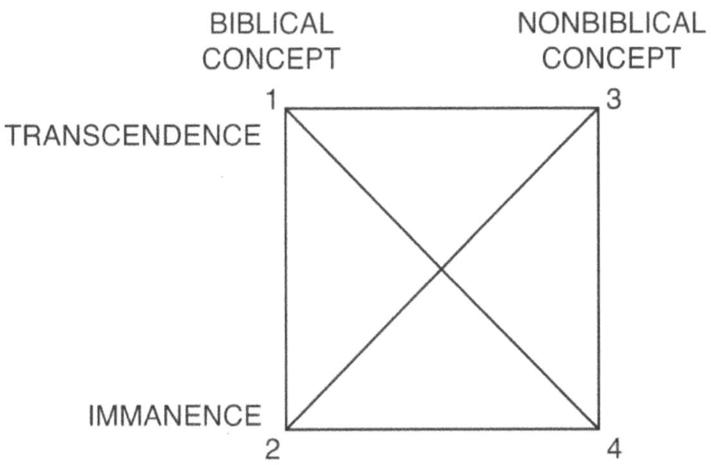

Fig. 1. The Square of Opposition: Transcendence and Immanence[14]

Frame mixes the first subset of the Square inventively to underscore the truth of the Christian worldview verses the inherent fallacies of non-Christian thought. The results are (1) Biblical Transcendence, (2) Biblical Immanence, (3) Non-Biblical Transcendence, and (4) Non-Biblical Immanence. Looking at the left side of the Square, we see that God is transcendent (biblical concept 1); he is exalted Lord and King. Enlisting the lordship attributes of CAP, God's transcendence is best associated with the lordship attributes of *control* and *authority*. However, God is also immanent (biblical concept 2), insofar as his *presence* is covenantally assured.

The right side of the Square illustrates the problem of emphasizing God's transcendence over his immanence (non-biblical concept 3). This category includes the legacy of the Gnostics, Rousseau, Marx, Nietzsche, the

Existentialists, and more. The right side of the Square also illustrates the non-biblical concept of immanence. Applied to epistemology, deistic and pantheistic thinkers and the professed antagonism of Ritschl and the German pietists toward any theological reflection on the transcendent nature of God are examples of this thinking.

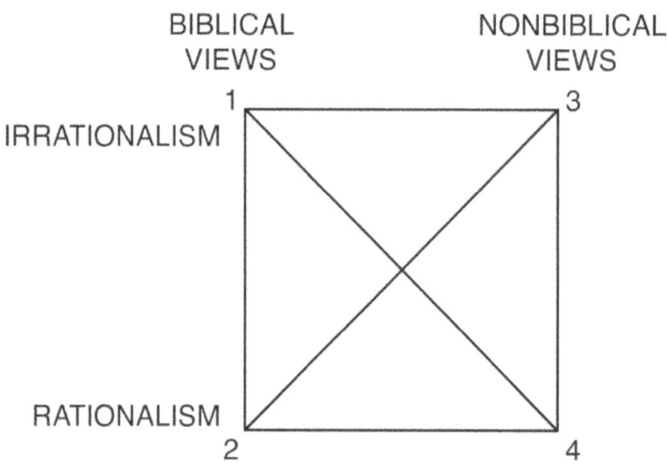

Fig. 2. The Square of Opposition: Irrationalism and Rationalism[15]

The Square can also be seen differently, according to the tension between irrationalism and rationalism.[16] Secularists who concentrate on either the teleological, the deontological, or the existential ethical task, or some combination thereof, create asymmetricality in thought. Either they establish *absolutes without content*, resulting in various forms of rationalism (non-biblical view 4) or *content without absolutes*, producing variant expressions of irrationalism (non-biblical view 3). For example, deontological ethics cannot find an absolute to justify duty. Plato, Locke, Rousseau, Nietzsche, and Hegel deny objective, propositional authority as the understructure for ethics.[17] They expostulate instead various forms of normativity, but they are unable to locate the absolute norm decisively (non-biblical view 4).

Conversely, Michel Foucault, Jean-François Lyotard, and Richard Rorty move us away from any theological reflection on the transcendent nature of God (non-biblical view 3), yet argue ideas in the form of norms.[18] Ironically, rationalism always alters to irrationalism, and vice versa. To urge the existence of an indeterminate norm is merely to ask people to follow the extension of the human psyche. To deny the existence of Absolutes is to deny the truth of that denial. All in all, Frame insists that non-Christian philosophical ethics up to the twenty-first century is bankrupt.

The Square is also meaningful for decidedly Christian thought. Because Christians reject autonomous reason, keeping their minds captive to the word of God, many modernists charge Christians with "irrationalism." Due to the reasonableness of Christian theism, Frame rejects this charge. At the same time, Frame seizes the opportunity to say that because God's knowledge is total and ours is not, there is a *form* of Christian irrationalism—a tacit acknowledgment that "human reason is limited, subservient to God's perfect reason" (biblical view 1).[19]

Then again, because Christians do make claims to absolute knowledge based on God's self-revelation, postmodernists often charge them with "rationalism." Once more, because of the limits of native reason, Frame rejects the implication but is amenable to a *form* of Christian rationalism, if it is stipulated "that through God's revelation [Christians] have access to real truth" (biblical view 2).[20] Accordingly, it is non-Christian systems of thought that are guilty of errant forms of irrationalism (the universe exists and operates by chance) and irrationalism (my thinking is sufficient).

Exemplifications of the Square

In the thought that the Square may require supplementary explanation, select voices from the field of secular ethics are here provided to illustrate its significance.

The central idea in the moral philosophy of Immanuel Kant is the categorical imperative. Standing in the deontological trend, he contends that the condition of morality is based on the idea that the moral law is absolutely and universally binding in all circumstances. In other words, the moral law is its own justification. The Königsberg master's first proposition of morals is that "One should act only on that maxim that can at the same time be willed to become a universal law."[21] Or, as Herman Bavinck characterized Kant, "You must—and that's it!"[22]

Yet unlike other deontologists, such as Plato, the early Greek Cynics, and the Stoics, Kant is a skeptic. Reality is unknowable to Kant. This real world he calls the "noumenal," or *Ding an sich* ("thing in itself"). All empirical knowledge is therefore knowledge of mere appearances.[23] How, then, can Kant sustain his categorical imperative? It is by drawing a distinction between hypothetical and categorical imperatives. Some ethical choices are hypothetical; for example, "*If* you walk the dog, *then* you may use a leash." Clearly, this imperative is universally non-binding, but other ethical decisions are hard and fast. How does Kant substantiate these? Frame explains, "An ethical principle is categorical if someone can consistently will its universal application."[24] Kant's favorite example is promises. If everyone were free to break a promise, they would have no meaning. Ethical imperatives are thus derived from the consistency of the nature of an idea together with its application.

Kant is in deep trouble before the Square. If the noumenal is impenetrable by reason, then we cannot have direct knowledge of God. Kant thus comes into conflict with concept 3 of the Square (non-biblical concept of transcendence). This leaves Kant to decipher the universe on his own terms, which brings him into conflict with concept 4: he conflates the Creator with himself, assuming sovereign authority to decide the world. As Frame puts it, "Kant pushes human autonomy to new heights, in effect identifying the mind of man with the mind of God—in his metaphysics, his epistemology, and his ethics."[25] According to Frame, Kant also violates views 3 and 4 of the Square.[26] "The rationalism and irrationalism of Kant's distinction between the phenomenal and the noumenal affect his ethics. If we cannot know the real world, how can we be sure of what our duties are? If our experience is virtually created by the mind, how can ethical norms be anything more than the human mind proclaiming duties to itself?"

Frame does not address Jürgen Habermas. However, this provides the opportunity to work with the Square in an original and constructive way. In our view, Habermas bridges both the deontological and the existential traditions of ethics. In his influential *The Structural Transformation of the Public Sphere*, Habermas developed the centerpiece of his position: the "public sphere"—a call to replace what he vituperated as "representational" culture—with *Öffentlichkeit* culture, that culture of public space outside state control where individuals can exchange views and knowledge and whose public reason can work as a check on state power.[27]

The public sphere that wants to bring objective reason to bear on politics, the arts and sciences, and more, is confronted by an impenetrable problem: it cannot show why people should do a certain thing, act a certain way, or seek a particular aesthetic. The amalgam of *Öffentlichkeit* culture is in essence the poll of unequally informed opinion, as much as individual people may appeal to reason. If there is a universal reason, then why do we need *Öffentlichkeit* culture? The fact that we need it demonstrates the unreliability of a public reason; indeed, the absence of it in the face of public subjectivity.

Habermas is trapped in Frame's irrational/rational tension. Frame makes an important point that could easily apply to Habermas: "Those who deny that worldview must seek objectivity in an unknowable realm (view 3), where the moral standard cannot be known at all, let alone objectively. They seek inwardness by making each person his own moral standard (view 4). But that dispenses with all objectivity and leaves us with nothing to internalize."[28]

Multiperspectivalism and Christian Ethical Methodology

Frame's sustained concern is not just with *tearing down* non-Christian ethics, but also with *building up* a positive basis for ethical decision-making methodology. As noted, his methodology (metaethic) includes normative, situational, and existential perspectives, as Scripture is their derivative source. He believes that his Christian ethical methodology thus abates the inherent irrational/rational circularity of the three major voices of secular ethics and provides a vision for a consistent visualization of life before God.

How so? If we take a very large view of Framian ethics as a whole, it is fair to say that a global, elemental consideration that comes to the fore in its organic wholeness is the essential lordship of God, which, to generalize, has a single focus: God's rightful claim on us as beings. The far-reaching claim comes to dominate all moral and ethical considerations on our part. The central thought is that the reification of a Christian ethical methodology accounts for all three principles of secular ethics (deontological, teleological, and existential) as perspectives—an ethic in which all three schools of thought are reconciled through divine lordship.[29] Seen from the angle of a secularized command ethic, narrative ethic, and virtue ethic, "A complete Christian ethic contains all three of these, and each includes the others perspectivally."[30] So his methodology envisages the normative, situational, and existential perspectives as covering the same subject matter of ethics but from different viewpoints or worldviews.

As a compelling expression of the same truth, the three perspectives—normative, situational, and existential—represent God's lordship attributes, or CAP, patent to us in his revelation. The method is quite flexible but is mainly focused on pedagogy. That is, since the three perspectives cover the same ground, the question of what ethical question one takes up under which perspective simply depends on which choice is most helpful in teaching the material to students and in personal research. The distilled essence of the method is this: "In general, a Christian ethical decision is the application of God's revelation (normative) to a problem (situational) by a person (existential)."[31]

With his decision-making methodology in place, Frame's "building up" has far-reaching implications for the creation. Under the situational ethic, which Frame interprets as similar to the secular teleological concern with "goal," he envisions the *telos* of life as encompassing the Cultural Mandate of Genesis 1:28 and the Great Commission of Matthew 28:18–20, by which "God and his people work together to bring transformation to people and to the world."[32] Contra Roman Catholic dualism and its doctrine of the twofold end, lordship effectuates a unitary claim on God's people, such that the "religious' life is not a monastic existence, but human life as a whole, directed to God's glory."[33] Truly, "There is no area of life where we are not called both to glorify God and to enjoy him forever."[34] Perspectivally, "We can think of glorifying God as normative, enjoying him as existential, and seeking his kingdom as historical and therefore situational."[35]

Continuity and Discontinuity between Frame and Secular Ethicists

Frame's comprehensive ethic raises an extremely important point regarding his view of non-Christian ethics. On one hand, because all non-Christian moral philosophies operate on "borrowed capital" from Christianity, one can always locate some gem of truth in them.[36] Hence, "Even the worst theology generally has some truth area of strength, some concern that is genuinely biblical."[37] This means that the variegated nature of non-Christian ethics, including the varied voices within the liberal Christian tradition, all find a voice in the perspectival approach. So, according to perspectivalism, Kant is right in postulating a normative aspect to ethics. Tillich is right that there is an existential aspect to ethics. Fletcher is right to affirm a situational component of ethics. So Kant, Tillich, and Fletcher make good points regarding the normative, existential, and situational component; they have each tapped into part of God's world.[38]

On the other hand, Frame thinks that the three secular ethical traditions misunderstand their own perspectives. In colloquy with Tillich, Frame can agree to an existential perspective. But that existential perspective is dependent on the other two, as Tillich would not admit. And all three perspectives must find meaning in the definition of God's word. So Tillich misconceives his own favorite perspective: the existential. Kant misconceives his own normative perspective because his norm is based in human autonomy, not in God's word. Thus, one's ultimate ethical concern is not merely incomplete but wrong, if it fails to embrace God's norms and facts. So Frame does not wholly dismiss secular thought, but his embrace of the antithesis between Christian and non-Christian thought overrides the possibility of complete unanimity.

John M. Frame and Richard B. Hays on Ethical Methodology

Entrée to the heart of Frame's Christian ethical method precipitates a fundamental query. He has insisted that an effective ethic is only discovered from the trove of Christian ideals. But this only elicits a deeper problem. "Whose Christian ethic?" One could be blindsided considerably should one undertake the prestigious enterprise of particularizing an ethic according to the lordship principle, only to discover a plethora of other voices in the same field of study, and all claiming conclusiveness or, at the very least, to point us in the right direction.

Why is Frame's procedure the better way? An instructive course of action would be to see how his work matches up in general terms to the work of another leading Christian ethicist. Owing to the deft hermeneutical gifts of Richard B. Hays and also because he has presented a structural approach to ethics that has shared interests with those of Frame, the forthcoming pages will concentrate on a corroborative study of these two thinkers.

In *The Moral Vision of the New Testament*, Richard B. Hays outlines a fourfold approach to New Testament ethics.[39] The multiplex schema represents a paradigmatically new method that grapples with the reality of the New Testament "text" without venturing into biblicism. Equally so, it ascertains the many ways the text is mediated by metaphor and narrative without venturing into the sort of deconstructive analysis that looks for "the world behind the text"—a procedure that historically has left us with little text to reconstruct for embodied living. An abstract of his approach includes the descriptive task, the synthetic task, the hermeneutical task, and the pragmatic task.

The *descriptive* task asks us "to explicate in detail the messages of the individual writings of the canon, without prematurely harmonizing them."[40] This first step is really exegetical in nature. The *synthetic* task moves on to know the basis of "coherence among the various witnesses," otherwise "what methods might allow us to give an appropriate account of this canonical coherence."[41] This second step is focused on the unity of texts. The *hermeneutical* task understands that the New Testament was written with a specific people and time in view and that helps us overcome "the temporal and cultural distance between ourselves and the text."[42] The *pragmatic* task is "embodying Scripture's imperatives in the life of the Christian community."[43]

From here, I want to investigate some shared and disparate representative points between Hays and Frame in their respective approaches to ethics. Correspondence of thought is seen in the developmental range of both proposals. Both Frame's three-part perspectivalism and Hays's fourfold account make plain that Christian ethics is a multifaceted undertaking that is dependent on the rich unity and diversity of both Scripture and human experience. A second similarity is that both plans are composed of parts that thrive in mutual dependence, or, as Hays says of his own method, "The four tasks interpenetrate one another."[44]

Although the two syllabi do not permit strict equivalence, in a rough sort of way the normative perspective and the descriptive task provide the ethicist with similar starting points, as both begin with what Scripture says. The normative perspective also shares a common interest with the synthetic task, as both take up principles that can account for the unity of Scripture. The situational perspective bears some affinity with the hermeneutical task, seeing that "the hermeneutical task is the cognitive or conceptual application of the New Testament's message to our situation."[45] The existential perspective looks something like the pragmatic task, which is "the enacted application of the New Testament's message in our situation."[46] In Hays, both the hermeneutical and the pragmatic tasks are most closely aligned, as both are governed largely by practical judgments. Thus, "It would be possible to group the two tasks together under the heading of application." On the pragmatic task alone, Hays echoes the Framian aphorism that "all theology is practice," in his insistence that "there can be no true understanding apart from lived obedience, and vice versa."[47] He means that the pragmatic task is not just what we do once we have deciphered Scripture's ethical priorities. Embodying Scripture's imperatives is rather an indispensable part of the interpretative process.

Paradigmatic tensions between Frame's perspectivalism and Hay's moral vision are far more sweeping. At the descriptive level, Hays is self-professedly reluctant to jump prematurely toward a strict harmonization of the New Testament canon. Any biblical theologian can understand this disinclination. However, Hays contends that such a harmonization is impeded by a "hidden complication," namely, that the explicit moral teachings of the New Testament texts are as much the product of the "community's *ethos*," as they are a manifestation of God's revealed truth.[48] Since the New Testament writers work with disparate symbols and social structures, we can speak only in hushed tones of the unity of the New Testament.[49]

The normative perspective of the lordship principle also consents to the vivification of community *ethos* in the formation of the New Testament canon. But for Frame, that rich community is found solely in the inter-Trinitarian life of God. Prolegomenous in his doctrine of Scripture is the fact that "God's word is God himself. God eternally communicates his love and purposes within the Trinity: Father to Son, Son to father, both to the Spirit, and the Spirit to both."[50] God's self-referential speech is essential for understanding how Frame views the reciprocity of God's self-communication and Scripture, for "by his grace and free decision he also speaks to his creatures. These communications do not exhaust his word, but they are truly his utterances, his expressions."[51] This positions the early Christian community not as producers of God's truth, but as *conveyers* of it. Frame does not therefore feel burdened to challenge the type of claim made by Hays that the earliest Christian communities were source-points of Scripture.[52] He simply traces Scripture from God to us.

This process forms the familiar CAP or, again, control, authority, and presence. It starts with the divine voice (normative) speaking to the prophets and the apostles (situational), who compose the written word under direct inspiration (existential). The normative, situational, and existential components are also apparent in this arrangement.[53] Given the limitation of this deliberation to ethics, a full description of Frame's doctrine of Scripture will have to wait. Of immediate concern is that we know that for Frame, "Scripture is sufficient to provide all the ultimate norms, all the normative premises, that we need to make ethical decisions."[54] All extra-biblical data, though participatory in answering ethical questions, must defer to this higher priority.

Hays's four-fold tasks are interrelated, yet the normative nature of New Testament ethics is not implied in the descriptive step: that all-important first step, in which the reader comes into contact with God's word. The answer to any ethical question must await further reflection. That is arrived at by making the descriptive task dependent on the outcomes produced by the other tasks with his model. As we will see in review of the next tasks, none ever arrive at an absolute ethical norm but each acts as a link in the chain of ethical indeterminacy.

This brings us to the synthetic task. Above all the tasks, the synthetic focuses on trying to achieve coherence among the voices of the New Testament canon. It does so by searching for a unifying set of "focal images" that arise most naturally from the texts and that make for a comprehensive characterization of all of the moral motifs in the canonical readings. For Hays, the most observable and comprehensive images that cohere the canon are *community*, *cross*, and *new creation.*

But why these three? Indeed, why images? Why not dogmas? In answer to the first question, Hays is firm "that no single principle can account for the Moral Vision of the New Testament writings."[55] He does speak of lordship, but not in a summative way. Frame utilizes the term as an abbreviation of the Bible's message. Hays understands lordship principally in the narrower Pauline sense, recorded in Romans 6—that decisive move of our allegiance from the dominion of sin to newness of life and obedience, and which is the effect of our participation in Christ's death.[56] As we will see in the approaching chapter on culture, Hays can move seamlessly from gospel *to* its cosmic and eschatological implications—a very Framian move. But he is far more at home when affirming that our ethical obligations move inescapably *from* the "cosmic context of what God has done in Christ."[57]

In reply to the second question, Hays tracks images, not dogmas, because the unity and sense of Scripture can be grasped *only* through an act of metaphorical imagination.[58] Here, Hays follows David Kelsey's premise in *The Uses of Scripture in Recent Theology* that every theological appraisal of Scripture must depend on "a single synoptic, imaginative judgment," in which the interpreter "tries to catch up what Christianity is basically all about."[59] Hays's imaginative reconstruction connecting us with the text is his three focal images.

In a review of the same book by Kelsey, Frame reacts to Kelsey's theological proposal of a complex *discrimen*. Here, Kelsey is acquiescing to a path previously set of R. C. Johnson, who explains *discrimen* as "a configuration of criteria that are in some way organically related to one another as reciprocal coefficients."[60] Kelsey reconfigures it slightly to mean "the conjunction of certain uses of Scripture and the presence of God."[61] The point is that Kelsey is looking for an interpretive matrix that combines the plain reading of Scripture with other premises, in some way unfixed to the plain reading of Scripture, in order to arrive at the meaning of the Bible, while remaining "theological-position neutral."[62] Without cataloguing everything Frame says of Kelsey's (and, by inference, Hays's) idea, this one response is ample.

> Yet if Scripture is "sufficient" with respect to any doctrine at all, it clearly must be "sufficient" in setting forth the norms for its own use. Even if we cannot set forth those norms exhaustively, somehow they must be there. We cannot accept Kelsey's apparent position that these norms are

> indeterminate, or that they are communicated through some divine influence apart from . . . Scripture. And certainly we cannot accept any claim that such a view is "theological position neutral!"[63]

At the heart of Hays's search for coherence is the human trait of "discernment."[64] Central to the formation of this judgment are the needs and responsibilities of the community of believers who form God's "primary sphere of moral concern"—even more primary than the individual.[65] We hear the readings together but not as receivers of an externally concretized set of rules of conduct. Rather, the needs of the community form the basis for a dynamic union of theology and ethics by which the word of the Lord is to be apprehended and appropriated faithfully.[66] Evidently, those looking for epistemological closure on moral teachings will not find it in Hays's synthetic task. The synthetic task benefits us as a "contingent interpretive performance" that presents only *one* "coherent moral vision in the texts." We are free to seek other visions using our own metaphorical imaginative judgments. The authoritative ground for ethics was settled for Frame once the pages of Scripture were open—in fact, before.

We have adduced that because the descriptive task is not enough to provide a definitive basis for ethics, the other tasks must be employed to arrive at a fully worked out conceptual framework. Even so, the hermeneutical task, which, to repeat, serves the purpose of identifying interpretive strategies for Christian ethics, is not meant by Hays to reach a standardizing of biblical ethics.[67] This is surely the case if we wish to uncover how ethical warrants function authoritatively within the limits of Scripture. "No matter how seriously the church may take the authority of the Bible, the slogan of *sola Scriptura* is both conceptually and practically untenable, because the interpretation of Scripture can never occur in a vacuum."[68] For this reason,

Hays procures other sources of authority, in order to arrive at a workable mode of hermeneutics. Those are *tradition*, *reason*, and *experience*.[69]

The need for these three sub-steps in the hermeneutical task is essential to carry out the hermeneutical "translation" of the New Testament. The hermeneutical task assumes that a given prerequisite for the search for any harmonizing idea is the strong acknowledgment of the necessary historical and cultural *distance* between us and the New Testament authors. "When we read Paul's letters to his churches, we are reading the mail of people who have been dead for nineteen hundred years. . . . Only historical ignorance or cultural chauvinism could lead us to suppose that no hermeneutical 'translation' is necessary for us to understand the texts."[70] This is why, in Hays's judgment, the New Testament cannot be received as a repository of pan-historical, dogmatic, moral claims. The translation process helps us make the voices from the past come alive in the present.

Frame agrees that the Christian ethicist must look to extra-biblical data when interpreting Scripture. He explains that "[W]hen we teach the word of God we do legitimately make use of extra-biblical knowledge . . . for we are called to apply Scripture to the contemporary world."[71] The lordship principle, in fact, envisions the value of normative, situational, and existential data forming a requisite *instrumentum laboris*—what Frame calls the "hermeneutical circle." This allied methodology suggests that Frame would be very comfortable with Hays's nomenclature of *tradition*, *reason*, and *experience.*[72] The main difference between hermeneutical translation and the hermeneutical circle is that "Scripture must remain primary," not just as *inceptum* but as *ultima ratio* among the hierarchy of norms.[73] It is thus tradition and reason leavened with autonomy and presumed to speak with parity alongside Scripture that he consistently opposes.

Yet this still leaves Frame with the *historical gap* between exegesis and contemporary ecclesiology and life. How, then, does Frame bridge it? He argues that (1) The modern ethicist has not left us without reliable ties to the original anthropological and cultural settings in which Scripture was first penned.[74] Hays also exploits the historical line of generational continuity, but differently. Rather than read the past as an anterior and settled basis of truth with consequential meaning for succeeding generations, the history of hermeneutics forms continuing points of posterior and reflective analyses for how Scripture can be re-read and reapplied. What we learn from Scripture is not what it meant and still means, but what it meant and *can* mean today.[75] (2) "The work of the Holy Spirit in illumination and demonstration is the supernatural factor that enables us to hear the words of Scripture as God's personal words *to us*" (italics added).[76] The Holy Spirit, to borrow from Hays, provides "the cognitive or conceptual application of the New Testament's message to our situation."
(3) "The ultimate answer to [the historical] difficulty is that in an important sense the word of Scripture is always contemporary. God speaks it in our hearing, our time, our culture. This fact does not take away our responsibility to interpret Scripture in the context it was first given. But it does eliminate the possibility that the historical gap might make the Word inaccessible to us."[77] To wit, the standardization of God's revealed will across the strands of time is contained in its Author.

A familiar chord is again struck by Hays's pragmatic task. He asks a highly legitimate question: "How shall the Christian community shape its life in obedience to the witnesses of the New Testament?" At face value, the question seems to be aimed at the practical implications of the New Testament. But when he answers his own question, we find that "No single, definitive answer can be given to such a question, because the community of faith continually confronts new circumstances that require us to work out our salvation with fear and trembling, forming fresh imaginative judgments—just as the New Testament writers themselves did—in response to the challenges of our time."[78] Each new generation of believers has accordingly its own job to seek out unique ethical solutions, for this is what "New Testament writers themselves did." The pragmatic task does not therefore end at fixed decisions but continues the work of the previous tasks *in search of* solutions.

Frame would acquiesce to the need for original ethical answers for we live in an original age. Nevertheless, he would add that to shape our lives *imaginatively* with no recourse to a "single, definitive answer" is to lead us away from the witness *of* the New Testament, to the witness set *by* the New Testament—for the purpose of creating ever-dynamic contours in ethics. The question for Hays, in that case, becomes at what point does the Christian community introduce self-serving leniency into its progressive development of what it understands to be ethical, in order to accommodate the interests of accelerating social change? In reacting to much feminist rhetoric, Hays correctly warns that private experience as a hermeneutical guide tends to be capitulatory to the political and social interests of the individual.[79] But can we say that he has answered this danger by replacing individual experience with the "focal image" of community or group experience? Without a definitive ethical answer at our disposal, at what point does group-think and its socially negative costs become a problem?

Here I think is the most fundamental problem with Hays's outline. Because it recognizes no absolute source for morality, the pragmatic task is able to arrive at ethical conclusions that contradict the descriptive task. A representative example is Hays on homosexuality. After recapping a plethora of biblical texts, he says under the descriptive task that homosexual behavior is sin.[80] But then under the pragmatic task, he asks, "Should persons of homosexual orientation be ordained?" He answers that "Strictures against homosexuality belong in the church's moral catechesis, not in its ordination requirements. It is arbitrary to single out homosexuality as a special sin that precludes ordination."[81] How did we go from one end of the spectrum to the other? For one, "The church has no analogous special rules to exclude from ordination the greedy or the self-righteous. Such matters are left to the discernment of the bodies charged with examining candidates for ordination; these bodies must determine whether the individual candidate has the gifts and graces requisite for ministry."[82]

Is this not a little bit like jury nullification? The facts are in, and the accused is clearly guilty of a pattern of sin, but the verdict is then left to "the discernment of the bodies"—that "imaginative judgment" of the community. Yet the church does have special rules that disqualify the greedy and the self-righteous from ordination.[83] Basic illogic is also evident. If strictures against homosexuality are for the church's catechesis, but not for its ordination requirements, how can we expect the ordained homosexual to catechize the youth accordingly?[84] Hays is right that there has never been a time when the community of the faithful has not partnered in reaching consensus on many doctrinal and ethical issues. But I am also aware of periods in the church's history when community assent has not led to a helpful *transmission* of the text, but to its *transformation*, and that into something wholly foreign to the plain reading of the text.

To Frame, it is obvious that people who are guilty and unrepentant of the nadir of depravity in Romans 1 should not become church officers. According to the *normative* perspective, "church officers are to be spiritually mature, to the point that they can be examples to the flock." Seen from the *situational* perspective, "people, who are gay, but closeted, presumably do not reveal themselves to the church, so the church cannot use their sexual orientation in determining their qualifications for office." Should people reveal their homosexual orientation, there is an *existential* perspective. "People whose 'orientation' is homosexual, but are committed to a celibate life and struggling with their sinful inclinations, may be considered by the church for ordination on a case-by-case basis."

Now, by means of the existential perspective, it looks as if Frame agrees with Hays that celibate homosexuals can be afforded a hearing for ordination. But there is a vastly important difference. It rests in Frame's nuanced position on sexual orientation. Writing on the seventh commandment, he insists that homosexuals must change to seek ordination. What may linger is their homosexual orientation. By "orientation," he means "a strong pattern of temptation."[85] That pattern is common to all regenerated children of God, as it takes any number of forms and is not sinful in itself. Temptations can always be resisted. However, if "orientation" refers to full-scale lust, then that is contrary to God's law and is sinful in itself.[86] Lust demands repentance. In either case, the ordinand must be born again. Hays believes that even if people do not become "straight" but continue even as prisoners of homosexual lust, they are eligible for ordination provided that they practice abstinence from lustful activity. All over again, we see how "the situational and existential perspectives may never be used to contradict the normative. In the end all three perspectives must lead to the same conclusion . . . there is nothing in the situational or existential perspectives that would lead us to rethink the normative in this case."[87]

Alternatively, Hays can produce a consistent outcome in ethics, even when the outcome is at variance with the larger witness of the Bible. For this example, we will look at his ethic on Christians serving in the military. On the descriptive level, he brings his remarkable interpretive skills to bear on a single passage: Matthew 5:38–48, which he calls "the central witness of the New Testament concerning violence."[88] Here Jesus says to "Love your enemies and pray for those who persecute you." Hays argues from this text against all war and Christian involvement in it especially. That Jesus did not require the centurion (Matt. 8:5–13; Luke 7:1–10) to leave his profession "suggests that the New Testament writers did not see participation in the army as sinful a priori."[89] However, the "central witness" of Matthew 5:38–48 must mean that the function of the stories of military men is like that of tax collectors and prostitutes: "so these stories about centurions cannot be read as endorsements of military careers."[90] Hays entertains the Old Testament holy war texts, but they are all easily discounted on the ground that "the New Testament vision trumps the Old Testament."[91]

Jesus' prescription against Christians brandishing weapons in time of war is further established by inducing the synthetic focal images. The call to non-violence is given to the *community* as a whole, so even though it is possible for a believer to be a soldier, that option "can only be seen as anomalous" within a people tasked with the vocation of suffering in the face of injustice.[92] Equally serious is the use of proof texts for physical defense, apart from the caveat that all such texts must be seen properly according to the "normativity of the cross," or else "we can be sure that the text is out of focus."[93] The determinative value of nonviolent behavior is further supported by the focal image of *new creation* that shapes the community eschatologically and prefigures the end of all war. The implication for all New Testament texts dealing even tangentially with brute warfare is that they "must therefore be read in this eschatological perspective. For example, even though Matthew 5:38–48 contains no explicit reference to eschatology, its directives must be read through the lens of the image of *new creation*."[94]

In the interests of space, I will skip over the hermeneutical and pragmatic tasks and return to Hays's discussion on homosexuality. I do so because here Hays offers practical advice on how to live in community with homosexuals that has meaning for military personnel and that finalizes what the remaining tasks say. Says Hays,

> Just as there are serious Christians who in good conscience believe in just war theory, so there are serious Christians who in good conscience believe that same-sex erotic activity is consonant with God's will. . . . I think that both groups are wrong, but in both cases the questions are so difficult that we should receive one another as brothers and sisters in Christ and work toward adjudicating our differences through reflecting together on the witness of Scripture.[95]

Despite Hays's acknowledgment that Jesus never called the centurion away from his job but did call the woman caught in adultery to "sin no more," that distinction seems to be lost on Hays, who clearly lumps together soldiers and eroticists as being in sin.

Frame's case for the ethics of warfare and military service develops out of the sixth commandment, "You shall not murder." So it should not surprise us that he elicits something close to Hays's eschatological prefigurement of *new creation*, pointing out that David was forbidden to build the temple because he was a man of war, and the temple anticipates a time of perfect peace with Jesus, the fulfillment of the temple.[96] Moreover, he also agrees with Hays that Matthew 10:34, "Do not think that I came to bring peace on the earth; I did not come to bring peace, but a sword," is a horatory metaphor to believers to stand strong in persecution.[97] But rather than brandish the Old Testament passages on *herem* warfare as anachronistic relative to the witness of the New Testament, he explains the Old Testament conflicts in a theocentric setting. "God wants it to be plain that Israel gains its victories, not through numbers, but through God's power."[98] Yet none of this provides an ethical blueprint for nations today.[99]

Divergently from Hays, Frame is willing to say that "[P]art of the meaning of just war is that Christian believers may fight in them. The allowance is based in the theocentric footing of the sixth commandment: God's delights in life and thus permits us to defend innocent life.[100] He cites the fact that John the Baptist confronted soldiers and told them not to extort, but never suggested that they should leave the army. The New Testament recognizes the extraordinary faith of the centurion, who said, gazing up at Jesus on the cross, "Truly this was a son of God." Conscientious objection is a real possibility for Frame, but it presupposes that there are *some* wars we do not need to object to.[101] Fundamentally, "a Christian will never advocate war unless it is a genuine responsibility of the civil magistrate, pursuing his office to protect the nation against hostile enemies."[102]

These differences on point are derivative of the larger theological contexts out of which both men work. Hays seems to want to do ethics out of specific biblical events (community, cross, new creation), rather than by a global examination of the whole Bible. Frame's issue with this approach, by and large, is that an ethic of any specific biblical event can only ever set a trajectory of biblical ideas in motion that support and circle back to that specific event. Thus, "An ethic of incarnation might focus on how we should follow Jesus' example by entering fully into the lives of others. . . . An ethic of atonement would focus on self-sacrificing love as the paradigm of love. . . . An eschatological ethic would see everything in the light of our future hope, including the rewards of heaven."[103]

When Hays explains that the purpose of involving centurions in the New Testament narrative is as a foil analogous to the account of tax collectors and prostitutes against unbelieving Israel, does that position arise naturally from the whole witness of the New Testament, or is it what "the New Testament's central message of peacemaking" demands of the reading?[104] We can go through all of Hays's rationales that call for an end to Christian participation in combat. But the question Frame would likely ask is, "What makes community, cross, and new creation the methodological guideline for deciding this issue?" As Hays encourages us all to construe our own focal images, who is to say that those are right?[105] And what is it about Matthew 5:38–48 that makes it "the central witness of the New Testament concerning violence," to wit, all other bible passages are to defer? As Frame cautions, "To derive from the event simply in itself is a case of the naturalistic fallacy."[106] Salient here for Frame is the fact that any event recorded in Scripture cannot be anything less than a matter of biblical law. To conceive ethics according to preferential biblical events—for example, creation, cross, and new creation—overlooks that an ethic based on one or more redemptive-historical events inevitably reverts to law when it seeks to define its specific standards.

One can retort that Frame is no different, in that he uses the lordship principle as his *lens* on Scripture and ethics. The difference, I think, is that control, authority, and presence differ significantly from community, cross, and new creation, in that the lordship principle is an all-embracing rubric for the whole message of the Bible, understood as a mandate from heaven to us. Hays's focal images represent one anthropologically based "vision" of the New Testament.

A Possible Shortfall in Frame's Lordship Principle

Yet there are also questions about Frame's existential perspective. He speaks of "human beings as revelation."[107] That would seem contradictory to the biblical truth that the apostles had authority as *recipients* of revelation (Ephesians 3:7–13; Galatians 2:8–9; and Romans 1:1–6) but not as sources of it. Yet Frame is steadfast that "The apostles place great weight on themselves as person-revelation."[108] There are global implications, given that all "Finite persons are also a means of God's revelation."[109] Deeper questions still emerge if we are to understand that triperspectivally, the normative, situational, and existential perspectives cover the same subject matter but from different viewpoints. Does Frame really want to say that finite people reveal the same subject matter as Scripture, only differently?

I agree with Frame that person-revelation can be a descriptive of a work of God. Theophanies—the incarnation, the inspiration, and illumination of the Spirit—are all divinely communicative, though in different ways.[110] As an appellation for people, I also concur that the *imago Dei* reveals important characteristics of God, although I am not content with Frame's idea that sin reveals God.[111] Yet none of this positions us at the center of what Frame really means by the revelatory character of persons.

Central most to the idea of person-revelation is Frame's familiar condensation that *theology is application.* So when he writes that "The apostles place great weight on themselves as person-revelation," it is in the context of the New Testament theme of *imitatio Christi.* Frame asks, for example, how are we to understand Jesus' declaration, "If anyone wishes to come after Me, he must deny himself, and take up his cross and follow Me" (Mark 8:34)? We can look up *deny* in a dictionary or a thesaurus and find more words, but these only repeat the first premise.

Where do we go from here? I understand what it means to "deny" oneself in the example set by Jesus and the apostles, for "language is part of life. To understand language, we must see what people do with it, how it is used."[112] According to the lordship triad, if God reveals himself "in events, words, and persons," then person-revelation is a necessary precondition for the acquirement of growth in grace. In speaking of person-revelation, it seems clear that Frame is reprising a central idea of his that "understanding the Word is applying it."[113]

Yet we are still left with questions for Frame. If theophany and the *imago Dei* are examples of person-revelation, then how are these forms of media substantially different from what the traditional division between special and general revelation has not already told us? And if he also means the self-evident idea that we can learn how to behave by observing mature believers, does this point provide enough content to warrant consideration of people as "revelation?" Or is this idea not better left to the topic of sanctification?

Frame would certainly reply that such examples are perspectives concomitant with the normative and situational perspectives. Although I think that this can be said convincingly of the existential perspective relative to all other subjects within his overall theology, in this particular case I am not entirely convinced that his types of person-revelation rise to the level of difference that would justify a separate perspective. While it is not my goal to eviscerate person-revelation, I question whether its occurrence under the existential perspective is not an attempt to fit certain data into the triperspectival paradigm for the sake of consistency.

The lordship principle is well thought-out as a macroscopic tool for theology. And the existential perspective offers a unique way of looking afresh at numerous God-person encounters from the anthropological position. But as is the case with all attempts to pare voluminous amounts of facts into a single synopsis, some parts can feel forced. Person-revelation may just be one such example.

Prior to the measurement of Frame and Hays on methodology, I noted Frame's strong opinion that the three schools of secular ethics (deontological, situational, and existential) are specious. Like the venerable Indian moral of the three "blind men and the elephant," each school thinks that it alone knows the truth. That has produced irresolvable perspectives in historical ethics. Frame contends that the constituents of historical secular ethics, variegated and often splintered though they be, find a unified and consistent reference point in triperspectivalism.[114] Nowhere is this coming together more evident than in his thought on the Decalogue.

Endnotes

---

1 *Proviso*: That the lordship triad accounts for the deficiencies of the deontological, teleological, and existential traditions in secular ethics, is strongly connoted by Frame in

DCL, 317: "The normative perspective can be seen as a Christian deontological ethic, the situational perspective as a Christian teleological ethic, and the existential perspective as a Christian existential ethic. These reflect the emphases of their non-Christian counterparts . . . but they bring these emphases together into a more coherent and fruitful unity in the context of our covenant relationship to God." That said, I do not find in Frame a premeditated effort to develop this idea in a sustained way, that is, to lay bare the unfinished thought of secular ethicists only to show how his ethical methodology finishes their work. Sustaining this idea is really my own burden, but one that seems unavoidable. In my conversation with Frame, he has agreed that this expansion is valid and needful.

2 *DCL*, 10.

3 Ibid.

4 DKG, 44.

5 C. Van Til, *The Defense of the Faith* (Philipsburg, NJ: P&R Publishing, [1955] 1963), 46. Also, *DG*, 185–187, and *DKG*, 44–48, are highly recommended reading on the relationship of knowing and obedience. In this vein, see also *DG*, 185–187, on the relationship of ethics to epistemology and metaphysics. *DCL*, xxvii and 354–355, makes explicit references to knowledge of God as a subdivision of ethics.

6 This statement made to a class at Westminster Theological Seminary, Philadelphia, on apologetics, at which I was in attendance. Elsewhere, he is unwilling to make ethics primary, but "there is a 'circular' relation between knowledge and obedience in Scripture. Neither is unilaterally prior to the other." *DKG*, 43.

7 *DCL*, 12.

8 Although we are here speaking of the multiperspectival system as applied to ethics as a metaethic that derives from Scripture, I think that Frame's real metaethic is Scripture itself. It is from that basis that the perspectival methodology in ethics is derived.

9 Bucer, cited by H. J. Selderhuis, *Marriage and Divorce in the Thought of Martin Bucer* (Kirksville, MO: Truman State University Press, 1999).

10 *DG*, 7. See also *DKG*, 81–85.

11 *DCL*, 239. Theology as application takes a somewhat different shape in Calvin, whose emphasis on *pietas* is almost entirely concerned with the indissoluble link between justification and sanctification. "John Calvin referred to his *Institutes of the Christian Religion* not as a *summa theologiae*, but as a *summa pietas*, for he was concerned to promote both sound doctrine and sincere piety." James Edward McGoldrick, "John Calvin, Practical Theologian: The Reformer's Spirituality," *The Outlook* 59, no. 6 (June 2009): 10–15.

12 *DCL*, 10.

13 For those who wish to undertake a deepened evaluation of the Square, see *DLC*, 41–53; *DKG*, 12–18; *DG*, 107–155; and *CVT*, 231–238.

14 Taken from *The Doctrine of the Christian Life* by John Frame, ISBN # 978-0-87552-796-3, page 42, P&R Publishing Co., P.O. Box 817, Phillipsburg, N.J., 08865, www.prpbooks.com.

15 Taken from *The Doctrine of the Christian Life*, ISBN # 978-0-87552-796-3, by John Frame, 43.
P&R Publishing Co., P.O. Box 817, Phillipsburg, N.J. 08865, www.prpbooks.com.
16 Although the two uses of the Square are close, the difference is one of stress. In my opinion, figure 2 emphasizes an epistemological perspective on ethics, while figure 1 of the Square focuses more on ethics relative to ontology. But again, there must be intersection between the two uses.
17 Frame treats these thinkers in *DCL*, 103–120.
18 Interaction with these thinkers is found in *DCL*, 88. I would add that the Christian tradition has not been exempt from the problems Frame enumerates in both versions of the Square. Justin Martyr, Clement of Alexandria, pseudo-Dionysius, and, in modern times, the "wholly other" of Barth and Bultmann maximized God's transcendence over his immanence. Alternatively, Schleiermacher internalized Christianity to such a radical degree that anyone could find God by simply looking within. We find this concept seminally expressed in Friedrich Schleirmacher's *Reden uber die Religion* (*To the Cultural Despises of Religion*).
19 *DCL*, 44.
20 Ibid.
21 I. Kant, *Grounding for the Metaphysics of Morals*, 3rd ed., trans. J. Ellington (Indianapolis: Hackett Publishing Co., 1993), vi.
22 H. Bavinck, *Essays on Religion, Science, and Society* (Grand Rapids, MI: Baker Academic, 2008), 262.
23 Representative quotes of Kant's view on this point are in Ellington's translation of Kant's *Grounding for the Metaphysics of Morals*, 52.
24 *DCL*, 112.
25 Ibid, 116. Frame adds, "There is a place for God in Kant's philosophy, but his God is not the source of moral norms. If God exists, for Kant, he exists in the noumenal realm." *DCL*, 115.
26 Ibid., 116.
27 See Jürgen Habermas, *The Structural Transformation of the Public Sphere*, trans. Thomas Burger (Cambridge: MIT Press, 1991). Influenced by American pragmatism, structural functionalism, and, to a lesser extent, post-structuralism, many of Habermas's central tenets are broadly Marxist in composition. It is through the complex dialectical process of reason and science that representational culture develops into the appearance of *Öffentlichkeit.*
28 *DCL*, 48.
29 See again n. 1 and *DCL*, 317, which describes these different ways of viewing the three principles of secular ethics.
30 *DCL*, 326. Frame deals extensively with these three ethical systems in Chapter 3 of *DCL*.
31 Ibid., 131.
32 Ibid., 307.
33 Ibid., 302.

34 Ibid.
35 Ibid., 307.
36 A term coined by Van Til's but used also by Frame, "borrowed capital" suggests that all non-Christian thought is parasitic on Christianity: regardless of its form, it must depend on God's order for verisimilitude. See, e.g., *AGG*, 72. That would include pagan ethical systems that pre-date Christianity, including Buddhism, Hinduism, and Jainism, in that these systems remain derivative of God's created order and self-disclosure since the beginning of creation.
37 *DKG*, 328.
38 Frame thus says that "[T]here is some truth in secular ethics because, despite its metaethic, it has encountered God's word in the self, in the world, and in the realm of norms (Rom. 1:32)." *DG*, 194. This idea is further predicated on his thought that the normative perspective is not limited to the propositional truth of Scripture. Even the empirical world and human subjectivity act as normative guides for ethical behavior, but far less so than does the Bible.
39 R. Hays, *The Moral Vision of the New Testament: Community, Cross, New Creation: A Contemporary Introduction to New Testament Ethics* (San Francisco: HarperSanFrancisico, 1996).
40 Ibid., 3. Hays is in the school of Stanley Hauerwas, who also resists the unity of the canon. "The narratives of Scripture were not meant to describe our world . . . but to change the world, including the one in which we now live." Stanley Hauerwas, "The Moral Authority of Scripture," in *From Christ to the Word: Introductory Readings in Christian Ethics*, ed. Wayne Bolton, Thomas D. Kennedy, and Allan Verhey (Grand Rapids, MI: Eerdmans, 1994), 135.
41 Hays, *Moral Vision*, 4.
42 Ibid., 5.
43 Ibid., 7.
44 Ibid., 3.
45 Ibid., 7.
46 Ibid.
47 Ibid., 7.
48 Ibid., 4. Hays is following a modernist line of hermeneutics made prominent by F. C. Baur, who, following Hegel, abandoned the effort to find "time-less truths" in the New Testament. In Baur's hands, the New Testament became the product of the earliest believing communities. George Ladd provides a helpful précis of the history of biblical interpretation, including the period of Baur and his followers, in the introduction to *A Theology of the New Testament* (Grand Rapids, MI: Wm. B. Eerdmans, 1974). Hauerwas also represents this trend. "The authority of Scripture derives its intelligibility from the existence of a community that knows its life depends on faithful remembering of God's care of his creation through the calling of Israel and the life of Jesus." Hauerwas, "The Moral Authority of Scripture," 34.
49 "Thus, the work of the historical critic entails reconstructing a 'thick description' of the symbolic world of the communities that produced and received the New Testament

writings." Hays, *Moral Authority*, 4. I think that makes any claim of absoluteness of the New Testament texts tenuous and the issue of coherence among the canonical writers problematic. As we will see, Hays does offer his own solution to the problem of coherence.
50 *DWG*, 48. On page 253 of *DWG*, Frame adds the lordship principles to this definition when he says that "the word of God is God himself, expressing himself through his lordship attributes of control, authority, and presence."
51 *DWG*, 48.
52 For Frame's brief remarks on textual criticism, see 232, 240, 253, 463, 536, and 544 of *DWG*.
53 See *DWG*, 239. That is not to suggest he is blind to the problem of harmonization or questions of factual consistency within the Bible. "Absolute ethical principle flows a *person* who is absolute. And only in the Bible do we find a God who is truly absolute and truly personal at the same time." *DWG*, 187, italics added. Frame is us away from titular "Bible problems" and toward a biblical worldview. If one presupposes the Bible to be the product of human effort, no amount of scientific harmonization can convince that it is "God-breathed." But if one works from the presupposition that the Bible *is* the word of God, then scholarship has its proper place in the study of so-called inconsistencies.
54 *DWG*, 231.
55 Hays, *Moral Vision*, 5.
56 Hays expresses this thought on pages 36–41, esp. page 39. The actual phrase he uses to reflect the Pauline meaning is "transfer of lordship."
57 Hays, *Moral Vision*, 39.
58 More recently, Hays has written on the role of the imagination in hermeneutics in *The Conversion of the Imagination: Paul As Interpreter of Israel's Scripture* (Grand Rapids, MI: Wm. B. Eerdmans, 2005).
59 D. Kelsey, *The Uses of Scripture in Recent Theology* (Philadelphia: Fortress Press, 1975), 159.
60 R. C. Johnson, *Authority in Protestant Theology* (Philadelphia: Westminster Press, 1959), 15.
61 Kelsey, *The Uses of Scripture in Recent Theology*, 160. See Frame's review of Kelsey's book online: "Review of Kelsey's *The Uses of Scripture in Recent Theology*, http://www.frame-poythress.org/review-of-kelseys-the-uses-of-scripture-in-recent-theology/.
62 Kelsey, *The Uses of Scripture in Recent Theology*, 166.
63 *DWG*, 483.
64 Not to be confused with the aforementioned "*discrimen*."
65 See Hays, *Moral Vision*, 196. Due to the limitations of space, the focal images of cross and new creation are not dealt with here.
66 It is for this reason that Hays views Ephesians and 1 Timothy as "pseudo-Pauline" epistles. Ephesians could not have been written by Paul because it underplays the community as a whole, emphasizing instead a "series of admonitions addressed to persons in particular roles within the household: wives/husbands, children/parents, slaves/masters." Hays, *Moral Vision*, 64. Also, 1 Timothy lacks Pauline authenticity because it "vigorously

promotes norms for the community," whereas "the writer is no longer thinking through ethical issues from their theological foundations. All that needs to be done is to guard the tradition entrusted by the apostle." *Moral Vision*, 71.

67 Because Hays is a biblical theologian, and Frame is a systematic theologian, my comparative study is a bit like comparing "apples to oranges." This disjunction is apparent when weighing Frame's situational perspective against Hays's hermeneutical task. Hays elicits the hermeneutical task as a way to discover a unifying set of ideas that bridge the biblical canon to us. In ethics, the situational perspective converges mainly on the data that makes up our outward environment, not internal biblical themes that are thought to function in the cross-cultural translation of Scripture. So I am working with limited overlap between the two men. To overcome this problem, a platform for conversation has been created by leaning more on Frame's perspectivalism relative to the doctrine of Scripture.

68 Hays, *Moral Vision,* 209.

69 For his complete explanation of these three sources, see *Moral Vision*, 210–211. By "experience," Hays means "the experience of the community of faith collectively." *Moral Vision*, 211.

70 Hays, *Moral Vision,* 6.

71 Frame, *The Academic Captivity of Theology* (Lakeland, FL: Whitefield Publications, 2012). In *DWG*, Frame, in addressing the logic of application, shows that a specific concern of the situational perspective is the mandatory use of non-biblical data. "Scripture contains no lessons on Hebrew or Greek grammar. To learn that, we must study extrabiblical information. Similarly, the other means that enable is to use Scripture, such as textual criticism, test editing, translation, publication, teaching, preaching, concordances, and commentaries, all depend on extrabiblical data." *DWG*, 232.

72 Case in point, on the level of tradition Frame himself makes great use of the Larger Catechism, in concert with Scripture, to reach ethical positions.

73 *DWG*, 232.

74 Frame says, "We learn from the previous generation, and the generation before then, all the way back to Bible time." Ibid., 295.

75 The reader is recommended to Chapters 40 and 42 of *DWG* for the processes by which Scripture reach us.

76 *DWG*, 309.

77 Ibid., 305.

78 Hays, *Moral Vision,* 313.

79 Exemplary is the critical insight conferred by feminism in subordinating Scriptural motifs on men and women to the discourse of modernity. See Hays, *Moral Vision*, 211. Hays is reluctant on this count because existentialist readings are not in accord with the synthetic "focal image" of *community*.

80 See Hays, *Moral Vision*, 389.

81 Ibid., 403.

82 Ibid.

83 See 1 Timothy 3 and Titus 1.

84 In fairness to Hays, he is not in favor of open-ended acceptance of homosexuality within the churches. For those who look for "unqualified acceptance of homosexuality seem to be operating with a simplistic anthropology that assumes whatever is must be good; they have a theology of creation but no theology of sin and redemption." Hays, *Moral Vision*, 402. But this just adds to the questions regarding the connectivity of his general theological formulation.
85 *DCL*, 760.
86 See Ibid., 760; 766–786. Frame advances ideas on homosexuality, genetic disposition, and science in "Living with Ourselves," 260–266 of *DCL*.
87 The previous quotes by Frame on homosexual ordination that are not footnoted are all part of an email to the author dated July 17, 2012, with some minor editing. It is important to note that in each case, Frame is interacting with my explanation to him about Hays's handling of the same issue.
88 Hays, *Moral Vision*, 335.
89 Ibid.
90 Ibid.
91 Ibid., 336.
92 Ibid., 337.
93 Ibid., 338.
94 Ibid., 338.
95 Ibid., 335.
96 See *DCL*, 704.
97 Cf. *DCL*, 705, and *Moral Vision*, 332–333.
98 *DCL*, 706.
99 See ibid., 706, for this point.
100 The whole of Frame's work on the sixth commandment, which involves many issues, hinges on God's lordship over life and death, as well as on God's delight in life. Consequently, human life, *innocent* human life especially, is to be protected, which is why Frame is dead set against abortion on demand. By the same standard, we may take life if it means protecting innocent lives (see *DCL*, 685). In either case, God's delight in life is not to be ratified as a static principle that forbids Christians from joining the military. Or, in an alternate view, is war always "violence"—the *unwarranted* exertion of force?
101 The notion that killing, even in self-defense, is never appropriate for Christians comes up in Frame's discussion of Anabaptism, which he thinks is manifestly unbiblical. See *DCL*, 606–610, 692, and 706–708.
102 *DCL*, 713.
103 Ibid., 931.
104 R. Hays, *The Moral Vision of the New Testament: Community, Cross, New Creation: A Contemporary Introduction to New Testament Ethics* (San Francisco: HarperSanFrancisico, 1996), 335.

105 Hays is thoughtful when he says, "The unifying images must be derived from the texts themselves, rather than superimposed artificially, and they must be capable of providing an interpretive framework that links and illumes the individual writings." *Moral Vision*, 5. My concern is his use of images as functionally independent devices that eventually stand between us and the text. Then we are in danger of losing Scripture's thematic consistency, in favor of criteria that pre-adapt us to equivocate on texts that do not conform to the model. The question is how to carefully relate image to metaphysics (biblically defined) to ensure that we are not venturing into some quasi-aesthetic ethic but are working from a purely theistic basis of revelation and analogy. Then all biblical data is regulatory of ethics, whereby we no longer need to decide between concepts and images to illumine the biblical texts.

106 *DCL*, 932. Identified with the analytic philosophy of E. G. Moore, the "naturalistic fallacy" (often called the Open Question Argument) vehemently argues against the extrapolation of a general ethic or fixed values, such as "good" or "goodness," from this simple premise. Frame exploits the idea to help support Christian theism over and against secular thought; e.g., *DCL*, 932.

107 The chapter title of Chapter 43, *DWG*. Cf., his definition of people *as a "means of divine communication*." *DWG*, 305.

108 Ibid., 318.

109 Ibid., 316.

110 See *DCL* for these categories, a section that appears to be echoed more thoroughly is Chapter 42 of *DWG*.

111 Frame: "Even sin, in one sense, images God, for sin is basically an attempt to be God, to replace God on the throne." *DWG*, 316. John is clear, however, that "This is the message we have heard from Him and announce to you, that God is Light, and in Him there is no darkness at all" (1 John 1:5). If sin is an image, an imitation is only ever a likeness of a principle source. In that case, to sin would imitate the devil, not God.

112 *DWG*, 305. This example shows the influence of Wittgenstein on Frame, as mentioned in Chapter 1.

113 *DWG*, 317. Frame distinguishes the lordship triad accordingly on page 304 of *DWG*. "Events" refer to the situational perspective, "words," to the normative perspective, and "persons," to the existential perspective.

114 See again n. 1 of this chapter on the point that this idea is nascent in Frame but lacks concerted development—something I wish to do.

Chapter 4

Lordship and the Ten Commandments

The contour of the theologian's ethic is an exposition of the Decalogue.[1] Of first concern are general observations on perspectivalism in relation to ethics. After this, attention will turn to select examples of how the lordship principle coalesces perspectivally the essential intendments of secular ethics.

The Decalogue represents a command ethic, not a narrative or virtue ethic. Nonetheless, the additional categories are accounted for seeing that the command ethic is aligned with the normative perspective, which, as a perspective, is able to include "all the ground that is covered by the other two approaches."[2] Viewed triperspectivally, the commandments thus form an aggregate moral vision for modern man. Presently, however, I am disposed to question why Frame's claim is unique. For viewed non-perspectivally, the present structure of the Decalogue already addresses virtually every area of life. That fact is even more basically evident in the intrinsic unity of the commands. Thus, we are not to "pick and choose" between commands. It was to prevent this very human tendency that God said through Moses, "*All* the commandments that I am commanding you today you shall be careful to do . . . (Deut. 8:1, italics added).

Frame can make the claim because in a conjoint expression of the unity of the Law, perspectivalism presses the unity of the Law further. There is cross-over or connectivity *between* the commands—for example, Deut. 8:1—but according to multiperspectivalism, there is also connectivity *within* the commands. The *élan vital* found in one is in another, and in all.[3]

Frame believes, therefore, that people who commit adultery are liars, while those who steal do so from a heart of covetousness. The fourth commandment, which prescribes rest and prohibits work on the seventh day, is violated by the misuse of our time during the whole week.[4] The perspectivally enriched unity of the Law is seen additionally in the fact that *each* law necessitates complete righteousness. Each law also forbids *all* sin, not just the sin singled out by individual laws.[5] Finally, the inter-unity of the commands finds rich expression in holy worship. Not just the second commandment, but *all* of the commandments are divine injunctions to worship. For "in all our relationships to God, we stand as worshippers."[6]

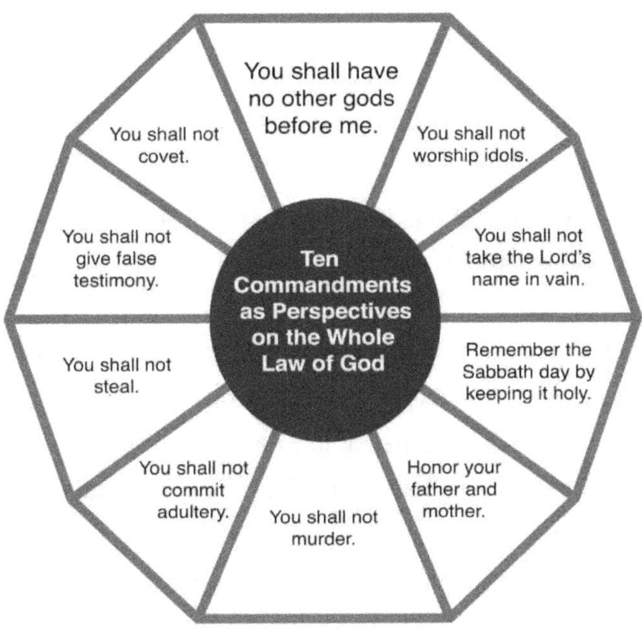

Fig. 3: The Ten Commandments as Perspectives on the Whole Law[7]

That the commandments stand together in mutual reciprocity prompts a unique arrangement, whereby Frame presents each law as a perspective on the whole of the Law.[8] The chart above enables us to read a familiar passage afresh: "For whoever keeps the whole law and yet stumbles in one point, he has become guilty of all" (James 2:10). Following Jesus, Frame locates the most important area of the inter-unity of the Decalogue in love: heart-felt love for God and for one's neighbors.[9] Love is the sum of the Law, for "love is central to the lives of God's people. It summarizes our entire obligation."[10] Taking this point through to lordship, love voices the elementary devotion of the vassal to the lord in a covenant. Says Frame, "So love should be defined triperspectivally as allegiance (normative perspective), as well as action (situational perspective), and affection (existential perspective)."[11]

With the love ethic as the condensation of the whole Law, it is apparent that the Christian command ethic is not a supercilious call to dispassionate and grudging obedience, similar to Kant's. It is a divine summons to intimate fellowship with the Lord.

Multiperspectivalism, thus far, in addition to pressing the unity of the Law further than traditional theology has taken it, most certainly stands in stark opposition to the modern trend to moderate and even dismiss the Ten Commandments in Christian ethics. This is what Enda McDonagh had in mind when he wrote that none of the great theologians "have given [love] the central architectonic place one might expect . . . In moral theology [love] received a very skimpy treatment."[12] Due to the extreme subjectivism, sentimentalism, and even eroticism that has accompanied love in the contiguous culture since the 60s, Stanley Hauerwas questions the validity of the virtue as definitive of Christian living. "If Christianity is primarily an ethic of love, I think it is wrong and clearly ought to be given up."[13]

Frame corrects such *dismissiveness* by pointing to what he terms the *ontological* stress and the *personal* stress of the love ethic. The ontological stress is seen in the fact that the Sinai encounter is instigated by the eternal God.[14] This makes the command an imperative of theology (normative) and provides it objective content. The temptation to marginalize even slightly the Decalogue is nipped in the bud.[15] Correlative to the ontological stress is the *personal* intent of the Sinai encounter: to possess our hearts that God might be our *summum bonum*. God is our chief end (teleological), and he changes us to be like him (existential). This objective attenuates the concern of those who are leery of love as *eros*.

In keeping with the depth and breadth of love, we cannot compartmentalize our love of a personal God and others. Yet neither must we love too scrutinizingly. Hence, Frame extends the discussion to incorporate "narrow" and "broad" applications of the commandments, or what could be called the *organic development* of the laws.[16] Here he is simply following a course previously mapped out by the Larger Catechism that works through the commandments according to their immediate and far-reaching applications. I'll provide examples in Frame of these twin emphases in upcoming sections.

These preliminary thoughts raise a deeper question still, though not new, but perhaps drawn more sharply in a postmodern age. Is it still feasible to speak in terms of a Lord who authoritatively insists on being worshipped? Those who react viscerally to the idea might want to pause and see the issue as Frame presents it perspectivally, especially as he presents it in light of the love ethic of the Decalogue. As we have reviewed, unique to multiperspectivalism is the fact that everything that constitutes control is in authority and presence, and everything that is tantamount to presence is in authority and control, and everything that amounts to authority is in control and presence. So God's control and authority are always gracious, loving, and merciful, while his grace, love, and mercy implement his control and authority for our good. Thus, Frame can say that "Sovereignty as I understand it is God's kingship or lordship. As such it embraces the three lordship attributes. It is important, I think, that we understand sovereignty (lordship) as control, authority, and presence, rather than (as writers often assume) bare control."[17]

With these generalities behind us, the subsequent facts will expound further on the initial assertion: that what historical ethics has torn asunder is reunited in Frame's perspectival method. While we cannot address each commandment, even more so, the macro or micro implications of each one, the following will provide examples of how key ethical topics find equilibrium in a single point of reference, once the subject matter is treated perspectivally. Subject matter will be treated according to three categories: absoluteness and content, objectivity and inwardness, and freedom and authority.[18]

Absoluteness plus Content

Now I have said that a leading trait of Frame's ethic is his critique of non-Christian moral systems and their inability to marry ethical absolutes with ethical *content.*[19] Ludwig Wittgenstein attempts to provide relevant content by bridging language and cognition, while denying the possibility of absolutes pertinent to both language and cognition. Thus, language cannot be conceived of as a device for communicating independently constituted (or individuated) thoughts. Instead, Wittgenstein conjectures, we cannot actually talk about concrete reality. We can only deal with concepts, pictures, models, words, and mathematics that touch reality. It is these forms of communication that *are* reality and reality is nothing more. These unsayable realities belong to the "mystical" realm.[20] Essentially, then, existence is meaning*less*. In this way, Wittgenstein gave academic respectability to the poetic muse of Shelly.

> He gave man speech, and speech created thought, which is the measure of the universe.

Quite conversely (and despite Wittgenstein's minimal influence on Frame), Frame solves Wittgenstein's fragmented worldview by locating the substratum of meaning and of morality in the God of meaning. The first table of the Law, outstandingly the first commandment: "You shall have no other gods before me" (Exod. 20:3), presents a normed and superlative case for exclusive love of God and all that he has said, because only he is Lord and he is Lord of everyone and everything.

However, it is with his translation and interpretation of "vanity" in the third commandment that lordship secures an inspirited place in our understanding of *universal meaning*.[21] Frame points out that "The term *shav',* translated 'in vain' can mean "empty, trivial, meaninglessness, as in Job 7:3."[22] Thus, "Meaninglessness is a form of falsehood, for the name of God is itself rich in meaning."[23] Therefore, not merely lies and profanity but any meaningless or empty statements about the universe are forbidden by the commandment. Meaningless declarations of fact about the world and false statements are in fact forms of idolatry, for both trivialize God. To imagine the creation as inherently opaque or to misuse anything in the whole of the creation is therefore to depersonalize God's name in the creation and to disobey the third commandment.

The lordship principle makes this point clear. *Control*: "naming is an exercise of sovereign control."[24] God is in the unique position to name himself, his people, thus "identifying his future with theirs," and to rule their environment.[25] *Authority*: just as fathers have the right to name their children, God's action of naming in Scripture reveals "God as the ultimate Lord."[26] *Presence*: existentially, because "God is also identified with his name" and God is in all things (though he is not confined to all things), his creation bears intrinsic meaning.[27]

Personal Annotations

Some of my own observations on the contemporary and fecundate cultural attitude inspired may be appropriate here. The deconstruction of normative views of language, instigated largely by Wittgenstein, has come to provide the basis for a critical narrative against self-styled group subordination and the promotion of free-speech advocacy for an open society. The wholly egalitarian construct of human identity sees old forms of morality and ethics as based in rhetorical constructs that are created, interpreted, or enforced in certain socially established ways. Foreseen beneficiaries of the new movement include people suffering racism, affirmative action, immigration reform, and civil rights for feminist and LGBTQ organizations.[28] The new literary mode, based in laws of speech neutrality, aims at the reversal of victim disadvantages as it defines them. But the egalitarian form of unity seeks to tear down biblical roles between men and woman, the biblical definition of marriage, and make all religions equal. In Europe, in particular, the literary advocacy is having an impact on European legal discourse.[29]

Although some of the issues raised—for example, civil rights and anti-racism—stem from the "borrowed capital" of Christianity, overall the modern movement raises serious ethical concerns about the correspondence of language to reality and thus reality itself. In fact, it means to undercut the positivist linkage of any absolute reality as a standard point of reference to a universal understanding of spoken language—assuming that this very connection is the cause of ongoing suppression of victimized people groups. The irony is that to accomplish this agenda, people must say that normative speech is *meaningless*, in order to assign it *new* meaning according to the dictates of an open society.[30]

However, God's naming of himself indicates his control, authority, and presence relative to his creation. Thus, according to Frame, to treat all things in the world as ultimately meaningless for the purpose of reassigning meaning to them according to the dictates of human reason is to treat God's name in vain. It is to provide the intellectual ground and social legitimization for the distortion of God's self-identification and his control over the world he has made. It is no coincidence that where language is viewed as culturally shaped and uncertain, the authority of God's lordship is also questioned.

Work and the Genesis Mandate

Accounting for both absoluteness and content, Frame locates a transcendent ethical norm in the prescription of the eighth commandment, specifically in its vaulting back to God's Cultural Mandate to the first couple to "work" the Garden. Set in the infrastructure of creation itself, Frame reasons here that the stable given of work "assumes that God has given to human beings ownership of property."[31]

The *narrow* meaning of the commandment is thus established in the rationale that "Stealing would have no meaning, unless there were a clear distinction between what belongs to me and what belongs to someone else."[32] The transmittal of property is not, however, absolute to man for "... ultimately all property belongs to God," with the coadunation that as stewards of God, we are "given responsibility to care for God's creation."[33]

Summing this dual thought, theft attains absolute meaning by virtue of the fact that "Scripture endorses the concept of private property, always with the *proviso* that God is the ultimate owner of creation and the one who has the ultimate authority over it."[34] The precepts of various forms of distributionist economics, based as they are in artificial state-monopoly, are therefore denied a rightful place in the Lord's order.

We can also look to the *broad* meaning of the eighth commandment for a centralization of the thematic marriage of absolute truth and ethical content. From the stable given of work, via the mandate of Genesis, Frame establishes that "The eighth commandment also presupposes a work ethic."[35] To ground a work ethic in the narrative of creation is to shift the historic Protestant work ethic, or Puritan work ethic, as Max Weber coined the phrase, away from John Calvin's emphasis that God's blessing of one's work or calling serves as a visible sign of one's redemption to a principle deriving from the material creation, yet without losing its distinctly supernatural, revelatory center.[36]

The same cannot be said of Mirosalv Volf, who, in *Work in the Spirit: Toward a Theology of Work*, wants to interpret our daily labor in a new paradigm, in which God's Spirit vivifies the new creation and acts as the source of *all* human ability and creativity. This is without reference to specifically Christian presuppositions, including those traditionally brought to bear on the creation mandate of Genesis. The significance of work, in his view, lay therefore within a *pneumatological* and eschatological framework that envisages all work as a doxological offering to God and that looks toward the consummation of the present age. All work that survives the test of God's judgment must be *assumed* to be in step with his purposes and therefore done with his aid (rationalism or non-biblical view 4 of the Square).[37] The problem is that Volf never defines the standard God will use to judge our work (irrationalism or non-biblical view 3 of the Square). More problematically, his dualistic paradigm, while holding out the prospect of judgment of work in the *future*, fails to provide a universally binding way to access the nature of theft *now*.

Objectivity plus Inwardness

Perspectivalism also alleges that "In the Christian worldview, moral standards are both objective and inward."[38] Now in Rudolph Bultmann's existentialism, obedience is the seminal criterion for determining the existence of faith. So much so, that Daniel Gallagher asseverates that "Bultmann interprets the terms 'faith' and 'obedience' to be interchangeable in the Pauline corpus."[39] Problematically, says Bultmann, the Lord of the past is unknowable.[40] "Obedience . . . is directed to the God whose existence is always presupposed. However, faith in Jesus Christ is not obedience to a Lord *who is known already*."[41] We are to know a Lord who is "presupposed," but obediential faith cannot act on a Lord "who is known already." One can already see the irrationalist/rationalist tension in Bultmann. Consequently, our obedience has no normative Christian standard that we can apply to real or hypothetical situations. In fact, Bultmann vociferously rejects such as norm.[42] In the end, Bultmann's objectivity gives way to inwardness without objectivity, and creates a problem no different in substance than the "piecemeal" approach of purely secular ethics.

How does Frame handle this specific dilemma? Drawing from the lordship principle, Frame's ethic avers that intellectual knowledge is propositional truth or "metaphysical" truth.[43] This truth is knowable and is known to its recipients (objectivity) in history. Thus Frame does not appeal to *Heilsgeschichte* or any form of metaphysical or epistemological dualism.

Metaphysical truth equates to the normative perspective and forms the basis for a deontological ethic.

But then also according to the lordship paradigm, there is ethical knowledge and its allied existential ethic (inwardness). The old saying is "Life is built on doctrine." Frame agrees but reverses the adage to say, "Doctrine is built on life."[44] We recall that one of Frame's main contributions to the field of ethics is his observation that ethics is foundational for metaphysics and epistemology.[45] The psychical basis for the postulation arises from the scholar averring that the intellect is an ethical organ. We learn by doing. In fact, Jesus said that people gain knowledge in an ethical environment. "He who has My commandments and keeps them is the one who loves Me; and he who loves Me will be loved by My Father, and I will love him and will *disclose* Myself to him" (John 14:21, italics added).[46] To "know" God, in the existential sense, is to be in intimate fellowship with him, much as Adam "knew" his wife is a prescient marker of knowing Christ in his fullness. In the New Testament, knowledge of God, the world, and the self is the result of walking in the Spirit. We walk in "faith working itself out through love" (Gal. 5:6).

A Practical Instance

An example of Frame's ability to match objectivity and inwardness in ethics may well look to his positions on birth control and genetic manipulation. Due to their relationship to human sexuality, he takes up these specific issues under the seventh commandment. Mankind has a normative command from God to "be fruitful and multiply" (Gen. 1:28). Yet there are situational and existential considerations that may permit a couple to limit the amount of children they plan to have. Per Frame,

> Reasons for birth control bear a high burden of proof. But it does seem to me that people might legitimately control births in order to guard the health of the mother or more effectively to minister to people in dangerous parts of the world. Such decisions should be made in the light of biblical principles, including . . . situational factors [situational perspective] and heart motives [existential perspective].[47] (words in brackets added)

In the debate over genetic engineering, conservatives typically warn against "playing God." Frame acknowledges this danger but provides situational and existential grounds for moving forward cautiously. Citing the fact that God is the Lord of creation, he exploits the Cultural Mandate of Genesis 1:28 to suggest that since we are called on to develop all of the earth's resource to the glory of God, and that our dominion requires imitation of God, then some genetic manipulation is permitted. Frame explains,

> But I know of no passage or principle of Scripture that ascribes to God alone the right to bring about changes in the human genome. On the contrary, the Cultural Mandate encourages human beings to be involved in the development of all the earth's resources for God's glory [situational perspective] and for their own dominion. Surely they cannot achieve that kind of dominion without also mastering themselves, without understanding and controlling developments within their own bodies [existential perspective].[48] (words in brackets added)

Clearly, Frame looks to the kind of general ethical Absolute Bultmann overlooks, while, at the same time, he values human, teleological, and existential considerations, once again demonstrating the ability of perspectivalism to arrive at a rounded ethic.

Genetic Manipulation: A Slippery Slope?

Although Frame offers well-reasoned restrictions on genetic manipulation, they seem oddly out of accord as he encourages the science "to improve certain kinds of intelligence or skills in people, or to improve the possibility that such gifted people will be conceived."[49] Plato's *Republic* advanced eugenics for a similar reason: to selectively breed for desirable qualities.[50] Plato also combined eugenics with population control by "exposing" undesirable babies.[51] Even if we were able to constrict eugenic manipulation of the human genome to the advancement of "gifted people," the unanswered question is what guarantee can society provide that breeding for the genetically superior will not turn into the nightmarish dystopia of Huxley's *Brave New World*? By Divine prerogative, we are each "fearfully and wonderfully made" (Ps. 139:14). The Cultural Mandate gives man dominion over lower nature, but for now I question its application in this way.

Freedom plus Authority

Under "freedom and authority," Frame has political philosophy principally in mind. His express concern is how the Bible can provide the type of balance the world needs between anarchy (freedom) and totalitarianism (authority).[52] An appropriate area of consideration is the contemporary perusal for social justice.

A Modern Moral Issue

In *A Theory of Justice*, John Rawls argues from a goal-oriented or narrative ethic (Frame's situational perspective) for an egalitarian form of liberty, in which individuals are guaranteed the greatest freedom compatible with the freedom of others.[53] His ethic also seeks to overturn inequality and to provide justice for the poor and disadvantaged, which, under the rule of fairness, ought to be established for all.[54] Yet Rawls cannot base his notion *a se* (independent) of raw subjectivity. In other words, he offers content with absoluteness, which leaves the "ought" of his system known as "Justice as Fairness" ambiguous and unconvincing. According to David Miller, Rawls's theory argues that the "Parties in the original position are supposed to be not only guided by a rational desire to promote their interests but also constrained by norms of reasonableness to ensure that they do not propose principles that some will be unable to accept."[55] But Vacek notes of systems such as Rawls's that society often confuses justice with love. "Respect for 'humanity' is mistaken for 'real, personal love.'"[56] What motivated the Good Samaritan was not social justice, but love for God and neighbor. Under the constraints of social justice theory, as espoused by Rawls, the neighbor is to be turned into a stranger when Jesus says to turn the stranger into a neighbor. Modern advocates for social justice would have us treat our neighbor with a universal impartiality that places him on the same level as someone we do not personally know or feel affection for.

Reintroducing Frame's idea that non-Christian ethics is utopian, I am reminded of the many instances in which nations that partition biblical principles become egalitarian. They want to help everyone by promoting for the general welfare and too often look to forms of socialism as the tool. Such powers are like an electric fence. An electric fence affects everyone who backs into it equally. What is the upshot? Governments seek to enforce the redistribution of wealth, even in the face of widespread resistance to the idea. But the fence is an impersonal force, incapable of heart-felt love or real discernment. Justice as fairness, especially as state-mandated policy, dulls society's sense of personal charity and replaces individual compassion with abstract equity.

Let us consider this perspectival alternative. With God's empathetic love as the basis, love and justice are united. We are commanded to love God and neighbor (deontological ethic). To show honor to parents and avoid murder, adultery, theft, lying to our neighbor, and coveting his possessions require in some sense these prerequisites as a desired goal and a plan to achieve them (teleological ethic). God's love makes the demonstration of our empathy (normative and situational perspectives) with fallen culture possible and gives it content, not only in the ontological sense, but, more important, in the human sense of intercession. In redemption, we are changed (existential perspective) to recognize the intercessory nature of Jesus' earthly ministry as the standard for the church in its work of social renovation. We lay down our lives for our brothers.

Socialized welfare is seen increasingly as a tool of social justice. Frame does not repudiate welfare but provides a biblical alternative. Let us focus on the fifth commandment. The *narrow* application of the fifth commandment appertains to our respect for parents. The underprivileged may be our parents. The fifth commandment thus addresses their needs through children's intercession: we are to care for our parents in their later years, thus providing an alternative to socialized welfare. So, comments Frame, "Welfare is first of all a family responsibility."[57]

More generalized forms of care and welfare are subsumed under Frame's *broad* view of the ninth commandment. Narrowly, the ninth commandment forbids bearing false witness against one's neighbor. Yet the panoptic connotation implies the opposite to Frame: we are to be faithful and true witnesses of Christ.[58] Our obedience helps us fulfill the Great Commission (Matthew 28:19–20). As the oppressed not only hear the gospel from us, but also see it incarnated in our actions, our transformed personal values align with the Lord's twin priorities of love and justice.[59] We humbly feed the hungry, tend to the sick, laugh with those who laugh, cry with those who cry, and mourn with those who mourn. When one weeps, the other tastes salt.

The Larger Problem

Freedom and authority may be approached even more broadly than politics and redistributionist economics. The struggle to find a satisfactory resolution between authority and freedom remains an uphill battle for contemporary Christian ethics generally.

Paul Tillich was a foundationalist. His dogmatics is based on a type of ontological-metaphysical "realism" of a sort that sees God as virtually synonymous with Being itself (otherwise, the Ultimate, the Absolute, the Unconditional). Tillich's criticism against the theistic God is that "He deprives me of my subjectivity because he is all-powerful and all-knowing. I revolt and make him into an object, but the revolt fails and becomes desperate. God appears as the invincible tyrant, the being in contrast with whom all other beings are without freedom and subjectivity."[60]

Since Tillich, postliberals and postmoderns in the West have rejected systems of foundationalism and push freedom to dizzying new heights. In distinguishing the non-foundationalist spirit of postmodernism, James A. Reimer can say "that we have come to recognize that there are numerous rationalities (each one intratextually coherent), and consequently, numerous understanding of ethics (virtue, goodness, justice, etc.)."[61] David H. Kelsey further clarifies the central idea of non-foundationalism.

> Thus, Scripture is not the starting-point for theology. Indeed, a theological system does not consist of "one long over-arching argument" resting on any starting-point, whether religious experience or religions text, but rather is a set of several different families of argument which, taken as a whole might be looked at in a quasi-aesthetic way as solicitation of mind and imagination to look at Christianity in a certain way.[62]

Postmodern theology rejects any ultimate, objective reference point for the ground of ethics. What is left is a "quasi-aesthetic way as solicitation of mind and imagination"—basically content-less, philosophical air that fails to anchor itself to real authority.[63] It is no wonder, then, that by the 1970s, M. F. Wiles could speak of the problem of trying to isolate "the beginning" of religious authority."[64]

The Answer According to the Lordship Principle

Frame contends that the inquiries of the past leading to a disjunction between divine authority and freedom in ethics find a way back through multiperspectivalism. Appealing to the *broad* connotation of the fifth commandment, the normative perspective of the command commits us to the authoritative voice of God. This idea may be viewed as having non-value in a politically correct age. Yet what are we to do with the common ethical vernacular of "right" and "wrong"? During the Nuremberg trials, Hitler's associates argued that they were just following orders. Well, they were. They had hoped that their peers would recognize they had no choice but demonstrate blind obedience to commands. But no one bought the lie. Why? Because, due to the "borrowed capital" of Christianity, we instinctively know that there is a limit to ethical claims. More, we are able to reason that for one to justify acts on the basis that one does not have a choice *is* a choice (irrational/rational tension). Frame is saying that the intuitive guide of reason and conscience is explicated further in Scripture (recall that we also have knowledge of the Word in our experience and in the self) and that this knowledge provides a bulwark against indiscriminate claims resulting in injury to others.[65]

Still, considering our innate knowledge of right and wrong, there is the role for the situational perspective. It comprises the teleological or narrative ethic and asks, "What are the best means of accomplishing God's purposes?"[66] Note that God commanded the primitive couple to "be fruitful and multiply" (Gen. 1:28). Yet concordant with this command, man is by nature a sexual being. Why does God order the man to do something *a posteriori* the fact that man can do nothing less than act in accordance with his purposeful nature? It is because not any procreation is permissible. The voice of the Lord sets the limits of authority, within which procreation is to take place. So we are to avoid adultery and fornication. The narrative ethic that focuses on changing the world through the development of peoples, races, and cultures is synthesized with a normative ethic, which asks, "What does Scripture say about this situation?"[67]

We also know instinctively to work and to develop all of the earth's resources, turning nature into culture; otherwise, no river would have a dam. And yet, for the same reason, God issued the second commandment, which cautions us to worship the God of nature and not nature itself. By impulse, we reject the Nuremberg defense. Yet in the sixth commandment, God commands *us* not to kill, which involves all disrespect for life, including abortion and euthanasia.[68] Once more, God's authority sets limits on us. God consistently commands us to do things we do by natural impulse so that we will remain bound to his ethical will. We thus change the world by submitting to the Law, which is also engraved on reason and conscience.

The existential perspective or virtue ethic is now crucial. If the law is engraved on the psychical life of people, but by sin we restrain ourselves from submitting to the Lord *in toto*, then this perspective asks, "How must I change if I am to do God's will?"[69] The answer is that "The atonement of Christ, applied to our hearts by the continuing work of the Spirit, renews us in the image of Christ (Eph. 4:24; Col. 3:10)."[70] Per usual, there are *ontological* and *personal* emphases to account for. Regarding the ontological, "Divine grace, atonement, and justification are certainly objective—realities occurring outside ourselves, which we cannot change."[71] Yet it is the personal emphasis that is phrased in such as a way as to surprise us. Frame quotes his former teacher Van Til, who said, "[T]he primary ethical duty for man is self-realization. . . . When man becomes truly the king of the universe the kingdom of God is realized, and when the kingdom of God is realized, God is glorified."[72]

Van Til expands on Christian "self-realization."[73] (1) "Man's will needs to become increasingly spontaneous in its reactivity." (2) "Man's will needs to become increasingly fixed in its self-determination." (3) "Man's will must increase in momentum." In an age of Art Nouveau forms of spirituality, including traditions of Eastern spirituality, nonduality, and recondite and meditative practices, one might be surprised to hear Van Til (and, by association, Frame) speak in such terms. But freedom is not antithetical to authority. True freedom is discovered in submission to authority: the Lord's authority.[74] *Spontaneity* is possible insofar as salvation has freed us to be the people God intended us to be. We can walk freely through the Garden of life, choosing to eat of any fruit we like, even on impulse, as long as the choice is not sinful.[75] Christianity permits improvisation within limits set for our protection and also to help us focus on what we ought to do in our love and service as a new creation to our Lord. *Self-determination* is not autonomy but an inalienable right: the God-given freedom to think, act, and "be" apart from social pressures and authoritarian constraint. And *momentum* is like unto a free-enterprise business, whose managers need to increase in "alertness, stability, and comprehensiveness of decision."[76] In short, authority and freedom come together in the Lord. So Tillich's critique of the theistic God that "He deprives me of my subjectivity" is flawed.[77] Frame would most certainly reply to Tillich, "So if the Son makes you free, you will be free indeed" (John 8:3).

Endnotes

1 Frame works from the position of the Ten Commandments in keeping with his high commitment to the historic Reformed faith, from which he looks to the Reformed catechisms and Calvin for inspiration. I must also note that by looking to the Decalogue as the basis for ethics, the theologian understands that such a life can only be lived in the power of the Holy Spirit. Thus, as a basis for Christian living, Frame follows Calvin's third use of the Law. Calvin writes, "The third use of the Law . . . has respect to believers in whose hearts the Spirit of God already flourishes and reigns. . . . For it is the best instrument for enabling them daily to learn with greater truth and certainty what that will of the Lord is which they aspire to follow, and to confirm them in this knowledge." *Institutes,* 2.7.12.
2 *DCL*, 385.
3 By "*élan vital*," I do not suggest that the commands are possessed by an impersonal, evolutionary force, such as Henri Bergson had in mind in his 1907 book *Creative Evolution*. Rather, I refer to that vital force of the person of God that interweaves all of the commands into an unbreakable corpus, as each and every person reveals his holy and righteous nature.
4 See *DCL*, 398.
5 See Ibid., 397.
6 Ibid., 411.
7 Taken from *The Doctrine of the Christian Life*, by John Frame ISBN # 978-0-87552-796-3, page 397
(P&R Publishing Co., P.O. Box 817, Phillipsburg, NJ 08865, www.prpbooks.com).
8 Here the word *perspective* should not be confused with Frame's general theory of perspectivalism.
9 Frame follows Augustine, who held that not only the Law and the Prophets, but everything in Scripture "tells of Christ and councils love" ("*Christum narrat et dilectionem monet*"). Augustine, *De Catechizandis Rudibus*, 4.8. Therefore, all Scripture hangs on the two great commands of love for God and love for neighbor. Cf. Augustine, *Contra Fastum*, 17.6.
10 *DCL*, 410.
11 Ibid., 333.
12 E. McDonagh, "Love," in *The New Dictionary of Theology*, ed. Joseph Komanchak (Wilmington, DE: Glazier, 1987), 602.
13 S. Hauerwas, "Love's Not All You Need," *Cross Currents* 172 (Summer–Fall 1972): 172.
14 See *DCL*, 387–390.
15 Here Frame pursues Kline's view that love of God is more of the nature of allegiance, in keeping with the suzerainty treaty of the ancient Near Eastern literary form, in which "The first stipulation, typically, was the requirement of exclusive loyalty." Ibid., 409.
16 See ibid., 399.
17 This quote came to me in an email dated June 29, 2010.

18 The three descriptors are joined by others and are found in *DCL*, 45–49. Although Frame limits his discussion of these groupings to express succinctly specific ethical interpretations of the Square, I will go further with them, for in them I find a means to coalesce copious and detailed accounts of ethical priorities in Frame in a short space.

19 E.g., "The non-Christian ethicist would like to believe, and would like others to believe, that he has moral standards without God. But he doesn't want to be bound by any rules. He wants to be autonomous. So he arrives at the paradoxical notion of absolutes without content: an appearance of moral principle, without any real moral principle at all." *DCL*, 46.

20 Hence, his two famous aphorisms read, "The limits of my language mean the limits of my world." "We cannot think what we cannot think; so what we cannot think we cannot say either." Ludwig Wittgenstein, *Tractatus Logico-Philosophicus* (1921), 5.6; 5.61. Influenced by Heidegger and Nietzsche, Jacques Derrida developed deconstruction as a technique for re-examining the fundamentals of writing and its consequences on philosophy in general, in order to uncovering the multiple interpretations of texts. Derrida suggests that all text has vagueness, and because of this, the likelihood of a definitive interpretation is not viable.

21 "You shall not take the name of the Lord your God in vain, for the Lord will not hold him guiltless who takes his name in vain" (Exodus 20:7).

22 *DCL*, 494.

23 Ibid., 495.

24 Ibid., 498.

25 Ibid., 490.

26 Ibid.

27 Ibid., 491.

28 Three excellent resources that relate deconstruction in language discourse to these movements are *Derrida and Legal Philosophy*, ed. Peter Goodrich, Florian Hoffman, Michelle Rosenfeld, and Cornelia Vismann (New York: Palgrave Macmillan, 2008), esp. 7–14; Elisabeth Weber, "Deconstruction Is Justice," *German Law Journal* 6 (2005): 179–184; and Benjamin P. Matthews, "Why Deconstruction Is Beneficial," *Flinders Journal of Law Reform* (2000): 105–126.

29 Uladzislau Belavusau develops a persuasive case for this in Belavusau, "Instrumentalisation of Freedom of Expression in Postmodern Legal Discourses," *European Journal of Legal Studies* 3, no. 1 (2010).

30 In Frame, this is yet another example of the rational/irrational tension inherent in all non-Christian ethical systems.

31 *DCL*, 797.

32 Ibid., 798.

33 Ibid., 797.

34 Ibid., 798.

35 Ibid.

36 For Weber's now famous views, see Weber, *The Protestant Work Ethic and the Spirit of Capitalism* (New York: Scribner, 1958). Alister McGrath covers the whole of the issue relative to Calvin and Weber in McGrath, *A Life of John Calvin: A Study in the Shaping of Western Culture* (London: Wiley-Blackwell, 1993), 219–246.

37 Hannah Arendt's work *The Human Condition* also attempts a sustained account of a positive and generalized philosophy of work using the themes of transfiguration and reification, ideas detached from Christian presuppositions. Her work is decidedly phenomenological, a profound influence exerted on her by Heidegger and Jaspers.

38 *DCL*, 48. Frame's description of "Objectivity and inwardness" is rather brief, but we find in it a source for a vast amount of his ethical thought. See ibid., 47–48.

39 D. Gallagher, "The Obedience of Faith: Barth, Bultmann, and Dei Verbum," *Journal for Christian Theological Research* 10 (2006): 55.

40 According to Bultmann, the resurrection is not literal *geschichte* ("history"). So he demythologizes faith by employing the concept of *Heilsgeschichte*—i.e., salvation history, or, more fundamentally, what historical events "mean" to people who experience them. As Heinrich Ott has presented, Bultmann's bifurcated ontology is only explained by the "hidden, personal, existential roots of his thinking." Heinrich Ott, *Geschichte und Heilsgeschichte in der Theologie Rudolf Bultmanns* (Tübingen: J. C. B. Mohr, 1955), 181. An excellent explanation and critique of Bultmann's cosmological dualism is found in David Cairns, "A Reappraisal of Bultmann's Theology," *Religious Studies* 17, no. 4 (December 1981): 469–485.

41 R. Bultmann, *pisteuô*, in *Theological Dictionary of the New Testament*, vol. 6, ed. G. Kittle (Grand Rapids, MI: Eerdmans, 1959), 211.

42 Consider his phrasing in a letter he wrote to Karl Barth in November 1952. "Now you have not convinced me that my formal view of myth is wrong. For my part I regard your material view as too narrow. For myth lives not only in stories of the gods but also in the world-view presupposed by them. The New Testament authors did not, of course, present 'general' cosmic relations and connections in the form of a story of the gods. But sharing the mythical world-view of their age, they tell the story of the Christ event as a story of the gods, as a myth." A personal letter to Karl Barth, Marburg, November 11–15, in *Karl Barth-Rudolf Bultmann Letters, 1922–1966*, ed. Bernd Jaspert (Grand Rapids, MI: Eerdmans, (1952), 96.

43 *DCL*, 352.

44 Ibid., 354.

45 See again the section in *DCL*, 355.

46 Elsewhere, Jesus said, "If anyone chooses to do God's will, he will find out whether my teaching comes from God or whether I speak on my own" (John 7:17, NIV). Besides the apologetic import of this passage, we glean that obedience from the heart to normative commands leads to true knowledge. No one will learn spiritual warfare unless one is in it.

47 *DCL*, 785.

48 Ibid., 789.

49 *DCL*, 790. Being sensitive to the issue, he offers seven criteria to guard against the misuse of the human genome. See *DCL*, 790–791. Chapter 37 of *DCL* shows Frame's emphatic "pro-life" stand.

50 "The bride and the bridegroom must set their minds to produce for the State children of the greatest possible goodness and beauty." *Republic*, 783e.

51 "The offspring of the inferior, and any of those of the other sort who are born defective, they will properly dispose of in secret, so that no one will know what has become of them. That is the condition of preserving the purity of the guardians' breed." *Republic*, 460c.

52 For this, see *DCL*, 48–49.

53 Frame has not written on Rawls, but as in the case of the prior work on Habermas, I will seize the opportunity to do some fresh constructive analysis via multiperspectivalism.

54 Rawls says that "one practicable aim of justice as fairness is to provide an acceptable philosophical and moral basis for democratic institutions and thus to address the question of how the claims of liberty and equality are to be understood." John Rawls, *Justice as Fairness: A Restatement*, ed. Erin Kelly (Cambridge: The Belknap Press of Harvard University Press, 1991), 5.

55 D. Miller, *Principles of Social Justice* (Cambridge, MA: Harvard University Press, 1999), 57.

56 E. C. Vacek, *Love, Human and Divine: The Heart of Christian Ethics* (Washington, DC: Georgetown University Press, 2004), 161.

57 *DCL*, 592.

58 See Matthew 10:33. Frame clearly takes the ninth commandment in broad terms when he injects into the language of the command the word *witnessing*, which does not appear in the original. Witnessing, of course, can be taken to mean the act of telling the truth, but traditionally witnessing is the act of public recognition of the Lord before people, the proclamation of the Good News (see Acts 8:4). Frame seems to acknowledge witnessing in terms of evangelism when he says, "'Witnessing' in Scripture is something you *are*, more than something you do. It involves not only speech, but actions as well. It is comprehensive." *DCL*, 398.

59 And we are reminded that the distilled meaning of the Decalogue balances God's concerns for love and justice as recorded by the prophet. "He has told you, O man, what is good; And what does the LORD require of you But to do justice, to love kindness, and to walk humbly with your God?" Micah 6:8.

60 P. Tillich, *Courage to Be*, 2nd ed. (New Haven, CT: Yale University Press, 2000), 185. For an excellent discussion on the directions in theology—one stemming from Tillich, the other from Barth; the former represented at the University of Chicago, the latter represented by the Yale Divinity School—see Terry D. Cooper, *Paul Tillich and Psychology: Historic and Contemporary Explorations in Theology, Psychotherapy, and Ethics* (Macon, GA: Mercer University Press, (1996), especially 195–197.

61 J. Reimer, *Paul Tillich: Theologian of Nature, Culture and Politics* (Munster, Germany: Lit Verlag, 2004), 168.

62 D. Kelsey, *The Uses of Scripture in Recent Theology* (Philadelphia: Fortress Press, 1975), 136–137.

63 I.e., Kant, Wittgenstein, Habermas, Moore, Arendt, and Rawls, and more, deny objective, propositional, Christian authority as the understructure for ethics, expostulating instead various forms of freedom, but are unable to authenticate these forms.

64 M. F. Wiles, "Religious Authority and Divine Action," *Religious Studies* 7, no. 1 (1971): 1–12.

65 Should one be called upon to harm another, "Scripture requires the believer to follow God, even when that action amounts to civil disobedience or revolt." *DCL*, 581.

66 Ibid., 33.

67 Ibid., 34.

68 We disdain one form of murder but embrace another. Why? The Socratic Paradox states that everyone seeks what is in his own best interest. So, murdering Jews is not in our interest, but if disposing of an unwanted fetus is in our interest, it is all too often expendable. It follows, then, that anyone who does wrong does so thinking it is good. For an exposition of the Socratic Paradox, see Gerasimos Santas, "The Socratic Paradoxes," *The Philosophical Review* 73, no. 2 (April 1964): 147–164.

69 *DCL*, 105.

70 Ibid., 321.

71 Ibid., 323.

72 C. Van Til, *In Defense of the Faith*, vol. 3: *Christian Theistic Ethics* (Phillipsburg: NJ: P&R Publishing, 1980). Also quoted in *DCL*, 323.

73 C. Van Til, *Christian Theistic Ethics*, 45–46.

74 Karl Barth said, "Rather, true freedom is freedom *for* God." Barth, *CD*, vol. 2/2, 552.

75 So "Our trust in God does not extinguish spontaneity, but rather fires it up." *DCL*, 323.

76 C. Van Til, *Christian Theistic Ethics*, 46. Also quoted in *DCL*, 323.

77 P. Tillich, *Courage to Be*, 185.

Chapter 5

Lordship, Ethics, and the Sacred Secular Distinction

The investigation on Framian ethics has thus far brought this book to a point of reflection on how quintessential ethical topics find symmetry in a single theological orientation when ethical issues are treated perspectivally. This is all in service to the larger question of how lordship shapes the perspectival approach to theology and ethics.

It is after deep and sustained study into Frame's treatment of the Decalogue that I believe I have discovered a latent but perceptible and resurfacing theme in his work: a disavowal of the sacred/secular distinction.[1] Although Frame's one kingdom stance is ubiquitous throughout his theology, especially his theology of culture, the specialized sub-theme of one kingdom thought—the sacred/secular distinction—is not something Frame mentions with consistency. So, clearly, the following pages offer original thought on Frame.

Although only major examples of this thematic strain in Frame are possible here, the book may well provide a point of inspiration for further academic study on how the sacred/secular distinction shapes a whole range of topics in Frame's corpus.

All Is "Holy" in the Regulative Principle of Worship

The second commandment declares, "You shall not make for yourself an idol, or any likeness of what is in heaven above or on the earth beneath or in the water under the earth. You shall not worship them or serve them; for I, the LORD your God, am a jealous God, visiting the iniquity of the fathers on the children, on the third and the fourth generations of those who hate Me, but showing lovingkindness to thousands, to those who love Me and keep My commandments" (Exodus 20:4–6).

To understand the express way the rejection of the sacred/secular distinction plays a major role in Frame's view of worship, a somewhat pared summation of the dispute between Frame and his interlocutors on worship is offered here.

Though the dispute has simmered somewhat since Frame came to teach at Reformed Theological Seminary in 2000, a major point Frame's critics have volleyed at him is that he takes an inconsistent stance on the second commandment. More specifically, they contend that he does not adhere to a strict interpretation of the Reformed Principle of Worship (RPW).[2] The critique of Frame has surfaced most pugnaciously in reply to his open advocacy of contemporary patterns and practices in congregational worship, which are set forth mainly in his books *Worship in Spirit and Truth* and *Contemporary Worship Music.*

The harshest response to Frame has come from Reg Barrow, who states that "Calvin would have excommunicated . . . Frame . . . without a second thought—given the idolatrous nature of [his] beliefs regarding public worship."[3] Also, Darryl Hart and Frame engaged in an email dialogue, in which Hart austerely reprimands, "For what [Frame] has really done is not only to take issue with the Puritan RPW. He has also set the Bible against the tradition to which he and I belong (as officers in the PCA and OPC, and as professors at Reformed seminaries)."[4] A more moderate tone is heard from T. David Gordon, who, in reply to Frame's article "Some Questions about the Regulative Principle," claims, among other things, that Frame's interaction with RPW is with "straw men which were then easily defeated."[5]

Replying to his critics, Frame claims to support RPW. "In my view, the Westminster Confession is entirely right in its regulative principle—that worship is limited to what God commands. But the methods used by the Puritans to discover and apply those commands need a theological overhaul."[6] Frame is saying that he agrees *in principle* with RPW, but *in practice* he is not at one with the historic Puritan expressions. This differentiation leads Frame to a number of personal emphases and positions on RPW.

(1) He thinks that Scripture specifically prescribes very little for post-Resurrection New Testament (NT) worship.[7] (2) He believes that some *elements* from the Old Testament (OT) are still in force; that we do not need a specific New Testament command to include, for example, choirs and instruments. He thus accepts the Reformed view of the continuity between the OT and the NT regarding the elements of worship.[8] Elements may be derived from Scripture, by specific text, theological principle, or approved example. (3) Once we agree on *what* to do in worship (the elements), we have to think about *how* to do them—for example, "expressions," "forms," and "circumstances," the latter of which Frame also calls "applications." For example, granted that we intend to preach, what should be the precise words of our sermons? The same can be said of prayers, hymns, etc. Frame

would have us give attention to what the *Westminster Confession* calls "all parts of the ordinary religious worship of God." Expressions, forms, and circumstances are determined to the degree that they (a) serve to apply a biblical element; (b) do not conflict with anything in Scripture. Again, this, of course, assumes that there is a valid distinction between elements and circumstances, something Frame does not always think is easy to separate. But still, for Frame, there is some value in using this distinction in a rough, pragmatic kind of way. Methodologically, therefore, he wants us to isolate the elements people do in worship, according to Scripture: pray, praise, offer sacrifice, read, preach, take sacraments, and so on. Then we explore the meaning of these, which will govern the specific things we do to carry out these mandates. The main thing is being able to say that *what* we do in Scripture is what God wants and being able to say that the *ways* in which we carry out these activities are pleasing to God.[9] (4) At this point, Frame can appear very Lutheran. In trying to weigh forms and circumstances, a major question will be, "Does Scripture *rule out* this or that?" In other words, even after we determine what Scripture *requires*, we must, in determining specifics, ask what Scripture *forbids*. (5) He thinks that the process of reasoning the selection of elements is not unlike the process of reasoning the choice of circumstances, forms, and expressions. (6) He believes that what actually distinguishes Reformed from Lutheran views of RPW is that Reformed people put all their emphasis on the selection of *elements*, while Lutherans focus their attention on determining what the Reformed call *circumstances*. The difference is mainly one of emphasis. (7) Frame does not draw a sharp distinction between worship in the narrow sense (Sabbatical worship) and worship in the broad sense (what Kuyper meant by "life is religion").

Although Frame holds to the continuity of OT and NT worship, point 5 above states that the process people use to determine the elements of corporate worship is not altogether different from the process people use to decipher the circumstances, forms, and expressions of the same. Frame's own process of reasoning leads him to affirm the use of contemporary musical styles led by praise bands, dance, and drama in NT worship.[10] His most fundamental problem with the traditionalist' classic interpretation of RPW is that much of what people claim to be biblical worship finds little support once weighed in the light of what Scripture *actually* says. And it is not ethical to go beyond Scripture. "So it is evident that Scripture must be our guide, in worship as in all of life."[11]

Frame's contenders claim that his logic blurs the distinction between elements and circumstances/forms/expressions—resulting in a new definition of RPW. For example, Brian McGraw, in confronting Frame, states confidently from Deuteronomy 12 that "This text alone ought to be enough to prove the regulative principle as taught in the Westminster Standards."[12] But could it be that McGraw is really saying that Frame's proclaimed adherence to the Westminster Standards is only alleged unless Frame's worship looks like McGraw's? Before I get to the exact issue of the sacred/secular distinction in all of this, a brief examination of McGraw's own logic may prove helpful toward an understanding of Frame's unwillingness to define RPW beyond what Scripture actually says.

Does Deuteronomy 12 offer the global statement on NT worship McGraw is looking for? Deuteronomy 12 speaks of the *place* of worship the Lord God will give the conquering Israelites (v. 11). In the same verse God specifies the sacrifices the people will bring, that is, "your burnt offerings and your sacrifices, your tithes and the contribution of your hand, and all your choice votive offerings which you will vow to the LORD." And the people are instructed to rejoice before the Lord while caring for the Levite (v. 13). They are prohibited from eating the blood of animals (v. 23). Regulations regarding the handling and consuming of burnt offerings are provided (v. 27). The chapter ends with a general warning to avoid the practices and abominations of the pagans, especially the offering of children in the fire to their gods (vss. 29-31).

Clearly, Deuteronomy 12 says nothing about preaching, teaching, prayer, exclusive psalmody, and the sacraments. It does not speak voluminously about the elements of worship, much less its forms, circumstances, and expressions. Verse 8 is clear that a man is not to devise worship according to "what is right in his own eyes." But we are presented with no clear template proposing regulations for all of the elements of Christian worship. It would appear that McGraw, in attempting to disprove Frame, must try to squeeze more nectar from the fruit than the fruit is able to yield.[13]

Now that we have a grasp of the overall dispute, on to my main objective, which again is to show how Frame's views on worship are motivated by a rejection of the sacred/secular distinction. Contra the speculation of Joseph A. Pipa that Frame's interpretation of RPW is essentially Lutheran, the exact opposite is the case. At the heart of Frame's interpretive theory lies a repudiation of the Lutheran sacred/secular distinction and an affirmation of the theological primacy of God's lordship over both the titular secular and the sacred.

Interacting with WCF 1.6, which specifies that "there are some circumstances concerning the worship of God, and government of the Church, common to human actions and societies," Frame says, regarding the specific words of prayers, for example, "Prayer is not common to human actions and societies."[14] According to Frame, the problem this creates for the traditional adherents of RPW is that they are prejudiced to interpret the "circumstances" of worship in a certain way, as if they, too, are God-inspired elements. Yet as Frame points out, this leads writer Michael Bushnell, who holds to the traditional view of RPW, to "distinguish between circumstances that have 'spiritual meaning' or 'sacred significance,' such as the words of prayers, and those that don't, such as the time and place of worship."[15] Frame detects in this sort of reshuffling a fear that should too much room be left for human reflection on what biblical worship should look like, this can only lead to an openness to ever new practices of circumstances, forms, and expressions. To tolerate a plurality of possible interpretations is not something traditionalists are wont to do.

But what, then, are we to make of the *non-sacred* aspects of corporate worship, such as the time and place of worship? In Frame, it is not possible to for any aspect of worship to be *common* or non-spiritual, as opposed to *holy* or spiritual. For instance, he says, "[I]f the leaders of a church schedule a worship service at an inappropriate time, say 4:00 a.m., this decision may greatly affect the quality of worship. The human spirit in Scripture is not something totally disconnected from the body." Referring back to WCF 1.6, "So even those aspects of worship that are 'common to human actions and societies' can make a spiritual difference. So although the distinction between holy and common is important in Scripture, I do not think it is helpful in distinguishing between elements, forms, and circumstances of worship."[16]

Frame brings us back to the decisive point raised: because God gives us little information for post-Resurrection worship, we are dependent on

Scripture for all that we do in worship. So it is not that Frame views the elements of worship on a par with circumstances and thus less important. Rather, he sees circumstances, forms, and expressions *as holy* as elements. All we do in worship must therefore be arrived at according to the sufficiency of Scripture and before the lordship of God. I conclude, then, that Frame's position on RPW is anything but Lutheran. It is motivated by his deep commitment to the dismantling of the sacred/secular distinction. The theological basis of that knocking down is lordship.

A Point of Consideration

Although there is much to commend Frame's reasoning on RPW, his common hermeneutic that rejects a sharp line between "narrow" and "broad" expressions of worship and that blends Sabbatical worship into "all of life" (point 7, above) could perhaps benefit from a clarification. Drawing heavily from Roman 12, Frame posits, "So the regulative principle for worship is no different from the regulative principle for the rest of life."[17] The lordship principle finds expression in the fact that "everything we do has spiritual significance."[18] Again, note Frame's abjuration of the sacred/secular division.

Countering Frame is T. David Gordon, who argues for the distinctive nature of Sunday worship and for the fact that not every act of worship to God during the week is appropriate for such worship. His logic goes like this.

> . . . giving my children a bath before bedtime is a matter which I believe gives glory to God (and a much-deserved rest to their mother!). It promotes their health, it calms them down for bed-time, and is "good, clean fun." However, as an officer in the church, I cannot bring a bathtub into our service

> of worship, place the girls in it, and give them a bath "to the glory of God," *requiring others* to observe the rite.[19]

Frame's hermeneutic that bridges congregational worship with life as worship is laudable, as it brings all of life before God *Coram Deo*. And Gordon has unfairly marginalized Frame in the above quote—for instance, Frame would not approve of bathtubs in worship. Nonetheless, Gordon exposes what could well be a weakness in Frame's hermeneutic: a conflation of the distinctiveness of corporate worship with the ordinary elements of life.

1 Corinthians 10:31, for example, is clear that we are to do all to the glory of God. Yet what we do in corporate worship does not necessarily draw direction from the same generalized set of duties. If that were so, then there would be no need for specific biblical injunctions on worship, only those that govern day-to-day relations between God and man. Frame is correct on the continuity between congregational worship and life. Readers of his might benefit if he were to present an equally clear set of directives regarding the discontinuity between the same.

Modern Application of Frame on Worship

There is an important point of application of Frame's theology of worship for post-Christian societies that have grown cold to the institutional Church. In the advance of major secular ideologies, I find adherence, in one form or another, to Nietzsche's doctrinaire statement "Let your will say: the overman *shall be* the meaning of the earth!"[20] And I wonder, is there yet hope for a Christian conception of life and of history in the West?

While it is true that *Christianity* is in decline, especially among Europeans, interest in *religion*, more broadly interpreted, is on the incline.[21] This suggests that the problem is not one of postmodern thought, if in fact we are to define "postmodern" as a mind-set in direct opposition to religion. Rather, the postmodern mind is increasingly open to the practice of spirituality on a number of different levels. The West's long march toward secularism is, in part, a reaction to state-controlled churches and dead traditions that fail to minister to people. "Monopoly churches get lazy," says Eva Hamberg, who, looking at Swedish data, drew a correlation between an increase in religious competition and a rise in church going. Europeans are deserting established churches, she says, "But this does not mean they are not religious."[22]

Frame's positions on the RPW may well provide religiously motivated Westerners with an impetus to take a fresh look at biblical worship. In the email debate between Frame and Hart mentioned previously, Frame charges that Hart's theology of worship blurs the lines between Scripture and tradition. He says, "The irony is that this very Regulative Principle clearly excludes what Hart seems to be saying elsewhere about the incorrigible authority of tradition."[23] If Frame is right that a narrow sectarianism has elevated theological and ecclesiastical "tradition" above Scripture, then rather than merely reject Christianity, Westerners must see that "the regulative principle is primarily a means of criticizing tradition." Even more emphatically, Frame calls us to ". . . use the regulative principle as needed to counter the dead weight of tradition."[24] So, as centuries-old churches, either ensconced in sacerdotal practices or long favored by the state, remain too detached from the people, Frame's Bible-centered blueprint for worship may just provide the sustained influence for the revitalization of Christian churches on the continent of Europe and throughout the West.[25]

The Fourth Commandment and the Intent of the Sabbath

A denunciation of the sacred/secular distinction is evident once more in Frame's handling of the fourth commandment, which directs us to "Remember the sabbath day, to keep it holy. Six days you shall labor and do all your work, but the seventh day is a sabbath of the LORD your God; *in it* you shall not do any work, you or your son or your daughter, your male or your female servant or your cattle or your sojourner who stays with you. For in six days the LORD made the heavens and the earth, the sea and all that is in them, and rested on the seventh day; therefore the LORD blessed the sabbath day and made it holy" (Exodus 20:8–11).

Different thinkers locate the decisive point of the fourth commandment in discrete ways: from "least Sabbatarian" to "most Sabbatarian."[26] In the latter thought of Meredith Kline, *discontinuity* between OT and NT administration is dominant. The disjunction arises "from a distinction that is very important to his theology, that between the holy and common."[27] This division produces "an order of common grace that mitigates the effects of the curse on the earth, but does not bring salvation. This includes the general culture, shared by believer and nonbeliever alike, particularly the institution of the state."[28] This dualism is seminal in the whole of Kline's thinking about church and society, a point I will probe further in the chapters on culture.

Important to note here, however, is that for Kline, his sacred/secular theorem positions the Sabbath in a *different form* for NT worship. Under the new covenant, we keep the Sabbath by worshipping God on the Lord's Day. But, according to Kline, we have no obligation to cease from work or recreation on the six previous days, in that these days are common, not holy.

So according to Kline's later view, the commandment under the new covenant administration does not call for the cessation of work, but the mandate to worship.[29] Kline does not even believe we are called to cease from work or recreation on the Lord's Day, except as far as such rest facilitates worship. His reason is that under the order of common grace, work is not holy but profane.

Frame concurs with Kline's *early* view that rest from work is the quintessence of the day, which in turn facilitates worship. Consequently, he rejects the later Klinean idea that imposes an "*order* of common grace" (italics added to stress that Frame does not reject the principle of common grace, but that the earth is ordered by it) and that insists upon a radical demarcation between holy and common in the new covenant period with its relegation of work to the area of the common.

Thus, with Frame, the cosmological bifurcation of Kline and others gives way to a robust holism, in which Sabbatical rest penetrates both cult and culture, not simply cult. This point of reference is most pronounced in Frame's view that Sabbath rest is a "creation ordinance" established for man pre-fall and marks the theological symbolism of the Sabbath (Genesis 2:2–3) as representing "a completion and celebration of man's cultural labors."[30] Continuity between pre-fall probation and post-fall forfeiting of the promise is thus in the continuous and systemically binding nature of what it means for all humans to exercise a "benevolent dominion."[31]

Yet the Sabbath is also based in redemption, for "Certainly in the postfall period it symbolizes the completion of God's redemptive purposes."[32] The eschatological timetable sees man's first rest from work as a prescient marker of the Day in which cultural work culminates in the restful and glorious freedom of the sons of God. But even here, there is no radical distinction between grace as opposed to works, or sacred in opposition to secular. The redemptive connotation of the Sabbath is in the context of "rest from the toil that sin has brought upon our working life," and not merely *rest* as pointing to our final rest from sin, as Calvin had taught.[33] With Sabbath interpreted as rest *from work*, and not just rest, even the redemptive significance of the Sabbath maintains its gracious center, while not losing its ties to our tilling of the soil, hard though it be for a time.[34]

The Fourth and Sixth Commandments and the Environment

I want to take a brief pause to look at just one way Frame applies his comprehensive understanding of the fourth commandment.

One of Frame's interests is in how Israel's Sabbath calendar required rest for the land, such that "the Sabbath years mandate ecological responsibility."[35] In particular, he thinks that the dominant anthropological theme of man as image bearer, who maintains the Sabbath calendar in an already defined order of creation, provides a systemic contour for a range of contemporary interests that seek environmental sustainability as a goal. If that be the case, then let's take in hand one specific ecological concern—the nascent industry of vertical farming.

The brainchild of Dickson Despommier, the plan proposes inner-city skyscrapers filled with floor upon floor producing crops year round as means to feed an anticipated 9.1 billion by 2050, 80 percent of which are expected to reside in urban areas.[36] Yet it may be that the new plan conflicts with Frame's thought that "Israel's Sabbath calendar has much to teach us."[37] For example, crop fields cannot be stacked one above the other without accommodating for blocked sunlight. Vertical farms' lighting must be supplied synthetically, consuming resource-intensive electricity, rather than free sunlight. For this reason God said, "Let there be light" (Gen. 1:3), before he said, "Let the land produce vegetation" (vs. 11). But closer to Frame's point, vertical farming looks to be in conflict with the honor due God that includes resting the land. To rest the land, as we do when we rotate crops or let the ground lie fallow periodically, is not a sectarian thought. It is a broadly human concern. To strip food-producing plants from the landscape only to grow them destitute of sunlight in vertical factory farms does not address the Achilles heel of agriculture: it is overworked and needs periodic rest.[38]

Frame's environmental ethic is echoed in his interpretation of the sixth commandment, "You shall not murder" (Exodus 20:13). The point of connectivity is in Frame's anthropocentric ethos that begins with the high valuation of the keeper of the Garden, who, under the Divine administration, is to "fill and subdue the earth."[39] Frame is here thinking of the "dominion mandate" of Genesis 1:26–28. Our shared dominion is, however, to be balanced by concern for non-rational animal and plant life. That is so because to value and to protect human life is to value the environment within which human life flourishes. "So man is to use the resources of the world, but is not to exploit them or deplete them."[40]

Under this command, Frame thus gives brief attention to how human dominion over the earth must consider animal mercy. Hence, "The human race itself has an interest in preserving species (some, at any rate), forests, wetlands, and the beauties of God's world."[41]

Frame's balanced environmental ethic is also helpful in that it avoids the extremes of environmental sentimentality and passivity. It accomplishes this by acknowledging God's laws that set limits on man's overconfidence. This is what Russell D. Moore was thinking when he wrote,

> I think Frame's basic structure of outlining Christian ethics according to the Ten Commandments is helpful. By rooting our ethical obligations here, he points us away from simple personal virtue or political action. Our environmental ethic is part of something much larger—a law that points us to final judgment (Rom. 2:14–16). This necessitates obedience and action, but it also makes them relative to human finitude, sin, and the sweep of redemptive history.[42]

As in the case of vertical farming, all technological advances are hit and miss at first. However, some eco-technical missteps are more often than not due to man's forgetfulness of his limits as a creature. Frame is most prophetic in his call to us to be "a responsible steward of the earth."[43] Efforts designed for the common good, though laudable, do not always take this goal into consideration.

The Fifth Commandment and Tripartite Relations

The fifth commandment pronounces, "Honor your father and your mother, that your days may be prolonged in the land which the LORD your God gives you" (Exodus 20:12). Commonly held divisions between family, church, and state are harmonized in the Larger Catechism, Q.124, which asks, "Who are meant by father and mother in the fifth commandment?" Answer: "By father and mother, in the fifth commandment, are meant, not only natural parents, but all superiors in age and gifts; and especially such as, by God's ordinance, are over us in place of authority, whether in family, church, or commonwealth."

In Frame, there is a synchronization of the three spheres (family, church, and state) that build upon the Larger Catechism. A lordship approach to theological anthropology avoids defining persons *in relationship to* three distinct entities, in other words, "who are meant" by the commandment. Instead, Frame begins with the *nature* of these three entities, and from there he speaks in terms of our responsibility to them. Frame's method of classification is thus one of *organic unity*, organized perspectivally, starting first with the family, which progressively finds its evolvement and complexity through history to church and state when the family has outgrown its ability to govern itself.[44] Any psychological or philosophical principle of contradiction that places the state lower than the original genera of church and family is omitted.

In "Toward a Theology of the State," Frame concludes that "This makes the state simply the government of the mega-family."[45] The addition of the church means "that we see the church and the state as extensions of the family."[46] Quite obviously, and to the point of this chapter, this theology presents an integral model of sphere-relatedness that again sets important challenges before the sacred/secular distinction and that calls for our common interest. For the question is no longer if the state should follow the voice of natural law, and the Church and the family the voice of Scripture. In their essence, all are uniformly mediums of God's thought, subservient to his authority revealed in nature and above all in Scripture.[47]

Now, on the express relationship of church and state, it is clear that Frame believes that the church is something different from the state. Yet that distinction is mainly one of function. For example, he agrees that the state is permitted to use physical force in carrying out its Divine mandate. The church is forbidden to do that, although individual Christians may become agents of the state and as such may use force. If the issue, however, is whether Christians (individual or corporately) may use force in converting people, of course the answer is no.

However, apart from the issue of functionality, Frame believes that the *nature* of both church and state find their ultimate constitution in God's revelation alone. Both may use natural revelation in the *application* of revelation to their circumstances, but it is special revelation that alone has authority over both institutions. So to say that the state's constitution is determined *exclusively* from reason and providence and *not at all* from Scripture is something Frame sees as seriously confused. For instance, he thinks that the church has the right to set forth authoritatively what Scripture says about public governance. And although the state may not formulate a creed for the church, he thinks that Christian rulers who are members of churches have the same right to exercise influence in creed-formation as do any other church members, but no more.[48]

A Question on a Perspectival View of the Fifth Commandment

Frame's organic interpretation of family, church, and state, which draws from the *historical continuity* of these areas, is helpful. What the scholar may not pay enough attention to is the *spiritual discontinuity* of the church relative to the family and state.[49] The fact is that the church is not just a historical outgrowth of the family. It is first the body of Christ (Ephesians 4:12–16). As we shall see under the seventh commandment, Frame does protect the mystical union of Christ and the church. But when we speak on the continuity of the church ought we not to speak first of the church as the living Body united forever with Christ? History may be the church's womb, but Christ is its head that gave it birth.

It is evident that Frame's historically synthetic hermeneutic wants to challenge the reflexive disjointing of family, church, and state, as is common to increasingly secularized societies. And I agree with his judgment that the charter and allegiance of the church and of the state are defined first and foremost by Scripture. The cultural and political implications of this allegiance are quite obviously far-reaching, and I do believe that Frame has these implications in mind in his construal of family, church and state.

However, another way to spell out the cultural and political implications of the church, apart from the family and the state, is in the powerful ministry of a people composed of all sexes, races, nations, cultures, and social classes (Ephesians 1:23; 2:15-16; 3:6; 5:30), as they are all united in Christ. For there is no division or distinction in the body of Christ between Jew and Gentile, slave and free, male and female. All are one in Christ (Galatians 3:28; Colossians 3:11). As God's principal means of establishing the Kingdom of God on earth, the church has been seen in all ages and will mature through the processes of redemptive history. But ultimately the church is not the product of any one historical point of reference, even the family. And we can expect the church to be all that God intends in its consummated state (Revelation 19:1–10).

Marriage: A Common Concern

The seventh commandment warns, "You shall not commit adultery" (Ex. 20:14). With the advance of secularization, sexual confusion, openness, and sexual abuse abounding everywhere, the importance of this commandment has been lost on modern societies.

What Frame calls the "broad meaning" of the commandment looks to adultery as a perspective on all aspects of human life. This is in conjunction with the fact that "all sin is unfaithfulness to God, spiritual adultery."[50] Because the fundamental structure of lordship always bears heavily on covenantal relations, he therefore reasons that "adultery is covenant treason."[51] That makes adultery in its broad meaning synonymous with idolatry. Frame can speak in terms of the association on account of the fact that the idolatrous practices of Israel broke the marriage relationship with Yahweh, thus incurring his jealousy.[52]

However, the obvious weight of the commandment is its "narrow meaning," which focuses on fidelity to one's spouse. Narrower still, the commandment, like the whole of the Decalogue, speaks to the darkest recesses of the human heart, from which every adulterous thought emanates, what Jesus called "lustful intent."[53] This, to Frame's way of thinking, is not the same as "lust," which is "something good, a God-given incentive to marriage."[54] I will revisit the idea of "sinful intent" in a bit.

How does the sacred/secular distinction find itself in the picture of Frame's thought on this specific commandment? Frame does speak of marriage in terms of its mystical connotations: that the bringing together of male and female images God's redemption of his people and the relationship of Christ to his church—all of which find fulfillment at the marriage feast of the lamb.[55] Still, the weight of his argument does not begin here—with its end infinitely ennobled in the more important realization of the New Covenant.[56] Nor is Frame's first concern to ground marriage in nature as a bulwark against various sorts of sexual license.[57] Of first importance to Frame is that marriage, and the sexual variations between men and women in that union, is expressly suitable to fulfill the Cultural Mandate: "the fundamental task of mankind, which is, first, to 'be fruitful and multiply and fill the earth' (Gen. 1:28)." Our attention to marriage (and family) is not, therefore, bidden on the basis of, or as mimetic of, empyreal grounds only. Instead, Frame presents marriage first as an ordinary building block of culture and thus essential for the advancement of worldwide civilizations. By setting marriage in the contexture of nature itself, Frame bridges sacred and secular strata, whereby creation's future is literally dependent on the continuing practice of marriage.

Frame thus prompts a viable answer to the question "Why should moderns care about the seventh commandment?" Should the answer that adulterous activity breaks the rich symbolism of Christ and his church not gain much attention in an increasingly secular age, we can remain on solid biblical ground by pointing out, for example, that a serious challenge facing European culture is the result of men and women rebuffing the creation ordinance. Fact is, the population of Europe is in steady decline. By 2050, it is expected to be around 664 million, nearly 10 percent smaller than its current size. The impact of this trend will be felt not only by European society and its economy, but also globally. In particular, the need to replenish the dwindling workforce will have long-term consequences on Europe's relations with its Middle Eastern and North African neighbors.[58]

What is the cause of Europe's population decline? "Europe's future demographic decline is not due to natural calamity. It is the result of women and men choosing to have fewer children than needed to ensure population replacement."[59] Behind this is the decline in the institution of marriage itself. Europeans are simply opting to marry late, or many of the European state class are giving up on marriage, choosing the good life they wish to enjoy without the burden of marital commitment or children, while still enjoying sex. As if to follow Sartre's notion of *pour soi* ("being for itself"), many Europeans (in fact, people worldwide) have rejected any inherent purpose to life established in nature or by God in order to live in radical freedom; to live in an "authentic" way that expresses autonomous freedom, our non-being. The advantages of an individualistic culture may be especially salient when immediate pleasure is an explicit goal.

But how does the individualistic formularization account for the interconnected world of which anthropology is its subject? As Frame clearly says, "Gender is fundamental to human life."[60] So marriage as a creation ordinance also speaks of our mutually shared commonality as humans. Cultural anthropology started with an interest in the evolution of culture on a global scale, including ways in which marriage and family grow in practice. Virtually, the academic study of man's origins stresses connectedness over "primitive isolates."[61]

Homosexuality

Once more, I ask the reader's patience as I leave aside the sacred/secular topic of this chapter to evaluate yet another issue of great import to modern societies—one that Frame treats biblically under the authority of the seventh commandment. It is homosexuality.[62]

One of Frame's positions on homosexuality may benefit if submitted to some clarification. Frame is firm that the sanctity and import of marriage must cause people to rethink misplaced sentiments affirming homosexual marriage. Now, there is much said these days about the distinction between homosexual act and orientation. Because Frame thinks that the term "orientation" is a fuzzy cultural term, he leaves room to interpret the meaning of the word. Thus, "If homosexual orientation is merely a strong pattern of temptation, it is not wrong in itself."[63] But, "On the other hand, if 'orientation' refers to lust, a desire that is contrary to God's law . . . then it is sinful in itself."[64]

So then, if by orientation we mean mere temptation, then that is not sin for it can be avoided. But if orientation is equal to lust, then it is always sin, even if one does not act on it. Lust is an infraction of the law of God, and Frame would say that this is true with respect to homosexuality or to any sin.[65]

Now, earlier I noted Frame's use of the term *lustful intent* from Matthew 5:28 (ESV). Certainly, none of us are like Jesus: *posit non peccare*. We all face degrees of temptation and are able to sin. Many homosexuals take this fact to mean that one can be a follower of Jesus Christ *as long as* one's lingering homosexual orientation is held in check.

What I am wondering is whether there is a way to clarify homosexual "orientation," given that Frame leaves open the meaning of the word. *Orientation* means "direction." Or it can mean "the state of being oriented."[66] That much is clear. However, by destroying the dominion of sin over us, Christ changes our basic orientation to sin. He makes us a "new creation" (2 Corinthians 5:17), though temptations remain. For anyone to suggest, then, that one can follow the new direction of the Spirit of Christ with a homosexual orientation seems paradoxical. The attempt to unite the two orientations encumbers one with the stresses of cognitive dissonance. Paul is clear that such a paradoxical reality exists in him relative to his sanctification (Romans 7:14–25) but not as he is "in Christ" (Romans 6:11). Even the process of sanctification has no room for the behavior (1 Corinthians 6:9). So wanting to clear up any confusion on terms, I would say that should homosexual orientation be understood as a "direction" of a person, it is always more than a "strong pattern of temptation" and is always culpable of "sinful intent."

In Romans 7:14–25, Paul speaks of the conflict of two natures, but this conflict is not between two equally opposing principles. V. 20 speaks of "indwelling" sin, lit. *oikeo*, which means "to dwell in." Yet Romans 8:11 speaks of the "in-indwelling" Spirit, lit. *enoikeo*. The additional "in" (*En*) means the old man and the new man are not equal powers. Rather, the Spirit is a deeper, more powerful presence in the life of the Christian. Based on Paul's discrimination between the two natures, we should not take "homosexual orientation" the same way we do "a strong pattern of temptation." This is not to minify the fact that although Christians are no longer under the dominion of sin, they still struggle with indwelling sin, for as Thomas Boston said of redemption, "It is a universal change. . . . Yet it is but an imperfect change. Though every part of man is renewed, there is no part of him perfectly renewed."[67] Evidentially, the subject is complex and presents a sustaining moral problem.

Covetousness and the Sacred/Secular Distinction

Let us now return to the main point of this discussion. Another place Frame's rejection of the sacred/secular distinction appears is in his views on the tenth commandment, which pronounces, "You shall not covet your neighbor's house; you shall not covet your neighbor's wife or his male servant or his female servant or his ox or his donkey or anything that belongs to your neighbor" (Exodus 20:17).[68]

Contemplating covetousness, Thomas Aquinas argued that the spontaneous desire for a thing does not qualify as sin. He maintained that only *dwelling* on a desire (*titillatio*) to the point of its completion is sin, but that unprompted desire that catches us "off guard" is not.[69] According to Frame, however, even a momentary spontaneous desire is enough to qualify as sin.[70] Certainly, any attempt to avoid impulsive desire would be an enthusiastic undertaking. How, then, does Frame justify his claim? Following Douma on total depravity, he says that "Our evil desires, even spontaneous ones, come 'from an evil heart.'"[71]

Frame's insightful comments on impulsive desire raise the theology of concupiscence.[72] Calvin was clear that concupiscence had affected more than our sexual appetite (Thomas).[73] It affected the whole person.[74] The classic Reformed position on concupiscence also includes original sin as a post-fall phenomenon that produces actual sins. Frame affirms original sin and that original sin involves concupiscence. However, Frame speaks in such a way as to variate him from Calvin, the relevance of which shall soon be made clear.

In an article, "Concupiscence: Sin and the Mother of Sin," R. Scott Clark, in explaining James 1:14–16, echoes the classic Protestant view. He says, "[I]t is clear from the Scriptures that concupiscence is sin, but according to James, [concupiscence] is more than that: it is also the seminary (seedbed) of sin. . . . Concupiscence (original sin) conceives actual sin and actual sin brings death.[75] Interpreting James further, Clark reasons, "Because of their corrupted desires, God does not grant their requests when they do pray. It is not as if, however, if they could somehow suspend their concupiscence, God would suddenly begin answering their prayers. Rather, their concupiscence is only more evidence of the fact of their friendship with the world (4:4) and that they do not have true, saving faith (2:14–26)."[76]

Scott is saying that we are never rid of concupiscence. He quotes Calvin to this effect.

> Thinking about the deadly mixture of God's Law and our sin, Calvin rejected any idea of sinless perfection in this life. "[I]f we go back to the remotest period, we shall not find a single saint who, clothed with a mortal body, ever attained to such perfection as to love the Lord with all his heart, and soul, and mind, and strength; and, on the other hand, not one who has not felt the power of concupiscence."[77]

Also supporting Clark's position is Larger Catechism, Q. 149. "No man is able, either of himself, or by any grace received in this life, perfectly to keep the commandments of God; but does daily break them in thought, word, and deed." How, then, is it possible to avoid sin? Scott explains, "It is not that we should not have intense desires. Indeed, God the Holy Spirit who 'dwells within us' does precisely that (*concupiscit Spiritus*), but he does not desire the sorts of things we do; rather he desires piety and holiness (4:5)."[78] On

Scott's reading, not all concupiscence is evil if our desires thirst after things above—spiritual things.

Frame envisions desires for holiness as proper. Contra Clark, however, basic human desires need not contain an element of sin. We can desire ice cream, sex, a family, to drive a luxurious car, to be a shipping magnate, and so forth, without coveting the *content* of our desire. So there are *natural* desires, and those are not sin. Desire turns to sin, according to Frame, *only* when we have "desires to get things by breaking God's law." So it is not wrong for Cornelius to desire a Maserati. It is wrong for him to desire to steal it, *even* if the thought of theft scarcely crosses his mind.[79] On this point, Larger Catechism, Q. 150, seems to bear out Frame: "All transgressions *of the law of God* are not equally heinous; but some sins in themselves, and by reason of several aggravations, are more heinous in the sight of God than others" (italics added).

So then, divergent from Thomas, Frame impeaches impromptu thoughts of evil. But spontaneous desires are sinful only *if and when* they break the Law. If one can avoid that, then no sin has been committed. Frame's position is sustained by biblical commands that compel the cessation of sin. Paul writes, "Become sober-minded as you ought, and stop sinning; for some have no knowledge of God. I speak *this* to your shame" (1 Cor. 15:34). And Jesus said to the woman at the well, ". . . sin no more" (John 8:11, see also 1 Peter 4:1). Common to these passages is that the divine directive is to be finished with sin. Covetousness understood this way is an *actual* sin of thought, word, and deed that can be avoided. In Calvin and Scott, concupiscence always leavens our choices, producing some presence of covetousness. Scott would have us avoid the problem by having us focus on "things above."

Much more can be said on the theology and history of concupiscence. The important point is that by locating covetousness in desire that breaks God's law, Frame indirectly raises a fresh way of thinking inimical to the sacred/secular distinction. For in Scott's reading of Calvin, for sin to be abated one must only set one's affections strictly on *spiritual* goals.[80] In Frame, however, one can desire *all things* compatible with God's good creation, providing one does not infract God's standards.

We should care about this point in the structure of Framian thought because it opens up to us a world of goodness minus the fear of retrenchment from the world. Christianity is not an *otherworld* religion that avoids sin only when the mind is attuned to the world of the transcendent. Rather, Christianity is an embodied life: free to explore its natural desires within the circumference of knowing God. Therefore, "Delight yourself in the LORD; And He will give you the desires of your heart" (Proverbs 37:4).

As Frame's writings have shown, he is adroit at a whole range of subjects in systematic theology and philosophy. That said, his early teaching career at Westminster Theological Seminary (Philadelphia) included the teaching of apologetics. Because my first exposure to the professor was in this setting, it is with great enthusiasm that I now turn to examine the Lordship principle as it guides Frame's resolute defense of the faith.

Endnotes

1 One might expect a study of the sacred/secular distinction under the heading of Frame's theology of culture, and be right, as shall be signified in the approaching areas on culture. But this abjuration, as it is replaced by a holistic understanding of God's lordship over all, is also plain in the manner in which Frame handles ethics.
2 The regulative principle states, "But the acceptable way of worshiping the true God is instituted by himself, and so limited by his own revealed will, that he may not be worshiped according to the imaginations and devices of men, or the suggestions of Satan, under any visible representation, or any other way not prescribed in the Holy Scripture." *Westminster Confession of Faith*, Chapter 21, Section 1. Obviously, a reading of the second commandment says nothing about praises bands, drama, dance, and other hotly debated practices for worship today. However, many Reformed folk are of the mind that RPW properly interprets the second commandment to mean that such practices are forbidden in corporate worship.
3 "Would John Calvin Excommunicate John Frame?" http://www.swrb.com/newslett/actualNLs/frameexc.htm.
4 "The Regulative Principle, Scripture, Tradition, and Culture," http://www.frame-poythress.org/frame_articles/1998HartDebate.htm; date of access: Jan. 15, 2015. In "Above the Battle," http://www.frame-poythress.org/frame_articles/2003Above.htm, Frame engages Marva Dawn, Horton, Muether, and Hart.
5 In the *Westminster Theological Journal* 54, no. 2 (Fall 1992): 358–359. See also T. David Gordon, "Some Answers about the Regulative Principle," www.tdgordon.net/theology/ecclesiology_worship.../frame_review.doc; date of access: Jan. 16, 2015. This originally appeared in *Westminster Theological Journal* 55 (Fall 1993): 321–329. Gordon is replying to Frame in "A Fresh Look at the Regulative Principle: A Broader View," http://www.frame-poythress.org/a-fresh-look-at-the-regulative-principle-a-broader-view/.
6 John M. Frame, *Worship in Spirit and Truth: A Refreshing Study of the Principles and Practice of Biblical Worship* (Phillipsburg, NJ: Presbyterian and Reformed Publishing Co., 1996), xiv–xv.
7 It is true that 1 Corinthians 14:26 is a clear prescription but incomplete. As well, the second commandment is incomplete and nondescript if taken as a mandate for all activities in Christian worship.
8 Curious is the fact that some understand Frame to mean "that no elements of OT worship are to carry over in NT worship without explicit NT warrant." Ryan McGraw, "A Critique of John Frame's 'Worship in Spirit and Truth,'" http://katekomen.gpts.edu/2010/06/critique-of-john-frames-worship-in.html date of access: Jan. 16, 2015. Not only does Frame deny the charge, but also even challenger Joseph Pipa finds twelve worship elements in *Worship in Spirit and Truth*: greetings and benedictions, reading of Scripture, preaching and teaching, Charismatic prophesy and

speaking in tongues (now ceased), prayer, song, vows, confession of faith, sacraments, church discipline, collections, offerings, and expressions of fellowship (the love feast and the holy kiss. Other elements could be included. See Joseph Pipa, "Worship in Spirit and Truth," http://www.the-highway.com/br_worship_in_spirit-truth.html; date of access: Jan. 16, 2015.

9 Frame states that rather than use any of the classic texts to substantiate RPW, as is commonly done, "I have based my defense of the regulative principle on fairly general considerations: the nature of worship as homage to God, the nature of revelation, the sufficiency of Scripture." *DCL*, 468.

10 On the subject of music for congregational use, Terry L. Johnson characterizes Frame's elocution that some current cultural trends in music ought to have a place in Reformed worship as a "*reductio ad absurdum*." See Terry L. Johnson, *Reformed Worship: Worship That Is According to Scripture*, 2nd ed. (Jackson, MS: Reformed Academic Press, 2000), 12, n. 14. For a contrary view that supports Frame and provides an extended examination of the historical development of exclusive psalmody under Calvin to the inclusion of hymns and spiritual songs in Protestant worship, see John Barber, "The Music God Likes in the Calvinist Tradition," in *The Kuyper Center Review* (Grand Rapids, MI: Eerdmans, 2013). Frame covers liturgical dance in *Worship in Spirit and Truth* (Phillipsburg, NJ: P&R Publishing, 1996), 131. On drama in corporate worship, see Idem., 94. Replying to Frame on liturgical dance, Joseph A. Pipa retorts, in, "Worship in Spirit and Truth," http://www.the-highway.com/br_worship_in_spirit-truth.html.

11 *DCL*, 468.

12 See Ryan McGraw, "A Critique of John Frame's 'Worship in Spirit and Truth,'" *Katekomen, The Online Journal of Greenville Presbyterian Theological College*, http://katekomen.gpts.edu/2010/06/critique-of-john-frames-worship-in.html; date of access: Jan. 18, 2015.

13 Frame analyzes a great many Bible passages in *DCL*, including Leviticus 10:1–21, 1 Samuel 13:13, and Jeremiah 7:31, only to say, "So these passages do not prove the regulative principle specifically. They do not prove that whatever is not prescribed is forbidden. They do show that God takes violations of his rules for worship very seriously." *DCL*, 470.

14 *DCL*, 471.

15 Ibid., 472.

16 Ibid., 473.

17 Ibid., 480. In *Dual Citizens: Worship and Life between the Already and the Not Yet* (Sanford, FL: Reformation Trust Publishing, 2009), author Jason Stellman pounces on Frame's broad view of worship early in his book, but he gives no attention to Frame's arguments. Frame has responded to Stellman in *The Escondido Theology: A Reformed Response to Two Kingdoms Theology* (Lakeland, FL: Whitefield Media Productions, 2011), 283–314.

18 *DCL*, 472. The two Scripture passages to which Frame eludes most often to prove this point are Roman 12:1–2, and his life verse, 1 Corinthians 10:31, "Whether you eat or drink, or whatever you do, do all to the glory of God."

19 *Westminster Theological Journal* 55 (Fall 1993): 321–329.
20 Friedrich Nietzsche, *Thus Spoke Zarathustra* (New York: Modern Library, 1995), Prologue, section 3, 125.
21 *Wall Street Journal*, "In Europe, God Is Not Dead," Saturday, July 14, 2007, http://online.wsj.com/article/SB118434936941966055.html; date of access: March 2, 2015.
22 Eva M. Hamberg and Thorleif Pettersen, "The Religious Market: Denominational Competition and Religious Participation in Contemporary Sweden, *Journal for the Scientific Study of Religion* 33, no. 3 (1994): 205–216.
23 "The Regulative Principle, Scripture, Tradition, and Culture," http://www.frame-poythress.org/frame_articles/1998HartDebate.htm; date of access: March 3, 2015.
24 *DCL*, 480.
25 All of what I have said here in no way discounts the fact that people attracted to "religion" are at the same time attracted to idols (Rom. 1). So I am not arguing for a dumbing down of the gospel to the level of people's innate religious attitudes. What I do think Frame's theology of worship offers us is a way to speak afresh to contemporary people, while remaining biblical in our approach.
26 For this historical and theological discussion of how Sabbath observance has been interpreted, see *DCL*, 513–527. Also, in this section I will not take in hand questions such as the change of the day of the Sabbath from Saturday to Sunday in the NT, openness to recreation on that day, and so on.
27 Ibid., 521.
28 Ibid.
29 This is the reverse of Kline's earlier view that envisaged the commandment as encouraging first rest from all of our labor and subordinately the worship of God as a benefit of that rest. Frame reviews Kline's earlier views in *DCL*, 523–524.
30 Ibid., 543. Frame refers to the Sabbath as a "creation ordinance" in *DCL*, 533. Note that Frame does not speak of work in general, but of work in terms of "cultural labors" toward the erection and advancement of worldwide civilizations. This is significant, in that the idea expresses his R1K view of culture, to be taken up in specific ways in the coming pages.
31 Ibid., 573.
32 Ibid., 533.
33 Ibid., 543. In Calvin, Sabbath rest is a means to an end: the worship of God. See John Calvin, *Sermons on the Ten Commandments*" ed. and trans. Benjamin W. Farley (Grand Rapids, MI: Baker, 1980), 108.
34 The most fundamental justification to observe the Sabbath, in Frame, is based in the Creator/creature relationship, which functions as a mimetic ideal for our Sabbath keeping responsibility. See *DCL*, 534.
35 *DCL*, 573.
36 See Dickson Despommier, *The Vertical Farm: Feeding the World in the 21st Century* (New York: Thomas Dunne Books, 2010).
37 *DCL*, 573.

38 This mirrors the land's enjoyment of Sabbath rest under the old biblical economy that included regulated fruit crops, whereby "The prohibition of harvesting any fruits for three years means simply that the entire organic matter produced by a tree during this time returns to the carbon cycle of that very soil. . . . Due to an input of organic matter equivalent to three consecutive sabbatical years, the fruit trees had a much better start and were bound to grant a higher yield." Hütterman, "Ecology in Ancient Judaism," in Neusner, *Encyclopaedia of Judaism*, vol. 4 (2000), 1727.

39John Frame, *The Doctrine of the Christian Life; A Theology of Lordship* (Phillipsburg, NJ: Presbyterian and Reformed, 2008), 744.

40 *DCL*, 744.

41 Ibid., 745. Evenhandedly, he notes on the same page, "But neither does Scripture justify the generalized suspicion of technology that is common in the secular environmental movement."

42 Russell D. Moore, "Re-Framing the Earth: Ecological Ethics in John Frame's *The Doctrine of the Christian Life*," paper presented at the Evangelical Theological Society, 2009 Annual Meeting, New Orleans, Louisiana.

43 *DCL*, 744.

44 See ibid., 595, on this point.

45 John M. Frame, "Toward a Theology of the State, part 2, http://thirdmill.org/towards-a-theology-of-the-state-part-2; date of access: March 4, 2015. Originally published in *Westminster Theological Journal* 51, no. 2 (Fall 1989): 199–226.

46 *DCL*, 595.

47 In appendix F of *DCL*, "Is Natural Revelation Sufficient to Govern Culture," Frame concludes, "So natural revelation is insufficient in our witness to the lordship of Christ." *DCL*, 955.

48 The bulk of this information came to me in an email from Frame dated October 31, 2013.

49 No one is in fact better at calling our attention to the metaphysical discontinuity in other areas; e.g., the Creator-creature distinction.

50 *DCL*, 747.

51 Ibid., 750.

52 See ibid., 415. Mutiperspectivally, the association is also firmly grounded in the way that the specific act of adultery in marriage triggers the attendant act of adultery in our relationship with God. Frame establishes this connection by reaching back to his deliberation on the fifth commandment. Supporting LC, Q. 124, which stipulates that our honor of father and mother has relevance for all authority relationships, Frame holds that disloyalty to parents can create a treasonous attitude to national authority. "But the family is more fundamental than the nation. It is the root of all corporate relationships. . . . As such, it reflects our fundamental relation to God, so that the mentality of rebellion is the same in both covenants." Ibid., 750.

53 Ibid., 767. Here Frame is quoting Matthew 5:28 in the English Standard Version.

54 Ibid., 766. His reading of 1 Corinthians 7:9 is that God does not condemn desire itself but "only a desire that cannot be controlled." Ibid., 767. This reading is supported by the

classic passage on the lust of heart, Matthew 5:28, where "to lust after" (KJV) translates the Greek word *epithumeo*.

55 See *DCL*, 748–751.

56 "God made man a relational being in his own image. Therefore, there is the need for intimate relationship within humankind (Genesis 2:18). Such a relationship is *also* necessary for the reproduction and multiplication of humankind (italics added). Walter A. Elwell, entry for "Marriage," in *Evangelical Dictionary of Biblical Theology*, http://www.studylight.org/dic/bed/view.cgi?n=464; date of access: March 5, 2015.

57 As Francis Foulkes, in looking to Genesis 2:24, says, "This statement from the creation story is the most profound and fundamental statement in the whole of Scripture concerning God's plan for marriage. It has been the ultimate bulwark of the church against the arguments for allowing polygamy. . . . it is the ultimate argument against promiscuity." Francis Foulkes, "Ephesians," *Tyndale New Testament Commentaries* (Downers Grove, IL: Inter-Varsity Press, 2008), 168.

58 These statistics are provided by Global Envision, "Fewer Babies Pose Difficult Challenges for Europe" (October 10, 2007). Given that these stats are now dated, the situation can only be more foreboding.

59 Ibid.

60 *DCL*, 748.

61 The term is found in Eric R. Wolf, *Europe and the People without History* (Berkeley: University of California Press), 13.

62 See my earlier discussion of homosexuality relative to the thought of Richard B. Hays, on pages 105-109.

63 *DCL*, 760.

64 Ibid.

65 See ibid., 767.

66 "Orientation," Merriam-Webster.com, 2011, http://www.merriam-webster.com/dictionary/orientation; date of access: March 7, 2015.

67 Thomas Boston, *Human Nature in Its Fourfold State* (London: The Banner of Truth Trust, reprint, 1964), 208–209.

68 Analysis on covetousness intersects with my previous talk on homosexual orientation.

69 "Matthew 5:28 says that if desire has excited the soul, there is no serious sin even if there is sin. But such excitement is an act of sexual lust. Therefore, not every act of sexual lust is a serious or mortal sin." Thomas Aquinas, *Summa Theologiae*, I–II, Q. XV, Art. 2, ad. 15.

70 He justifies this view, for one, because the word of God goes as far as to judge our "evil thoughts and imaginations" (Gen. 6:5; 8:21)." *DCL*, 848. This only strengthens the question as to how "a strong pattern of temptation" (short of desire or lust) to homosexuality can avoid sin. Are we to assume that such a powerful inclination is able to avoid an unplanned impulsive desire for a person of the same sex?

71 Douma, *The Ten Commandments*, trans. Nelson D. Kloosterman (Phillipsburg, NJ: P&R Publishing Co., 1996), 351.

72 Frame does not use the term in *DCL* because he is not prone "to introduce a historical technical term for its own sake" and also because he thinks "concupiscence is ambiguous." In an email to the author, dated December 27, 2011.
73 Roman Catholic thought stipulates that concupiscence preceded the Fall: it was a disharmony between reason and affection that had to be remedied (even before the Fall) by a divine gift of grace, the *donum superadditum*. The Protestant theologians consistently defined concupiscence as a post-fall phenomenon.
74 "[T]hat everything which is in man, from the intellect to the will, from the soul even to the flesh, is defiled and pervaded with this concupiscence; or, to express it more briefly, that the whole man is in himself nothing else than concupiscence." *Institutes* 2.1.8.
75 R. Scott Clark, "Concupiscence: Sin and the Mother of Sin," *at* http://www.modernreformation.org/default.php?page=articledisplay&var1=ArtRead&var2=361&var3=issuedisplay&var4=IssRead&var5=37; date of access: March 11, 2015.
76 Ibid.
77 Scott, quoting *Institutes* 2.7.5.
78 Clark, "Concupiscence: Sin and the Mother of Sin."
79 *DCL*, 848. To this, I can add that Scripture judges "the thoughts and intentions of the heart" (Hebrews 4:12).
80 It is not clear how concupiscence does not shape even our intense desires for piety and holiness, if we are always under its power.

Chapter 6

Lordship and Presuppositional Apologetics

Christian apologetics is "the discipline that teaches Christians how to give a reason for their hope."[1] The field of theology finds support in 1 Peter 3:15–16, which records, "but sanctify Christ as Lord in your hearts, always *being* ready to make a defense to everyone who asks you to give an account for the hope that is in you, yet with gentleness and reverence; and keep a good conscience so that in the thing in which you are slandered, those who revile your good behavior in Christ will be put to shame." The defense of the faith contends for the truth of God against objections, exposing the perceived flaws of the secular challenge to Christianity, in the hope that interlocutors will be drawn by the Word and Spirit of God to the knowledge of the truth. Despite this centralized concern of apologetics, generally speaking, the nisus among Reformed theologians has been toward a solipsism of sorts: in this case, a supreme occupation with defending a particularized defense of one apologetic method over and against other methods. This *desert island* apologetics misses the central issue: apologetics as a tool for the world-wide proclamation of the evangel.[2]

I will offer a constructive and comparative analysis between Frame's presuppositional model of apologetics and other apologetic methodologies, but at the forefront of this discussion comes the need for a broadened understanding of Frame's most significant input into the present subject.

Frame's Important Contribution

Although rightly credited as a leading defender, analyst, and critic of the apologetics of Cornelius Van Til, Frame's most outstanding and indeed helpful contribution vis-à-vis apologetics is his consistent ability to center our attention on apologetics as a tool for carrying out the Lord's Great Commission (see Matt. 28:18–20). As he says, "Our apologetics must be pervaded by a sense of Christ's lordship . . . and this demands *diligent preparation* so that we may be able to obey our Lord's Great Commission."[3] While the designation *presuppositional apologetics* is most often associated with Frame, the lordship principle provides a missional point of departure that can just as easily lead Frame to call his approach "evangelistic apologetics."[4]

Frame's evangelistic and confessional emphasis also challenges the idea that apologetics is prolegomena to theology. The Princeton school of apologetics argued as if apologetics could be separated from the biblical *kerygma*. B. B. Warfield is representative of the tradition that sees apologetics as laying the foundation for theology. In an article on apologetics, he says, "It is, in other words, the function of apologetics to investigate, explicate, and establish the grounds on which a theology . . . is possible."[5] In the same expose, he notes that "Apologetics supplies to Christian men the systematically organized basis on which the faith of Christian men must rest." For Warfield and the Old Princeton School, apologetics is not an evangelistic proclamation of the gospel but is narrowly limited to studies that lay the rational foundation for the vindication of the evangel. Against this view, Frame secures the closest possible connection between apologetics and the New Testament *kerygma*. The weight Frame gives to evangelistic priorities in apologetics knows no equal within the contemporary Reformed community. This claim will be examined further.

The Triperspectival Emphasis

As is everything in Framian theology, evangelistic apologetics is shaped by the perspectival approach. The relationship between apologetics and perspectivalism is found in the simple fact that the Christian *apologia* necessarily involves epistemology. One must engage the mind of the person to whom one is presenting the parts of the Christian faith. This engagement is most easily facilitated perspectivally. Why so?

In much the same way that he critiques the history of secular ethics, Frame contends that secular epistemologies have found it hard to relate sense experience, reason, and feelings in their accounts of human knowledge. They have also been perplexed by the relation of the subject (the knower), the object (what the knower knows), and the norms or rules of knowledge (logic, reason, etc.). Perspectivalism, Frame believes, abates these deficiencies.[6] Through the lenses of the three perspectives, the knowing subject comes into contact with the objects of knowledge, particularly the primacy of God's revelation. The *norm* is God's authoritative revelation, the *subject* is the person who lives in the face of God, and the *situation* is the world as God has made it and controls it.[7] So the three aspects of knowledge correspond to the attributes of God's lordship. The task of the apologist is to uphold God's authoritative norm within a given human situation, made up of people who are uniquely created in God's image. Take away one of those, and there is no basis for knowledge at all, with the result that apologetics falls to the ground.

I may put the matter this way. In the "normative perspective," the apologist asks the question, "What do God's norms direct the unbeliever to believe?" In the "situational perspective," we ask, "What are the facts relevant to his or her belief?" In the "existential perspective," we ask, "What belief is most satisfying to a believing heart?" The normative perspective calls the unbeliever to faith on the norm of Christ and his gospel. The situational perspective seeks to contextualize the gospel according to the situation within which people live. And the existential perspective takes into account the relationship of the gospel to the internal temperament and proclivities of those whom we are engaging. I will revisit these ideas.

The following will formulate more amply Frame's contribution to apologetics and its intensely proximate relationship to the lordship principle, most fundamentally expressed by his perspectival approach to theology. Precisely in connection with this goal, the following material will develop three related categories of apologetics, or what Frame calls the "general shape" of a biblical apologetic. They are (1) "The fear of the Lord is the beginning of knowledge (Prov. 1:7) . . . indeed, wisdom and knowledge are summed up in Jesus Christ." (2) Though God is known through his creation, people repress this knowledge (Rom. 1:18-32) until God renews their minds (Rom. 12:2)" (3) "The apologist should press upon the non-Christian the evidence that God is clearly revealed in nature . . . in the context of a biblical worldview . . . and should present the Gospel . . . using Scripture's own arguments (as (1 Cor. 15:1–11 and other arguments) that follow scriptural leads."[8]

The heart of Frame's apologetic procedure is points 2 and 3. This asseveration is supported by an episodic encounter with the theologian, in which he interjected himself into a circle of students at Westminster

Theological Seminary (Philadelphia) who were in the throes of discussion—a group that included me— to ask, "What are you guys talking about?" One man replied "Van Til." That prompted Frame to say, "All of Van Til can be boiled down to two points: all men know God but suppress the truth in unrighteousness, and the only way to approach them is to pull the rug right out from under them." In other words, denial of the existence of God is a self-deceptive act, before which the apologist must press the truth of God in the belief that only that truth can transform hardened hearts. Frame went on to explain to the students that his distillation of this specific area of Van Tilian apologetics is centroidal to his own method.

Fear of the Lord and Transcendental Argument

Frame's first apologetic concern is with the fear of the Lord as the alpha of true knowledge of God. In his entire corpus, *Jehovah* is equivalent to Lord and serves to unite all biblical passages regarding God's lordship attributes of control, authority, and presence (CAP).[9] Even though preceding sections of this work have been clear that Frame's thought is altogether covenantal, the transcendence of the Lord, his aseity and otherness, are always preclusion to his nearness to his people.

Most critical of apologetics, then, is that "there is no continuum between God and creation. There are no degrees of divinity: God is divine, and we are not. There are no degrees of reality, either."[10] Reverential fear of the Lord is thus a controlling motive in the lives of those who hear the evangel in matters both spiritual and moral.[11] Concomitantly, God's transcendence serves as the supreme basis for the axial proof of God in Frame's apologetic: the transcendental argument for God (TAG).

The proof begins with the presupposition that the self-existent God of Scripture is wholly different from us and is the source of all reality, truth, knowledge, meaning, actuality, and possibility. The presupposition is presented to a doubter mainly via *negativa*, viz., by simply reversing it and stating that "Without God there is no meaning (truth, rationality, etc.); therefore, God exists."[12] TAG can thus claim that even the possibility of rational predication is impossible apart from God, "because without him it would not be possible to reason, to think or even to attach a predicate to a subject (predication.)"[13] Van Til expressed this proposition using the analogy of a child slapping her father in the face while sitting in his lap. Just as the child's attack on her father is made possible only by the support of the father, so also the atheist is only able to deny God because God gives the atheist life and breath. The striking correlative conclusion is that atheism presupposes theism.

The corollary finds philosophical precedence. Since Gotlob Frege (1848–1925) and his early work in the role of presuppositions in semantics, the phenomenon of presupposition has been proposed in modern analytic philosophy by P. F. Strawson and Bas van Fraasen and others, to say not only that A presupposes B, but also not-A implies B. According to the original proposal presented by Strawson: *S* presupposes a statement *S*, if and only if the truth of *S* is a precondition of the truth-or-falsity of *S*."[14] The Strawsonian presupposition is typically considered in the literature in the subsequent form: (1) *P* presupposes *Q* if and only if *Q* is true provided *P* is true or *P* is false. Applied to apologetic argument, God's existence is implied (or proved) either by the assertion or the denial of causality. In modern Reformed circles, Van Til was the first to put forth TAG.

It follows, then, that in actual apologetics, TAG has two steps: one defensive, the other offensive.

The first step is to ask the unbeliever to assume the truth of Christianity "for the sake of argument," so that the Christian can present the inherent rationale of the claims of Scripture.

The second step is for the Christian to assume the position of the non-Christian "for the sake of argument" and then to present a *reductio*—that is, demonstrate the absurdity of the unbeliever's worldview taken to its logical outcome.[15] For example, the theist can argue before the non-theist, "Your very denial of God assumes God. Your only recourse is to repent." Frame follows his former teacher on the dominant themes linking the Christian worldview to predication: that God is the author of all meaning and rationality.

However, according to the original Van Tilian proposition, Frame demurs somewhat on the strength of the falsity of atheism to presuppose its object. For if atheism is incoherent as a system, Frame wonders how atheism can provide a logical line of reference to that which is coherent. He does, however, assume the use of *reductio* though reservedly.[16] I will explore Frame's reservations on this point in more detail in upcoming sections.

Now I have proposed that Frame's doctrinal/doxastic commitments are *sui generis*, insofar as are appurtenant to the Great Commission. Already this point positions Frame somewhere in the spectrum of Reformed apologists and epistemologists with apologetic interest. Yet the claim requires further support. Given that TAG remains a standard point of departure for Reformed apologetics, this is an apt point in our discussion to buttress the claim. Far from exhaustive, the following will present a comparative study of Frame, Cornelius Van Til, Francis Schaeffer, and Greg L. Bahnsen on apologetics—all the while, bearing in mind the premise that Frame's apologetic goals enhance evangelistic priorities more than what we find in these other apologists.

Frame and Van Til on Transcendental Argument for God (TAG)

Van Til used to explain that argument for Christianity achieves certainty only if it is tenaciously transcendental or presuppositional.[17] He was inclined this way because in his mind it was the only argument that avoided *neutrality*.[18] Van Til's strong reprimand of E. J. Carnell and J. Oliver Buswell demonstrates his position.[19] It is not that Van Til was wholly against the use of Christian theistic evidences. He opposed their use in the sphere of rational impartiality. Presenting Christianity before the natural logic of fallen man as reasonable and probable—a choice among other possible options—was to present evidence as a *brute fact.*[20]

Deeper still, it forces the apologist to reduce one of the horns of the dilemma: God's incomprehensibility and sovereignty or man's finite knowledge and total depravity. One is sacrificed to the other when one ventures from transcendental polemics and introduces irrationalism and rationalism into the Christian apologetic. The apologist can introduce irrationalism into Christian teaching by falsely assuming that the unbeliever has some determinative power to understand the workings of the universe, when in fact autonomous reason cannot decipher any part of the universe definitively.[21] The apologist can inject some rationalism into the discussion when he looks outside Scripture to reason and history to answer detractors of Christianity.[22]

Van Til circumvented the irrationalist/rationalist pitfalls of apologetics by insisting that theory meet practice—in other words, that apologetics not serve as prologue to theological study. We should not seek to establish the *reasonableness* of theism before presenting theism but should present the claims of theism as a challenge to non-Christian thinking *in toto* from the start. Instead of striving to establish the authenticity of theism first and then advancing arguments in support of it, Van Til says, "[I]t is Christian theism *as a unit* that we seek to defend. We do not seek to defend theism in apologetics and Christianity in evidences, but we seek to defend Christian theism in both courses" (italics added).[23]

The earlier period of Frame's academic career saw him in agreement with Van Til. In time, however, his view changed. Mainly, Frame's problem was that in Van Til's hands, TAG follows a negative line of reasoning only. More specifically is his concern with the words "as a unit" from Van Til's argumentation cited just above. Viz., Frame questions the practicality of presenting TAG as a *complete* defense of Christianity. He does not believe, as did Van Til, that the whole of Christian theism can be proved by a single theistic argument, regardless of how well it may articulate the whole of the biblical doctrine of God. It is not Frame's goal to cast doubt on TAG but to sharpen it.[24] He does so by enlisting the assistance of supplementary arguments of a more traditional kind, in the belief that their use does not kowtow to the secular mind.

Closely consociated with this evolvement is the Framian distinction between *presupposition* and *premise*. Van Til held that the presupposition of any defense of Christianity must match the premise of the specific argument in view, or else one's orthodox position would be emasculated by one's pragmatism. No longer willing to marry presupposition to premise, the latter Frame embraces a more expansive set of positive or direct expostulations.[25] Using the argument from design, as an example, I interpret him to mean that the premise "There is design in the universe" does not *necessitate* the presupposition that the God of Scripture is responsible for its design. However, the use of the premise does not infer inescapably that one is guilty of autonomous reasoning. Rather, a Christian can exploit the *premise* that the universe displays design on the basis of the *presupposition* that God is responsible for its design, and remain on safe ground. The same can be said for any positive argument for God. I think that Frame's paying new attention to Van Til's position is the genesis of his evolvement on *broad circular argumentation.*[26]

To the point at hand, Frame's readiness to enlist supporting argumentation, beyond what Van Til was willing to do, is the result of his great knack at recognizing that the practice of evangelistic apologetics often requires extemporaneity. The utterance of the gospel is not straitjacketed but *person-variable.*[27] By that phrase, Frame means that the apologist is to be protean in a creative sense when declaring the lordship of Christ over specific areas of people's lives. As Frame says, "Since proof is 'person variable,' we are particularly interested in choosing an argumentative approach that makes contact with the individual or group we are talking to."[28] The difference with Van Til is further motivated by Frame's *normative* perspective of apologetics, or apologetics as proof, which will be investigated in an upcoming section.

The person-variability of TAG is forcefully applied to the extent that the apologist-evangelist bears in mind specific spiritual strongholds in the lives of his listeners. Or, as Frame says, "[Jesus] didn't specifically describe all the areas of his lordship to every inquirer; he restricted himself to mentioning those areas which were of particular temptation to each individual."[29] The classical arguments for God may also be employed in the person-variable nature of apologetics. Some, in the illusions they entertain in their self-absorbed autonomy, may need to hear the cosmological argument, while God may use the teleological argument as a means to cause others to pause and think. Alertness to specific barricades in people's lives where lordship is of particular offense, combined with use of the traditional apologetic arguments when needed, affords the evangelist a full arsenal that he can wield with creativity and flexibility.

Van Til may well reply to Frame that the use of person-variability in apologetics is not coeval with the conjunction of presupposition and practice. However, anyone with any experience in personal evangelism knows full well the importance of spontaneity. Frame's honing of TAG is not in the least a call to cater to autonomous reason or to use the *blockhouse method* of apologetics.[30] Rather, he seeks to follow the model of evangelistic apologetics exampled by Jesus of Nazareth. Seen from this angle, the use of *both* transcendental argument *and* classical evidences is not mutually exclusive.

Frame and Francis Schaeffer

I am saying that Frame's work in academic apologetics demonstrates greater value for evangelism than what I find in Van Til, Schaeffer, and Bahnsen. Now Frame himself has credited Francis Schaeffer not in the first place as an academic but as "a smart evangelist."[31] So, is continued argumentation to prove Frame's superior evangelistic priorities a threat to hoist with one's own petard? Strong indicators to support the claim exist.

But before investigating this assertion further, let us ask, "How has Schaeffer influenced Frame?"

In an article, Schaeffer viewed himself as a bridge between the apologetics of Van Til and the more traditional/classical apologetics, mainly that of Buswell—a bridge that Van Til would have rejected.[32] The Schaeffer article also had a profound effect on Frame. It facilitated his acceptance of the justifiable use of reasonable arguments as a means to waylay the unbeliever's inconsistency—for example, "So you believe in logic, but if you really believed in logic you'd be a Christian theist."

Thus, he says, "[Schaeffer's] emphasis on *both* presuppositions *and* verifications is important; possibly even an advance over Van Til in emphasis."[33] For Frame, verification includes all presuppositions "by tests of coherence, factual adequacy, and practical life."[34] The process of verification is triperspectival. "Epistemologically, it goes like this: (1) We presuppose the norms or standards for knowledge, (2) we apply these to the evidences and facts, and (3) we adopt those conclusions which we believe are warranted. (1) is normative, (2) situational, (3) existential . . . These are perspectivally related: error on one of these will lead logically to error in the others. That's the approach I developed in DKG."[35] The *antithesis* between the believer and the unbeliever (or between the non-believer and God) is something that Frame is thus willing to exploit.[36]

Still, there are problematic areas in the Schaeffer apologetic that differentiate him from Frame and hinder his goal of evangelism. (1) Schaeffer maintains a faulty history of philosophy. He claims that Plato and Aristotle embraced objective truth verses falsity, and that this antithesis was the accepted distinction in philosophy until the emergence of Hegel. After this, philosophy is marked by irrationalism, an "escape from reason."[37] It is the Greek antithesis (truth vs. falsity) that must be recovered in order to reach modern man with the gospel. (2) Based on (1), Schaeffer gives indication to a neutral idea of truth, apart from Scripture. Because people are capable of entertaining the Greek idea of antithesis, Schaeffer does not eschew the fact that the natural mind cannot discern *fully* right and wrong. In other words, "Schaeffer does not make explicit the natural man's rejection of all legitimate standards of verification."[38] (3) Based on (2), the effect of his thinking in evangelism is that "he calls men to a neutral notion of truth apart from Scripture, which believers and unbelievers share in common."[39] That is, he contends that before people can rightly understand the gospel, the apologist must practice a type of pre-evangelism: to help people see the antithesis as the Greeks saw it, to accept the necessity of absolute truth, and from that reconstructed foundation, apply the gospel.[40] Cf. the Old Princeton School mentioned earlier, which viewed apologetics as laying the rational groundwork for the proclamation of the biblical *kerygma*.

Although Frame agrees with Schaeffer that verification is useful, he critiques Schaeffer for trusting natural reason with the ability to verify tests of coherence, factual adequacy, and adequacy for practical life, apart from God's lordship over all minds as revealed in Scripture.[41] As Frame sees it, verification is useful but *only* as we presuppose the standards or norms for knowledge from Scripture. According to William Edgar, "Schaeffer's system requires us to submit Christianity to natural theology, rather than affirm it as self-authenticating."[42] Frame wants us to seek verification *presuppositionally* and also in the realm of *broad argumentation.* In other words, to reason in such a way that is compatible with the conclusion.

How does Schaeffer's system hurt his evangelistic aims? Edgar provides clarification in speaking of Van Til's problem with Schaeffer's "torn book" analogy. The substance of the analogy is that of man who finds a mutilated book in his attic with only some recognizable information. Shortly thereafter, the man discovers the rest of the book in the attic, information that unlocks the meaning of the whole book. The mutilated section represents the order of the universe and the rest of the book stands for the Bible. According to Edgar, Van Til believed that the natural mind can no more discern the truth of nature than the truth of the Bible. Schaeffer errs, as Edgar points out, because he "makes concessions to natural theology, according to which general revelation provides knowledge of God, which is good enough as far as it goes, but needs completion."[43]

Although in one place Schaeffer affirms man's ungodly suppression of the message of nature, he belies this when he says that natural reason does not invent the order of the universe but "recognizes it."[44] In Schaeffer's view, then, natural man is competent to judge whether Scripture is the appropriate complement to general revelation. Edgar counters that Schaeffer's distinction "is not especially convincing since the Bible teaches that we cannot even recognize the 'order' without new hearts. Reason without regeneration is not even competent to judge what has been observed."[45] Frame joins Van Til and Edgar: "I believe that Schaefer was rather unclear on some important matters, particularly the existence of a distinctively biblical concept of truth."[46] Frame avoids Schaeffer's pitfall in evangelistic apologetics by always maintaining a biblical concept of truth, which, more than Schaeffer, does far more to make unbelievers aware of their helplessness before, and in need of, the biblical God.

Frame and Greg L. Bahnsen

Comparing and contrasting Frame and Bahnsen on TAG is much like doing the same with Frame and Van Til. Throughout his teaching ministry, Bahnsen was doggedly Van Tilian. So in what follows there is some bleed-over from my review of Frame and Van Til. The important areas of continuity between Frame and Bahnsen are that both claim the presuppositional heritage together with TAG. The differences between the two thinkers are, according to Frame, a matter of degree, although Bahnsen viewed the differences with Frame more disapprovingly. On the eve of Bahnsen's last visit to the hospital, just before his death, he replied to an email from Frame, in which Frame wished him well. Bahnsen ended with the words, "I still disagree with you on the transcendental argument."

From Frame's perspective, the difference in degree can be summed in two points. First, whereas Schaeffer underestimated the antithesis between believer and non-believer, Bahnsen overestimated it. On propositional knowledge, Frame asks whether the unbeliever "can never utter a true statement, such as 'the sky is blue'?" He answers, "On that question, I do not believe that Van Til ever arrived at a clear answer, nor did Bahnsen."[47]

Second, Bahnsen holds to an extremely narrow view of what constitutes transcendental argument. He is not willing to accept any supplemental argumentation, out of his belief that the premise of, say, any traditional argument for God must be based on autonomous thinking. For him, any inference from the world to God, directly or heuristically, cannot be properly transcendental. He therefore spends much of his academic prowess critiquing other presuppositionalists (i.e., "desert island apologetics"), whom he suspects of arguing autonomously. Bahnsen is much like his mentor Van Til—engaged in movement battles. Frame remarks, "At a number of points, I think that Van Til and Bahnsen should have given more benefit of the doubt to [Clark, Carnell, and Schaeffer] by interpreting them in more favorable ways."[48] Frame is saying that Van Til and Bahnsen should have focused more on the antithesis between God and the fallen human heart for the purpose of proper evangelism, and not among themselves and other apologists.

The gaping inconsistency in Bahnsen's dismantling of Clark, Carnell, and Schaeffer is that transcendental argument is an argument. It is an argument for the existence of God that is always of the general form "X, therefore God." In the debate with Gordon Stein, he does seem to be saying that "physical laws, therefore God"; "logic, therefore God"; and "morality, therefore God."[49] But is not this line of reasoning broadly circular, if not a form of traditional argumentation?

By way of further annotation of Frame, it a very fine line that Bahnsen draws with the objects of his scorn. On one hand, he is critical of apologists for their use of evidence or reason, but it is not a problem for him to use the argument from design. This seems permissible because in his mind, his arguments are consistent with his conclusions.

Yet how can Bahnsen know with certainty that Carnell, for example, was not arguing in a way consistent his conclusions? It almost seems as though he (and Van Til) is psychoanalyzing these other men. In many cases, however, one could read Clark, Carnell, and Buswell as though they were espousing TAG.

In dialogue with Don Collett, Frame makes some points that are equally appropriate for Bahnsen. Collett joins Van Til and Bahnsen in the assumption that the traditional apologetics of Aquinas, Joseph Butler, and William Paley fall short of TAG in its lead thesis that God is the transcendental condition of predication.[50] Instead, Collett claims that these men present being, causality, or purpose and then, on the strength of autonomous reasoning, strive to prove the God of Scripture. Van Til, Bahnsen, and Collett hold that a god who can be reached by independent reason is not the God of Scripture. Collett, et al., looking to Strawson and van Fraasen, encourage a very limited use of *modus ponens* (if A, then B) and *modus tollens* (if not-A, then B) in the use of TAG.

Frame individuates himself from Collett in two ways. To begin with, he does not limit *modus ponens* so narrowly. He joins Collett in the propriety of the argument from cause. But he also insists that such reasoning avoid tautology. Should an unbeliever sniff at the causal argument, Collett wants us to repeat TAG until it hits its mark. But here is where the primacy of the Great Commission reveals itself again in Frame's thought. He worries that committed opposition will not be persuaded by the recycling of an argument when they are steadfastly against the first premise: God.

What is his solution? Frame asks, "How do we prove that God is the transcendental ground of causality? We need to establish the first premise. How do we do that? By showing that it is meaningless to speak of causality unless God exists. How do we do that? Perhaps by showing (with traditional apologists) that an infinite series of causes is unintelligible, and that to deny that infinite series is to affirm God."[51] Frame is saying that is possible to use traditional arguments to reach a transcendental conclusion *as long as* God's lordship is sustained in all argumentation.

The transmission from Collett to Bahnsen's inconsistency is conspicuous. Citing the Stein debate, if Bahnsen can say, "Logic, therefore God," then Frame can say, "Morality, therefore God," or, "An infinite series of causes is unintelligible, therefore God," as do the traditional apologists. The difference evidentially lay in the detail that Bahnsen is dead set against *appealing* to natural logic but not against *using* logic in apologetics, and he confuses the two. Frame seems more consistent about the difference, whereby he permits the use of logic in apologetics, and again for the purpose of better evangelism.

The contrast with Collett finds an analogous point of comparison with Strawson. Not only does Frame, like Strawson, hold that "logic implies God, but that logic presupposes God," but also Frame can show that God is the presupposition of logic with more force to the extent that we draw out further implications from the first premise—for example, Bahnsen's argument that logic implies God's existence.[52] Now a potential problem may loom. To the degree one extends the argument backward, or more broadly circular, one may run the risk of slipping away from the ground of the Christian epistemology altogether. Yet we have found no evidence of such slippage in Frame's work. Picture a man standing in front of a mirror with a mirror behind him. He sees an infinite series of images of himself. But should he step out of the line of mirrors, he loses his perception. As long as the apologist remains in the line of reasoning that is consistent with the conclusion, he can use an infinite series of arguments, which will only enhance the transcendental nature of his stance. But should he move away from his fundamental presupposition, he will lose his way. Frame never moves.

Frame's Problem with "Reductio"

Now, earlier I said that Frame has reservations about using *reductio* in apologetic argumentation. That raises the use of *modus tollens* and a further difference with Collett. Frame accepts the syllogism: *if not-A, then God exists*, and that that means that God "is the transcendental ground of all intelligibility and nonintelligibility, meaningfulness and meaninglessness." However, if the negative argument is all we can say, he demurs. "This dissolves, for me, the original meaning and attractiveness of transcendental argument. . . . Do we really want to say that even a meaningless, unintelligible world would presuppose God? . . . I must reluctantly conclude that at this point the transcendentalizing of apologetics implodes into nonsense."[53]

Driving Frame's hesitancy on *modus tollens* is a deeper issue still. Although the Strawson-Bahnsen-Collett formulation is valid to illustrate the lordship aspect of *authority* in epistemology, it will not, by itself, according to Frame, convince any skeptic. I have arrived back at my main point: Frame's concern is with the practical import for the Great Commission.

Notwithstanding the *reduction ad absurdum* of *modus tollens*, and the problematic area of *modus ponens*, as Frame sees it, there is hope. He confers that both *modus ponens* and *modus tollens* are useful in apologetics, as long as "we can establish these premises and the logic leading to their conclusions.[54] To convince, "we need to look to traditional logic and evidence."[55] Of course, I cannot say that TAG, as a comprehensive argument, and as proffered by Strawson/Bahnsen/Collett, has failed to convince skeptics. What I do know is that if the Bahnsen/Stein debate is an indicator, TAG functions more aptly as a means to silence scoffers than it does to lead them to a saving knowledge of Christ. Frame gives every indication that his difference with Bahnsen hinges on this critical point.

Some additional commentary may be helpful at separating out some of the issues before us. TAG is important for it defends the particular elements of Christianity with an awareness of the connectivity of each element in the overall Christian system of truth. However, it cannot be overlooked that in its historical genesis, the argument was arrived at largely for negative reasons. Tracing our steps back to Kant, he attempted to answer what he saw as the errors of Continental Rationalism and British Empiricism in the idea that the conditions and analysis of knowledge are substantiated in the transcendental aesthetic and the transcendental analytic. Van Til also estimated Empiricism and Rationalism adversely but for expressly theological reasons. Yet the result ends with Van Til adopting transcendental thinking: a middle way. I think of a man driving on a highway. Wanting to avoid the speedsters in the far left lane and the slow pokes in the far right lane, he chooses the middle road.

We can say, and correctly, that TAG is biblical. But lest we forget our place as presuppositionalists in historical theology; that is that the transcendental apologetic was born as a reactionary movement, it will continue to provide a reactionary answer. It will serve well to silence unbelievers but not to enliven them to amazing grace. It is this point that reinforces Frame's points about extended argumentation. The fact that a man is in the center lane of the highway does mean he must stay there. Traffic conditions in either the far left or the far right lanes of the highway change and allow him to move about. The Strawson/Bahnsen/Collett maxims would have the man remain in the middle lane indefinitely. For the purpose of enhanced evangelization,

Frame directs us to take advantage of the two other lanes: logic and evidence, when conditions allow for it (and even might insist on it) but always with deference to the Lord of all logic and evidence. In the end, we will arrive at the same transcendental goal as those who remain in the middle lane but perhaps with more effectiveness. Thus, as I first pointed out, "[Frame's] critical account of Van Til allows us to take a somewhat less apocalyptic view of methodological differences among apologists, so that we can indeed concentrate on fulfilling the Great Commission."[56]

The Parable of the Fish[57]

A further reflection on TAG begins with what may appear to be an odd question. "Does a fish know it's in water?" The obvious mental response is, "Well, maybe it's not *conscious* of the water, but in some way the fish knows it's in water." Then after further thought, we might conclude, "The only way to know for sure would be to ask the fish." We say, "Mr. Fish, do you know you are in water?" The fish flips its tail, "No." We muse silently, "Hmm, this fish is unwilling to acknowledge that water is the source of all reality, truth, knowledge, meaning, actuality, and predication in his life." So we press the argument. "Mr. Fish, 'Wet, therefore water.'" Another flip of the tail tells us, "I don't believe in water." But we are ready. "Mr. Fish, even your negation of the possibility of water is made possible by the water." The fish is unmoved. Ah, but as it turns out, this is no ordinary fish. It is a flying fish. It is just then that we notice a great tuna slowly approaching the fish from behind. We stand waiting to see what will happen. Suddenly, the fish also notices the tuna and on the wing of the air leaps from the water to save its life and repeats his flying acrobatics until the tuna retreats. We think, "Wait, there may be a possibility of reasoning with the fish." We try once more. "Mr. Fish, to spare your life you just flew out of the water. Surely you noticed the difference between the water and the air. So you must know that you in water, right?" The fish appears motionless. He's thinking. "A double flip of the tail now tells us that he acknowledges the fact that he has been in water all along." We are satisfied, and so is the fish.

Obviously, men and fish cannot communicate on a rational level, but let us assume that our ability to talk with the fish is something like Frame's *point of contact* in apologetics.[58] Yet with what important tool do the point of contact and the powerful moving of the Spirit work to convert sinners? The gospel. Paul says, "For I am not ashamed of the gospel, for it is the power of God for salvation to everyone who believes, to the Jew first and also to the Greek" (vs. 16). And what is the intent of the gospel in people's lives? It is to change dead spiritual hearts and to produce new creations: Christians—all to the glory of God.

In the parable of the fish, the fish is all people, the water is God's universe, the first argument is TAG, and the use of extended argument is Frame's employment of TAG, which includes logic and evidence. In all of the movement battles over what constitutes proper transcendental argument, it is rare to find in the literature on the subject the straightforward biblical idea that the gospel is what changes people, not argumentation—regardless of whether it is narrow, broad, Strawsonian, or something else. What made the fish jump from the water? The tuna. Why do men jump from the biblical God? They perceive God as a threat to their autonomy. It was never our job to convince the flying fish he was in water but to warn him of the danger of the tuna. Likewise, the pressing need before the church is not to persuade men that God is the transcendental ground of intelligibility, but to warn them "Repent, for the Kingdom of heaven is at hand" (Matthew 3:2); to declare "that Christ died for our sins according to the Scriptures, and that

He was buried, and that He was raised on the third day according to the Scriptures" (1 Corinthians 15:3–4).

Our argument, designed to get the fish to concede he was in water, also fell short of God's expectation. Our hope should also have been to see his fish nature changed. Only the gospel can make new creations out of God-haters. Frame, though he is a figure in the parable of the fish, also stands outside the parable. He is clear that TAG is not our *witness* to unbelievers but "is a way of *illustrating* the role of divine authority in Christian epistemology" (italics mine).[59] The core of the Christian message is that "we hear and believe the message of the gospel."[60] Making the gospel of utmost priority and TAG more of an illustration in apologetics is further evidence of the superior position of the Great Commission in Frame's thought.

Endnotes

1 *AGG*, 1. The word *apologetics* derives from the Greek word ἀπολογία, which means "speaking in defense."
2 By this term, I refer to the tendency among many apologists to defend what they feel is the best form for apologetics, rather than simply doing apologetics, which, according to 1 Peter 3:15–16, is the paramount concern of the defense of the faith.
3 *DKG*, 358. Similarly, says Frame, "Apologetics and preaching are not two different things. Both are attempting to reach unbelievers for Christ." *AGG*, 16. See also pages 53–55 of *AGG* for Frame's evangelistic stress in apologetics.
4 *AGG*, 74. He makes a special case for the priority of the defense of the faith over apologetics as an abstract discipline in an article titled "Apologetics." See http://www.frame-poythress.org/frame_articles/2005Apologetics.html; date of access: March 14, 2012.
5 B. B. Warfield, "Apologetics," in *The New Schaff-Herzog Encyclopedia of Religious Knowledge*, ed. Samuel Macauley Jackson (New York: Funk and Wagnalls Company, 1908), 233. Retrieved at http://www.monergism.com/thethreshold/sdg/warfield/warfield_apologetics.html; date of access: Feb. 16, 2012.
6 Ibid., 15–20.
7 Frame examines this sequence in ibid., 62–63.
8 These points are adapted from John M. Frame, "Apologetics," retrieved from http://www.frame-poythress.org/frame_articles/2005Apologetics.html; date of access: March 14, 2012. The entirety of this chapter will use this three-fold formula as an outline.
9 The title "Lord" is a rendering of the work *kurios*, which the New Testament authors used to render the Hebrew IHWH. However, in Chapters 2 and 3 of *DG*, Frame goes to quite a bit of length to correlate Yahweh with Lord. See *DG*, 37 especially.
10 *DG*, 217.
11 Jehovah declares to Moses, "Oh that they had such a heart in them, that they would fear Me and keep all My commandments always, that it may be well with them and with their sons forever" (Deut. 5:29)!
12 *AGG*, 70.
13 Ibid., 70–71.
14 P. Strawson, *Introduction to Logical Theory* (London: Methuen & CO., 1952), 49. According to Frege, "If anything is asserted there is always an obvious presupposition. The simple or compound proper names used have a reference. If one therefore asserts 'Kepler died in misery,' there is presupposition that the name 'Kepler' designates something." First published in *Zeitscheift für Philosophie and philosophische Kritik,* Philosophie und philosophische Kritik, 100:34. English translation of the article is *Translations from the Philosophical Writings of Gottlob Frege*, ed. Peter Geach and Max Black (this piece translated by Max Black) (Oxford: Blackwell, 1952), 56–78. For a general review of Frege's theory, see Theo M. V. Janssen, "Frege, Contextuality, and Compositionality," *Journal of Logic, Language and Information* 10, no. 1: 115–136. Also helpful are P. F.

Strawson, "Identifying Reference and Truth-Values," *Theoria* 3 (1964): 96–118; Bas van Fraassen, "Presupposition, Implication, and Self-Reference," *Journal of Philosophy* 65 (1968): 136–152; Bas van Fraassen, "Truth and Paradoxical Consequences," in *The Paradox of the Liar*, ed. R. L. Martin (New Haven, CT: Yale University Press, 1970); and D. Wilson, *Presuppositions and Non-Truth-Conditional Semantics* (London: Academic Press, 1975).

15 The second step is, for Van Til, the essence of offensive apologetics. It is the lack of constructive empirical evidence in Van Til's exploitation of the positive side of TAG that gives it a negative tone.

16 For Frame's use of reduction, see Frame, *Speaking the Truth in Love: The Theology of John M. Frame*, ed. John J. Hughes (Phillipsburg, NJ: P&R Publishing, 2009), 963, fn. 2.

17 Van Til used "certainty" against the backdrop of the impossibility of a proposition being false. He stressed that Christian truth is certain and should be presented as certain, not as merely probable. Frame, however, is willing to use the language of "probability," not in reference to the certainty of God, but to the nature of our arguments, which sometimes fall short of absolute certainty. See *AGG*, 86, and *DKG*, 136. Also worth noting is that in his enduring exposition of Van Til, John Frame makes a critical distinction between the Presuppositionalism of Kant, Fichte, Schelling, Hegel, and more, pointing to the fact that Van Til's presuppositions were not hypothetical but categorical. In this sense, the "pre" in presuppositional really meant "pre-eminent" to Van Til. See *CVT*, 131–138.

18 In both Van Til and Frame, the word *neutrality* represents an area of dialogue with the unbeliever that assumes God's absence: a sphere of argument that does not presuppose the living God. Frame says that Van Til was not against all use of evidence, but only on the basis of such neutrality, a subject I will explore later in this book.

19 Cornelius Van Til, "Presuppositionalism," *The Bible Today* 4, no. 7 (April 1949): 218–228.

20 In Van Til and Frame, a "brute fact" supposedly exists in time and space independently of God or man's interpretation. Van Til especially thought that other apologists had treated evidence this way, as existing independently from God and therefore as a means to lead non-believers to the knowledge of God.

21 This tendency typically happens when the apologist answers the charge that Christianity is guilty of rationalism—i.e., that the Christian faith is an extension of one's opinion.

22 This can happen when the apologist attempts to answer the charge that Christianity is guilty of irrationalism—i.e., that Christians take everything on faith, etc., minus science.

23 C. Van Til, "Christian Theistic Evidences," vol. 6, in *In Defense of the Faith* (Phillipsburg, NJ: P&R Publishing, 1978), i.

24 A full reading of Frame's concerns with the transcendental argument is in *AGG*, 71–75.

25 *AGG*, 80 extrapolates this idea.

26 "Narrow circular" argumentation is of the type that affirms, "The Bible is true because it says so." Frame's hesitation on this line of argument centers on the fact that although "all valid deductive syllogisms are circular in the sense that the conclusion is already implicit in the premises" narrow reasoning contracts the space between conclusion and premise so severely that "it almost begs the unbeliever to challenge the premises." Ibid., 62, n. 7. In

its place, he recommends "broad circular" argumentation, in which the argument is expanded outward, but always remains faithful to Christian presuppositions. See Ibid., 10.
27 In *DKG*, 347 and 382, Frame admits his indebtedness to George Mavrode's *Belief in God* (New York: Random House, 1970), for his concept of person-variability.
28 *AGG*, 67.
29 Ibid., 64–67.
30 The "blockhouse method" is what Van Til called any apologetic methodology that starts with beliefs thought to be held in common between believers and unbelievers and then attempts to supplement that common ground with additional ideas. I have demonstrated that Frame is not open to this approach. Rather, he accepts that the theistic argument should have a transcendental starting point and goal. But thinking evangelistically, and with biblical example before him, he allows for some latitude in the presentation of theism as a unit.
31 In an email to the author, dated August 21, 2009.
32 More on this debate is available in Francis Schaeffer, "A Review of a Review," *The Bible Today* 42, no. 1 (October 1948). This longstanding work is currently available at http://www.pcahistory.org/documents/schaefferreview.html. Frame calls Schaeffer's middle road "Modified Presuppositionalism."
33 J. M. Frame, "Some Thoughts on Schaeffer's Apologetics," 2010; electronically filed at http://www.frame-poythress.org/some-thoughts-on-schaeffers-apologetics/; date of access: Sept. 11, 2011.
34 The test of coherence seeks to know whether or not consistency is present in the Christian defense. This is the most basic verification, behind which are tests for facular adequacy—i.e., fact-claims made by Scripture. For example, skeptics may ask, "What of the variant accounts of the same event recorded in the Bible?" How many women visited the empty tomb?" A question based in practical adequacy may ask, "Does Christianity work for us?" *DWG*. Accessed Aug. 24, 2012.
35 Frame, "*Some Thoughts on Schaeffer's Apologetics*."
36 In Van Til and Frame, "antithesis" represents the opposition between Christian and non-Christian thought. See John M. Frame, *Cornelius Van Til: An Analysis of His Thought* (Phillipsburg, NJ: P&R Publishing, 1995), 187–213. Van Til resisted the use of verification as a point of contact with unbelievers. However, it is Frame's belief that Van Til would have approved of his use of verification if he understood its use in the area of "broad circular" argumentation, which, for Frame, can in fact avoid the pitfalls of impartial appeals to logic.
37 Francis Schaeffer, *The God Who Is There* (Downers Grove, IL: Intervarsity Press, 1968), 1–29. I think that Schaeffer made too much of irrationalism and not enough of the rationalism in modern culture. Frame balances both, as seen in his Square of Opposition (see chapters on Framian ethics).
38 *DWG*.
39 Ibid. Date of access: Aug. 24, 2012.
40 "Before a man is ready to become a Christian, he must have a proper understanding of truth, whether he has fully analyzed his concept of truth or not. All people, whether they

realize it or not, function in the framework of some concept of truth. Our concept of truth will radically affect our understanding of what it means to become a Christian. We are concerned at this point, not with the *content* of truth so much as with the *concept* of what truth is." Schaeffer, *The God Who Is There*, 143.

41 Per Schaeffer, "[T]ruth is not *ultimately* related even to the Scriptures." Schaeffer, *The God Who Is There*, 157. Bryan A. Follis notes that Schaeffer is not denying the high role of Scripture but is saying that it is related to something behind it, namely the nature of God. "For Schaeffer the final screen of Christian truth is that which is in relationship to what exists and ultimately to the God who exists." Bryan A. Follis, *Truth with Love: The Apologetics of Francis A. Schaeffer* (Wheaton, IL: Crossway Books, 2006), 91. William Edgar is not so gracious to Schaeffer. "Curiously, Schaeffer does not strictly equate either the Scripture or God with the truth. The truth, in fact, is not '*ultimately* related' to the Scriptures. God himself is what he calls 'the final screen of truth.' Thus, God is 'behind' the truth, but is not equated with truth itself." See http://www.chaleteagle.org/cybershelter/Study/95040A.htm; date of access: Aug. 3, 2012. Originally published as William Edgar, "Two Christian Warriors: Cornelius Van Til and Francis A. Schaeffer Compared," *Westminster Theological Journal* 57, no. 1 (Spring 1995): 57–80. Edgar is perhaps pressing Schaeffer's position too far when he says that Schaeffer does not equate God with truth, or else to what "final screen" would Schaeffer be referring?

42 W. Edgar, "Two Christian Warriors." Date of access: Aug. 3, 2012. On the self-authenticating nature of the voice of God in Scripture, see Greg L. Bahnsen, *Van Til's Apologetic: Reading and Analysis* (Phillipsburg, NJ: P&R Publishing, (1998), 209–219, 715.

43 W. Edgar, "Two Christian Warriors." Date of access: Aug. 11, 2012.

44 The point is well made throughout this set of sermons, collected in Francis A. Schaeffer, *Death in the City* (Downers Grove, IL: Inter-Varsity, 1969). "Just as a scientist does not create the order in the universe but does recognize it, so reason does not create the answer but simply recognizes it. Of course this does not mean that reason will necessarily *receive* the answer. Each person has to *choose* to receive God's truth. But God's truth is clear." Francis A. Schaeffer and C. Everett Koop, *Whatever Happened to the Human Race?* (Old Tappan, NJ: Fleming Revell, 1979), 152.

45 W. Edgar, "Two Christian Warriors." Date of access: Aug. 11, 2012.

46 *DWG*.

47 Ibid., 182. Van Til, in fact, admitted that the antithesis with respect to the unbeliever is a hard point to clarify. How can an unbeliever "know" God but not "know God"? He admits that the unbeliever is simply a mixture of truth and error. See Cornelius Van Til, *An Introduction to Systematic Theology* (Phillipsburg, NJ: P&R Publishing, 1974), 26–27.

48 J. M. Frame, "Review of Bahnsen, *Presuppositional Apologetics: Stated and Defended*, in *John Frame's Selected Shorter Writings* 1 (Phillipsburg, NJ: P&R Publishing, 2014), 183. Bahnsen's rebukes of Clark, Carnell, and Schaeffer are in ibid., 137–260. It is also true that Frame also admired Bahnsen's effort, seen more toward the end of his life, of "taking it to the streets." Bahnsen had become less a defender of theonomy and of Van Til

against other apologists and more of an active apologete. Sadly, after he found his niche, he died soon afterward. Frame recounts, "I applauded, however, his new outward emphasis as taking seriously the Great Commission." In an email to the author, February 29, 2012. This suggests that Frame is not alone as the standard-bearer of evangelistic apologetics. However, I do not think, likely due to his shortened life, that Bahnsen carried that commitment through as consistently as has Frame.

49 Frame states this differently in "Reply to Don Collett on Transcendental Argument," at http://www.frame-poythress.org/frame_articles/2003ReplytoCollett.htm. Originally published in *Westminster Theological Journal* 65 (2003): 307–309.

50 In one place, Frame purports a more open posture toward Thomas Aquinas. Contra Van Til, he did not think that Thomas was attempting to make causality perfectly knowable as a precondition to knowing God. Rather, Frame takes from Thomas the exact opposite point: that causality is unintelligible without a first cause and that only God is that first cause. See *Speaking the Truth in Love*, 962–963. But this point is confusing, for elsewhere Frame is critical of Thomas. He quotes Robert Dabney, who observes of Thomas's thought, "For faith presupposes natural knowledge, even as grace presupposes nature and perfection the perfectible. It involves reasoning from God's effect to his nature, without the aid of revelation, and under the assumption that God's effects are better known to us than he is." Robert L. Dabney, *Lectures in Systematic Theology* (Grand Rapids, MI: Zondervan, 1878; reprint 1972), 1, 2, 2, Reply, Obj. 1. "In other words," Frame concludes, "Aquinas is recommending autonomous reasoning, which is self-consciously removed from the authority of God's Word, enabling us to argue from the same premises of Plato and Aristotle." *DG*, 225.

51 J. M. Frame, "Responding to Some Articles," in *Speaking the Truth in Love: The Theology of John M. Frame,* ed. J. Hughes (Phillipsburg, NJ: P&R Publishing, 2009), 965.

52 J. M. Frame, "Reply to Collett on Transcendental Argument," 2003, http://www.frame-poythress.org/reply-to-don-collett-on-transcendental-argument/; date of access: Sept. 12, 2012. Or more fully, "Start with Bahnsen's argument that logic implies God's existence. Then argue that without logic, no predication is possible. Then we can use something like this syllogism: If predication is possible, then logic is reliable. If logic is reliable, then God exists. This syllogism shows . . . that without God neither logic nor anything else is intelligible, a transcendental conclusion." Frame, ibid.; date of access: Sept. 26, 2012.

53 J. M. Frame, "Responding to Some Articles," 967.

54 Ibid. So, then, Frame's characterization of *modus tollens*, that it leads to "nonsense," is only true insofar as it is used as a stand-alone argument. With proper support, Frame is for it.

55 Ibid.

56 Retrieved from John M. Frame, "Van Til: A Reassessment," http://www.frame-poythress.org/frame_articles/Reassessment.htm; date of access: Aug. 27, 2012.

57 The parable is original.

58 Frame and Van Til hold that nature provides the unbeliever with knowledge of the existence of the covenantal God, before whom he abjures sinfully. This knowledge is our "point of contact" in the apologetic setting. For this, see *AGG*, 82–85, and *DKG*, 365–368.

Point of contact can be viewed according to all three perspectives. This idea interacts with Frame's twin concept of *persuasion and proof*, elaborated in *AGG*, 62–64, That is, although all arguments for Christianity *ought* to persuade, not all proofs *need* to persuade. The apologist need not therefore be burdened with second-guessing the effectiveness of argumentation. Rather, the success of any line of reasoning "depends on the Spirit. The Spirit bears witness to the Word. Insofar as an argument conveys biblical content, the Spirit bears witness through such an argument." In an email to the author, dated December 14, 2013.

59 J. M. Frame, "Responding to Some Articles," 967.

60 *DCL*, 141.

Chapter 7

Lordship and Epistemology in Apologetics

The Fall of Man and Self-Deception

I am reviewing and expanding the three related categories of Framian apologetics enumerated earlier. I now move to point two: "Though God is known through his creation, people repress this knowledge (Rom. 1:18–32) until God's grace renews their minds (Rom. 12:2)."

Presuppositions

Framian apologetics is evangelistic apologetics. Evangelism raises questions such as "What are we to say to the unbeliever?" "And how do we say it?" Implicit in these practical questions are theoretical and foundational questions. "What can the apologist presuppose about the unbeliever's knowledge of God?" Answers to these types of questions are invaluable for apologetic interaction, for with them we know how best to witness to the unbeliever, and without them, we are groping in the dark. Paul lays down the first of our first principles in the light of a very explicit epistemological concern, when he declares,

> For the wrath of God is revealed from heaven against all ungodliness and unrighteousness of men who suppress the truth in unrighteousness, because that which is known about God is evident within them; for God made it evident to them. For since the creation of the world His invisible attributes,

> His eternal power and divine nature, have been clearly seen, being understood through what has been made, so that they are without excuse. (Romans 1:18–20)

According to Mounce, God's wrath (*orge*) is his divine displeasure with sin.[1] "Ungodliness" and "unrighteousness," according to Constable, refer to "injustice toward other human beings," while the "truth" refers to "truth that people know about God (cf. v. 25).[2] They suppress this truth by their wickedness."[3] But, says Cranfield, "God has revealed His wrath as well as His righteousness (v. 17) from heaven in the gospel."[4] In the unfolding drama of history, God reveals hatred toward sin and his judgment of sin with the effect that "the moral devolution of humanity is not just a natural consequence of man's sinning but also a result of God's judgment of sinners."[5] As much as the passage speaks to man's intrinsic knowledge of God in a general sense, and that his turning from God to sin will be judged at the *eschaton*, the loosening of men's sin as described in vss. 18–32 is the *present* judgment of God; that is, "God gave them over in the lusts of their hearts to impurity" (v. 24).

In Frame, it is the former emphasis that is typical, though the latter thought is not altogether absent. He finds in Romans 1:18–20 a form of knowledge in unbelievers that undermines their avowal of God. Their suppression of God is analogous to self-deception. In other words, although non-Christians make claim to an independent, modern mode of inquiry into reality whereby they find God wanting, the Spirit's scrutiny unmasks a prima facie knowledge in the unbeliever that exposes an immediate self-consciousness of God. The non-Christian conceals this knowledge while exercising autolatry: worship of self, and idolatry: worship of what else God has made (vss. 23–25).[6]

Barth on Romans 1

Karl Barth drew a very different conclusion than did Frame from the *locus classicus* of natural theology. "It is impossible to draw from [Romans 1:18–20] a statement (which can then be advanced as timeless, general, and abstract truth) concerning a natural union with God or knowledge of God on the part of man in himself and as such."[7] Barth's reaction is due to the dialectical nature of his logic and his view of the transcendence and unknowableness of God. Berkouwer can thus say of Barth on this very matter, "There is no original revelation of God through the work of his hands: the text of the cosmos is itself dumb, but the light of revelation in Christ *shines into the cosmos* and only then does the Scripture speak of a subsidiary line."[8]

Frame's contestation with Barth is easily drawn. "The point is not that unbelievers are simply ignorant of the truth. Rather, God has revealed himself to each person with unmistakable clarity, both in creation (Ps. 19; Rom. 1:18–21) and in man's own nature (Gen. 1:26ff). In one sense, the unbeliever knows God (Rom. 1:21). At some level of his consciousness or unconsciousness, that knowledge remains."[9] Frame thus sees in Paul the religiously momentous point that all unregenerate men know God so undeniably and unmistakably from natural revelation that they are left with no defense for their faithless response to the truth concerning Him. To Frame, then, lordship is not only the grand presupposition of the apologist's presentation, but also the grand fact the apologist presupposes about the sinner's moral suppression of God.

Calvin spoke of a *divinitatis sensum* ("awareness of divinity") and *semen religionis* ("seed of religion") in each man.[10] He uses the terms first to explain the universality of non-Christian religions, even in the furthest reaches of undeveloped societies, and how it is that all men are conscious of the difference between good and evil. So man has no excuse before God. Negatively, he draws from this first premise a second: God-consciousness in the form of superstition and idolatry is a sign of men's turning away from the true God and of their own condemnation, "because they have failed to honor him and to consecrate their lives to his will."[11]

McGrath on Romans 1

Alister McGrath takes the opposite position from that of Barth. He finds in natural theology a great deal of grist for the mill to build a case for Christianity.[12] For McGrath, the natural world is in fact full of "clues" that point to God. The apologist can use these clues to show how Christianity "makes better sense of things than its rivals."[13] In fact, "Our task is to help people realize that the Christian faith is so exciting and wonderful that nothing else can compare to it." [14]That priority leads McGrath to a type of perspectival arrangement in apologetics similar to Frame's. One such example is his use of Plato's cave illustration. That someone comes into the cave to explain what the real world looks like corresponds roughly to Frame's normative perspective. That the structure of the cave itself contains clues to a world beyond the cave may relate to Frame's situational perspective, while the prisoner's intuition of a better world outside of the cave is more or less equivalent to Frame's existential perspective.[15] Notwithstanding this similarity, the precise failure of McGrath's project is his lack of attention to Paul's teaching in Romans 1 on self-deception: that apart from regenerating grace, the secular mind can only suppress the truth of God in its experience of the created order. Unfortunately, McGrath fails to offer any interaction with, or answer to, this truth. Furthermore, I think that Christianity is not just the *best* explanation of the natural world but the ONLY explanation.

The Difficult Nature of the Problem

Explaining "self-deception" has nonetheless proved notoriously difficult. As Bahnsen clarifies, "It is more than just a bit odd, is it not, to say that someone believes what he does not believe!"[16] The idea is surely contra Descartes's view that the mind is fully transparent to itself. We could conceive of a subconscious realm where religious beliefs can reside, though we are not conscious of them. So people might know God without knowing that they know God. However, the plausibility of this suggestion draws currency from studies on the human psyche since the nineteenth century—for example, Freudianism. Or is it that the whole of our beliefs are noncurrent: we are only conscious of a very limited number of our beliefs at a given time and they must be brought to consciousness? Typically, we say that people who once consciously believed something, then forgot it, but later become conscious of it again did not stop believing in the intervening period of forgetfulness.

Frame's Covenantal View of Romans 1

Frame joins other self-consciously Reformed theologians to seek a solution to the difficulty in the noetic effects of the fall. As far as the limitations of the present discussion go, a laconic description of the noetic effects of Adam's massive transgression encompasses the metaphysical and ethical dimensions of knowledge. Metaphysically, man did not cease to be the image of God after the fall, or else he would cease to be man. Historic Reformed theology teaches that all men are created in the *imago Dei*.

Hence, all men are capable of rationality, intuition, love, work, marriage, and more. Such things are hard-wired in all people. Ethically, the fall brought about the loss of that original righteousness, holiness, and truth the first man once enjoyed. However, we would be wrong to assume that the post-fall loss has not affected man's metaphysical constitution. What remains in the fallen creature is not fully functional as God intended at creation but, too, has been defaced, so that even man's rationality, interpretation of beauty, and love are fundamentally self-centered, rather than God-centered. This is something of the metaphysical/ethical dilemma posed by the fall.

At this juncture, Frame sets the traditional answer within a broader context. I know that lordship is a covenantal concept and that according to Frame not just believers but "everything and everybody is in covenant with God (cf. Isa 24:5: all the 'inhabitants of the earth' have broken the 'everlasting covenant')."[17] So when Paul reveals that unbelievers know God (Romans 1:19), Frame understands that to mean that they know not only *that* God exits, but also *who* God is: their covenant head. This places men's suppression of God in a brighter light. Now we see that not only are they simply unhappy with the idea that God is, but also they are unwilling to meet their covenant responsibilities. I can elicit from this expanded understanding that the biblical imagery of man as the *imago Dei*, though the image can be perceived economically in terms of freedom, rationality, personality, and so on, and that such human endowments can be compartmentalized according to "moral" or "natural"; man as the image of God is best understood as what man IS in living relationship with God. Man as image of God is always man-in-relationship to God—the one whose "is-ness" exists as he exists in covenant relationship to God. It is not that the image of God is as much *in* man, but rather the Bible speaks of man *as* the image of God. What does this mean for apologetics? It means, according to Frame, that "each man has a basic orientation either for or against God, and that this basic orientation will determine whether the specific acts of his life are pleasing to God or not."[18] The purpose of Framian apologetics, in the larger context of lordship, is thus to remind man of the covenant into which God placed him as *imago Dei* and to challenge him to reorient his total being God-ward.[19]

Herein lies a vastly important aspect of Frame's lordship theology. It is that all non-Christian judgments about God are not intellectual judgments alone but are *morally* determined. A wrong judgment about God is one we *ought not* to make, while a right judgment about God is one we *ought* to make. In the previous chapters on ethics, the reductionist statement was made that in Frame's thought, "everything boils down to a matter of ethics." The epistemological question (what do we know that the unbeliever knows?) provides us with the determinative reason why ethics assumes an antecedent, or controlling, position in Frame's view of things. It is that man's epistemological deprivation is consequent to disobedience, and only obedience can solve his epistemological return to sanity. Jesus said, "He who has My commandments and keeps them is the one who loves Me; and he who loves Me will be loved by My Father, and I will love him and will disclose Myself to him" (John 14:21). Here love and obedience, not intellectual knowledge, open Jesus' disclosure of himself to us.

In summing this section, what we can presuppose about unbelievers? (1) That nature has revealed to them the reality of God with axiomatic clarity. (2) That this revelation is not merely clear, but known to them. (3) There are no atheists. (4) That their knowledge, though it incorporates *that* God exists, has more to do with a self-conscious renunciation of *who* God is—

covenant head and Lord. (4) That their renunciation is a *moral* determination to practice self-deception.

Frame and Ligonier

We are talking about the apologetic encounter, beginning with the question of what epistemological baseline (ethically determined) we can rightfully presuppose in the unbeliever, and how this presuppositional approach informs our evangelistic dialogue with him. And I have mentioned the metaphysical/ethical dilemma posed by the fall. Now it appears that Frame brings a nuanced position to these ideas. I will explore his stance in the context of his defense of Cornelius Van Til before a group of writers associated with Ligonier Ministries.[20]

In an article titled "Van Til and the Ligonier Apologetic," Frame seeks to defend Van Tilian apologetics against a host of charges levied by the Ligonier group, who maintain the classical form of apologetics: evidences and logic aimed at showing the rational necessity of God. A full synopsis of the article is not my point. The cardinal issue at hand is that on one essential issue, Frame takes a point midway between the classical position of the Ligonier apologetic (TLA) and the transcendental method as espoused by Van Til. This matter is especially important regarding what Frame thinks unbelievers *know* about God in a state of self-deception.

TLA submits that in coming to know the God of Scripture, we must begin with ourselves, or what some have called "the primacy of the intellect," while Van Til wants us to start with God.[21] What does this divarication mean? The issue centers on what natural reason can understand properly in the light of evidences. In saying that we must begin with ourselves, TLA wants us to appeal to the unbeliever's reason, for "One simply cannot start outside himself. To begin outside oneself, one would first have to depart from himself."[22]

Per Frame, TLA claims that "Van Til abandons apologetics, refusing to reason with unbelievers" and that Frame is unwilling to enter rational discourse with any unbeliever.[23] But the marginalization is unfair. The actual difference between Van Til and Frame versus TLA on this subtle point is not over the *use* of reason, but over the *role* of reason. The presuppositionalists demand that reason remain subservient to the *standard* of evidences, whereby God's voice binds the selection of the criterion of truth the apologist uses, while TLA encourages argument outside that standard and as a means to build a case for God.

From the vantage point of the presuppositionalists, the divide focalizes on the fact that the unbeliever suppresses not only the proofs for God, but also the criterion of the proofs. It is not that the unbeliever lacks the psychological faculties to hear and to negotiate the demands of a multiplicity of different systems of logic. He lacks the *will* to respect each point, and the end-point, of syllogistic logicality leading to true knowledge of God. He *cannot* even admit that logic itself is part of the world God has made because he *will* not. This does not infer that Van Til emasculates the self or reason. "[T]he self is the 'proximate,' but not the 'ultimate' starting point."[24] The "ultimate starting" point is God, before whom the unbeliever must be called to account. Much like Frame, then, Van Til presents presuppositional apologetics as an *ethical* necessity.[25]

TLA responds that to present an apologetic that sets the discussion in such a way that asks the unbeliever to think about God as the ultimate standard of knowledge before he knows that God exists is contradictory. That is because the unbeliever cannot recognize God as the ultimate standard *until* he knows that God exists. We must therefore adopt some temporary, provisional standard in our apologetic as a means to reason with the unbeliever about the reality of God. After which point the provisional standard, like the third stage of *Apollo 16*, can be dropped, leaving the unbeliever to ride the heights of true knowledge of God. The provisional standard includes the law of noncontradiction, the law of causality, and the basic reliability of sense perception.

In my opinion, the call for an *ad interim* standard of verification is out of accord with Paul's point in Romans 1:18–20 that the unbeliever has already arrived at a decision—one against the God of the covenant. Evidences may be presented, but as K. Scott Oliphint has said, "The problem is not with the *evidence*, but with the '*receptacle*,' (i.e., the sinful person) to which the evidence constantly (through creation) comes."[26] So the *whole man*, his entire direction, his whole way of interpreting facts is subverted, darkened, so that man is now *non posse non peccare*. This is what Van Til means by "starting with God" (a point TLA completely misses). Frame clarifies that the "pre" in presuppositional is not a reference to temporal precedence—that is, something one should believe about God before one believes anything else about God. Rather, the prefix "should be understood mainly as an indicator of ethical eminence (e.g., *pre*eminence)" in the defense of the faith.[27]

Frame's Distinctive Standpoint

This leads us to Frame's "nuanced position." Frame is less critical than Van Til of the ability of the fallen intellect to arrive at true conclusions about God. In reply to the Ligonier group, he states,

> In any case, I grant what I think they want me to, that people sometimes reach true conclusions about God without the witness of the Spirit. Van Til's writings do pose some difficulty here. He does clearly recognize that unbelievers know the truth (Rom 1:21) and that they sometimes reach true conclusions "in spite of themselves," i.e., in spite of their unbelieving presuppositions. However, there are points at which he seems to say that unbelief always leads to intellectual error and that no propositional truth is possible apart from the Spirit's witness.[28]

What does Frame mean when he says that unbelievers can arrive at true conclusions about God without the Holy Spirit?

> When I make statements like this I usually have the Pharisees in mind. . . . The Pharisees believed such propositions as "God exists," "God revealed himself to Moses," "God's law is normative for our lives," "Sin must be atoned by blood sacrifice," "There will be a general resurrection on the last day." But the general judgment of the Gospels is that most of these were unregenerate. That leads us to consider that Satan himself is doubtless even more orthodox.[29]

So the statement refers to "propositional truths"—the very thing Van Til has in view when criticizing even natural man's ability to know properly the flowers of the field.[30] We have seen Frame make this same point with

Bahnsen when he asks whether unbelievers cannot say properly that the sky is blue. Frame's point is well taken. If unbelievers cannot so much as say rightly that 2 + 2 = 4, then all possible lines of communication with them are broken. It is a mystery, then, that Frame has been so roundly criticized by R. C. Sproul and the Ligonier group as a Fideist.[31] But are the propositional conclusions of non-Christians "true," as Frame suggests?

I have said that the results of the fall have affected men *in toto*, not only ethically, but also metaphysically and epistemologically. Now a *proposition* is a philosophical term used in formal logic to describe the content of assertions that are understood to be non-linguistic abstractions drawn from sentences that can be evaluated as either true or false. For instance, "All water is wet" is a common proposition. When I use the term "propositional truth," I am working with truth claims that can be stated and analyzed in forms that fit into what is called in logic: propositional-form.

Yet some categorical syllogisms can be problematic. For example, according to Aristotle's term logic a proposition refers to a kind of sentence, in which one affirms or denies the predicate of a subject. An illustration would be "All men are created mortal." The conclusion would then follow that "Socrates is a man," thus "Socrates is mortal." Now if we say, "All men are mortal" and "Jesus of Nazareth is a man," where does this proposition lead us? To theological error.

Propositional logic should therefore seek to express *complete propositions*, or TRUE truth, as Francis Schaeffer said. I am inclined to see in Van Til (and Bahnsen) this sort of reasoning. Flowers and gravity are interrelated to the God of flowers and gravity. In that Jesus *is* the truth, true propositions are such because the subject and the predicate of any sentence find meaning in him. Did the Pharisees and Satan make "true" propositional statements, as Frame indicates?

On one level, Frame is correct. Christian and non-Christian agree that 2 + 2 = 4. However, when lambasting the Pharisees, Jesus decried, "You are of your father the devil, and you want to do the desires of your father. He was a murderer from the beginning, and does not stand in the truth because there is no truth in him. Whenever he speaks a lie, he speaks from his own nature, for he is a liar and the father of lies" (John 8:44). This statement comes after Jesus' encounter with Satan in the wilderness, in which the evil one quoted the Old Testament *accurately* (Matthew 4:1–11). Yet Jesus says of him (and by way of inference the Pharisees) that he "does not stand in the truth because there is *no* truth in him" (italics added). We may elicit from this statement of Jesus' that for one to speak the truth requires one to "stand" in the truth—to stand in the Son of God, something an unbeliever cannot do.

Considering this fine distinction, is there a better way to propose Frame's idea that non-Christians can reach true conclusions about God without the enabling of the Holy Spirit? Perhaps I can say it this way: that although men can say 2 + 2 = 4 in a way that is *right*, they cannot say it in a way that is *true*—that is, TRUE truth. Bearing this principle in mind may permit us to *both* reason with the unbeliever in the context of evidences *and* do so from a wholly presuppositional point of view.[32] I think that Frame would agree with our noetic distinction; otherwise, why would he agree with Edgar against Schaeffer? Explicative of this very distinction is also his statement that "If a person is a non-believer, then evidently he needs to be born again by God's Spirit before he can apply the Word of God to his life."[33] Thus, it is that the witness-bearing power of the Spirit that operates conjointly *fides quae creditor*—that is, with the content of the faith. But the Holy Spirit also imparts *fides qua creditor*—in other words, the faith by which the content of the gospel is believed.

Univocal or Analogical Knowledge?

As a matter of first principles in evangelistic apologetics, I have asked, "What does the unbeliever know about God?" However, the biblical apologetic is shaped not only by what Scripture says the unbeliever knows, but also by what it reveals he *can* know, is capable of knowing, as a believer. We must remember that we are ambassadors of the biblical God, with whom we expect people to walk unto glory. So we might also ask, "Is it our hope that the cynic can know God *as* God knows himself or can he only know God reflectively in a creaturely way?" This is the univocal/analogical problem in Christian epistemology. The question arises in the context of the structure of human thought. It bears its own unique dilemma. If we stress too excessively that knowledge of God is univocal, we run the risk of lowering the incomprehensible God to the level of the finite and make God as one of us. But if we stress too emphatically knowledge of God *per analogiam*, we may very well deprive God of all likeness to the humanity he has created, with the result that all we are left with is a barren abstraction.[34]

To a considerable extent, the argument took fertile shape in the debate of the 1940s between Cornelius Van Til and Gordon H. Clark. It is a matter of regret that I can only provide an abbreviated review of the controversy. Van Til was jealous to protect the Creator/creature distinction, both in reality, or what Frame, in harmony with his lordship priority, calls "two-levels of reality," and in knowledge.[35] Frame stands with Van Til: "God's thoughts are the originals of which ours, at best, are only copies, images."[36] Earlier,

Herman Bavinck said, "There is no knowledge of God as he is in himself. We are human and he is the Lord our God. . . . he infinitely transcends our picture of him, our ideas of him, our language concerning him. He is not comparable to any creature."[37] This led Bavinck to verify a staple of Continental Reformed thought: the *archetype/ectype* distinction in epistemology.[38]

Clark, conversely, feared that if man's knowledge was derivative of God's, then this would lead to skepticism. Van Til, however, insisted that redeemed analogical *sapentia*, though incomprehensive and derivative, is nonetheless *true* knowledge.[39] Bavinck puts it like this, "Ectypal knowledge must not be seen as merely symbolic, a product of poetic imagination. . . . While our knowledge of him is accommodated and limited, it is no less real, true, and trustworthy."[40] In addition, Van Til held that redeemed human knowledge is *partial*—or, as he used to say, "non-exhaustive." Clark, although also eager to protect God's lordship, says that God knows more than we do, but the *quality* of our knowledge can be the same as his. Van Til argued that both the *quality* and the *quantity* of God's archetypal knowledge differ from our ectypal knowledge. Finally, both men agree that all knowledge is given by natural and special revelation. But for Clark, that revelation is propositional, in the sense that it always conveys univocal truth. Clark interprets John 1:1 to mean, "In the beginning was Logic, and Logic was with God, and Logic was God. . . . In logic was life and the life was the light of men."[41] Clark then makes the stunning admission that "Logic is God."[42] Clark does not mean that human logic is God, but that God thinking is logic and that the connection of his logic to ours is univocal. The source of univocal knowledge is the Bible. "What is said in Scripture is God's thought" and since our logic is univocal of God's, there exists a direct continuum from God's thought, to Scripture, to us. Van Til and Frame deny such an epistemological continuum.[43]

For Van Til, God's revelation to man is always *accommodated* truth. Accommodated revelation is *coherent* to man, but true coherence does not afford identity of *content* between the revelation God gives and what man receives.[44] Herein is a precursor to Frame's covenantal lordship principle. Because man cannot know God *in se*, but always and forever as a servant (analogically), even now in the face of Scripture, "Man knows in subordination to God; he knows as the covenant-keeper."[45] A vaulting back to the thought of Girolamo Zanchi is observable, in which the Italian Reformer distinguishes between univocal, equivocal, and analogical knowledge of God.[46] According to the analogical relation, God has priority over man: what perfection exists ontologically and epistemologically exists in God principally and in man secondarily.

Toward a Resolution

In deliberating on this debate, I ought to acknowledge that Clark and Van Til were not in binary opposition, especially as Van Til had thought. But at least the specter of error is apparent in Clark's seminal idea that "The intelligibility of the Scriptures presupposes logic."[47] Anticipating a critique of his views based on Isaiah 55:8–9, which stipulates that God's thoughts are not our thoughts, Clark replies, "If for example, we think that David was King of Israel, and God's thoughts are not ours, then it follows that God does not think David was King of Israel. David in God's mind was perchance prime minister of Babylon."[48]

In an important essay, Nathan Pitchford succeeds in countering Clark's biblical example.

> On the contrary, given the basic legitimacy of the system, it is entirely possible to prove that God's knowledge is in actuality analogical to what we understand by Nebuchadnezzar's being King of Babylon; because God himself framed the symbolical/analogical essence of human language as well as the corresponding and uniform human apprehension which it awakens. In other words, if the Possessor of absolute knowledge is also the Framer of a symbolic representation of that absolute knowledge, he is entirely capable of making the analogical an accurate reflection of the absolute.[49]

Thus, analogical knowledge does not cast one into the morass of ambiguity, as Clark suggests. A Clarkian might reply, "The only way to prove that our knowledge is analogical is to have univocal knowledge." Frame responds, "Given my definition of analogical i.e., ultimate standard, I would say that we can prove that our knowledge is analogical simply by Scripture. Clark himself, were he willing to use Van Til's definition of analogical, would certainly have agreed with that method of proof."[50] It seems there may have been more unanimity of thought between the two men than has been assumed—a matter future scholarship may wish to clarify.

The value of these present observations is seen in relation to 1 Peter 3:15, "but sanctify Christ as Lord in your hearts, always being ready to make a defense to everyone who asks you to give an account for the hope that is in you, yet with gentleness and reverence." The Greek word translated as "hope" is *elpis*. Emphasizing as it does the idea of "expectation," Peter speaks in terms of an essentially unified eschatological hope of the Old

Testament, a hope that has as its single focus the Day of the Lord. Peter's interest is that his readers be invariably prepared to defend their joyful, confident expectation of eternal salvation. Clark's viewpoint, by stressing as it does the evidential claims that add to our assurance of the gospel account, and thus the systematic conception of epistemological certainty, lacks consensus with the coming kingdom of God, which, in the New Testament, is held in successive episodes: one part present; the other part future. It is in the midst of the already/not yet manifestation of the kingdom that Peter can thus call us to purity of heart and zealous expression of a "living hope" (1:3).

This life is one of mutual sharing in the sufferings of Christ. With even greater faith, then, the sufferings of each Christian hasten the Parousia, not by mechanically reducing a fixed number of sufferings yet outstanding, but by bringing the members of Christ into serious self-reflection on the seeming polarity between evil and salvation. The connection is this. Peter would have us settle on the rationale or "reasonableness" of the delay of the return of Christ, in the understanding that suffering for the gospel in the *interim* period serves as a means to advance the gospel. Especially as we are asked, "Where is this coming he promised?"(2 Peter 3:3), our apologetic in all "gentleness and reverence" (1 Peter 3:15) points questioners to a distinct reality, one that is in us, has changed us, yet which forms a proleptically shaped community of faith and that apprehends the present within its larger *telos*. The Day will reveal all. Then conjectural self-reflection will cease, and only true knowledge will prevail. Then, and only then, we will know the Lord fully, even as we have been known fully. Our "living hope" is a faithful response in real time, amid real suffering for Christ, looking to a real future. But it is hope, not sight. The analogical interpretation of redeemed knowledge best fits the biblical description.

Endnotes

1 R. Mounce, "Romans," in *The New American Commentary* (Nashville: Holman Reference, 1975), 76–77.
2 T. Constable, "Notes on Romans," 1999, http://www.soniclight.com/constable/notes/pdf/romans.pdf; date of access: February 25, 2012.
3 Date of access: Feb. 24, 2012.
4 C. E. B. Cranfield, *A Critical and Exegetical Commentary on the Epistle to the Romans*, 6th ed. (London: Bloomsbury T&T Clark, 2000), 109–110.
5 T. Constable, "Notes on Romans."
6 In Van Til, it is self-consciousness that presupposes God-consciousness.
7 Barth, *CD* 2/1, 121. Barth's rejection of natural theology was felt in his disavowal of plausible proofs in apologetics. He said, "Faith is rather a freedom, a permission. It is permitted to be so—that the believer in God's Word may hold on to this Word in everything, *in spite of all that contradicts it*. It is so: we never believe 'on account of,' never 'because of'; we awake to faith in spite of everything. Think of the men in the Bible. They did not come to faith by reason of any kind of proofs, but one day they were so placed that they might believe and then had to believe *in spite of everything*. . . . When we believe, we must believe *in spite of God's hiddenness*. This hiddenness of God necessarily reminds us of our human limitation. We do not believe out of our personal reason and power. *Anyone who really believes knows that.*" Karl Barth, *Dogmatics in Outline* (Harper Perennial, 1959), 20.
8 G. C. Berkouwer, *General Revelation* (Grand Rapids, MI: Eerdmans, 1955), 30.
9 *AGG*, 7–8. Though speaking in a different context, I think that Frame's words are still apt for answering Barth.
10 "There is within the human mind, and indeed by natural instinct, an awareness of divinity." *Institutes* 1.3.4. In theological literature dealing with the doctrine of man, *sensus divinatus* is often preferred to *divinitatis sensum*. The term *semen religionis* ("seed of religion") refers generally to a numinous awareness of God and is near in meaning to *divinitatis sensum*, as it speaks to man's moral response to God. "As experience shows, God has sown a seed of religion in all men. But scarcely one man in a hundred is met with who fosters it, once received, in his heart, and none in whom it ripens—much less shows fruit in season." *Institutes*, 1.4.1.
11 J. Calvin, *Institutes of the Christian Religion*, trans. Ford Lewis Battles (Philadelphia: Westminster Press, 1960), 1.3.1.
12 A. McGrath, *Mere Apologetics: How to Help Seekers and Skeptics Find Faith* (Ida, MI: Baker Books, 2012).
13 Ibid., 19. Elsewhere, he says, "Like all narrative, the Christian story cannot be 'proved' by objective rational or scientific means. It has to be by its ability to make more sense of things," 141. As the title of McGrath's work shows, his apologetic is highly indebted to C. S. Lewis, whose moral proof for God also spoke of right and wrong as "clues to the

meaning of the universe." See Lewis, *Mere Christianity* (New York: McMillan Publishing Company, 1952), Chapter 2.

14 A. McGrath, *Mere Apologetics: How to Help Seekers and Skeptics Find Faith* (Ida, MI: Baker Books, 2012), 19.

15 For his multifaceted approach to Plato's cave analogy, see ibid., 148–152.

16 G. Bahnsen, Greg L. Bahnsen, "The Crucial Concept of Self-Deception in Presuppositional Apologetics," http://www.cmfnow.com/articles/PA207.htm; date of access: March 13, 2012. First published in the *Westminster Theological Journal* 57 (1995): 1–31.

17 *DKG*, 102. The question naturally arises in this context. How can it be that everyone is "covenantally" responsible to God? Frame illuminates, "Romans 1:18–20 teaches that fallen men know *that* God is. But their knowledge is also of his 'invisible attributes' and 'divine nature' (v. 20). They also have a *personal* knowledge of God—i.e., they know *him*, not just information about him (vs. 21, 32)." Like Van Til, Frame thinks it is impractical to say that someone can knows *that* God is but is completely ignorant about *who* he is. But can we go as far as to say that fallen men know that they are in covenant with God and therefore are covenant-breakers? Paul never uses the term *covenant* in Rom. 1. In any case, it is important here to formulate some understanding of what *covenant* means. Covenant is a Lord/servant relationship, and clearly the sinners of Rom.1 understand that. Furthermore, covenants in Scripture all have the same essential elements: God's name, historical prologue (grace), stipulations, sanctions, and administration. In Rom. 1, fallen men know who God is (the name). They have the responsibility (stipulations) to obey and worship God—always a covenantal responsibility in Scripture. Those responsibilities are accompanied by blessings for obedience and curses for disobedience (covenant sanctions). Clearly, what happens in Rom. 1 is that God administers curses for disobedience. Now there is no "historical prologue" in Rom. 1, but, interestingly, Paul brings in something like this in Acts 14:17 and 17:24–30: the historical prologue (previous grace) is the fact that God has given to people the benefit of living in his world within fixed "bounds of habitation" and "fruitful seasons." They ought to be grateful for such unmerited favor and should worship the true God alone." Edited version of an email reply from Frame to me, Jan. 15, 2012.

18 J. M. Frame, *The Amsterdam Philosophy* (Phillipsburg, NJ: Harmony Press, 1972), 23. The completed paper by Frame is also now accessible at http://www.frame-poythress.org/frame_books/1972Amsterdam.htm.

19 G. C. Berkouwer laid great stress on this very idea. See *Man: The Image of God* (Grand Rapids, MI: Eerdmans, 1962), especially 114.

20 This is an international multimedia outreach started by R. C. Sproul in 1971 in Ligonier, Pennsylvania.

21 J. M. Frame, "Van Til and the Ligonier Apologetic," *Westminster Theological Journal* 47, no. 2 (Fall 1985), 285. The entire article is reprinted in *AGG*, 219–243. The "primacy of the intellect" is a term first coined by Herman Bavinck. "Aristotle already affirmed that God was the Blessed One, because he was the unity of thinking and thought and completely

above all craving, striving, and willing." Herman Bavinck, *Reformed Dogmatics*, vol. 2 (Grand Rapids, MI: Baker Academic, 2009), 211.

22 J. M. Frame, "Van Til and the Ligonier Apologetic," 283, quoting R. C. Sproul, John Gerstner, and Arthur Lindsley, *Classical Apologetics* (Grand Rapids, MI: Zondervan, 1984), 212.

23 J. M. Frame, "Van Til and the Ligonier Apologetic," 284, quoting R. C. Sproul, *Classical Apologetics*, 227.

24 J. M. Frame, "Van Til and the Ligonier Apologetic," 283.

25 Quite fairly, Frame cites the Ligonier group's affirmation that the "The intellectual problem is caused by the moral problem, not the moral problem by the intellectual one." Frame, ibid., 292, quoting R. C. Sproul, *Classical Apologetics*, 5. But he goes on to say that the group does not stress the intellectual deficiency in man strongly enough.

26 S. Oliphint, *Covenantal Apologetics: Principles & Practice in Defense of Our Faith* (Wheaton, IL: Crossway, 2013), 46. Italics are his.

27 *AGG*, 13, n. 16.

28 J. M. Frame, "Van Til and the Ligonier Apologetic," *Westminster Theological Journal* 47, no. 2 (Fall 1985): 291.

29 In an email to the author, dated Dec. 9, 2012.

30 Van Til's full quote is, "This implies that [the unbeliever] knows nothing truly as he ought to know it. . . . the "natural man" is not only basically mistaken in his notions about religion and God, but is as basically mistaken in his notions about atoms and the laws of gravitation. . . . Now it may seem as though it is straining at a gnat to insist on the point that the natural man does not even know the flowers truly, as long as it is maintained that he does not know God truly. The point is, however, that unless we maintain that the natural man does not know the flowers truly, we cannot logically maintain that he does not know God truly. All knowledge is inter-related." Van Til, *An Introduction to Systematic Theology*, 26.

31 See R. C. Sproul, John Gerstner, and Arthur Lindsley, *Classical Apologetics* (Grand Rapids, MI: Zondervan, 1984), 299, 301.

32 The Puritan Divine John Owen expressed the same thought. "The difference between believers and unbelievers as to knowledge is not so much in the *matter* of their knowledge, as in the *manner* of their knowing." John Owen, *The Mortification of Sin* (Edinburgh, Scotland, and Carlisle, PA: Banner of Truth, abridged edition, 2004), 98.

33 *DCL*, 32. Cf., *DKG*, 143. In addition, cf., Frame's response to William Lane Craig, in *Five Views on Apologetics*, ed. Stanley N. Gundry and Steven B. Cowen (Grand Rapids, MI: Zondervan, 2002), 74–81.

34 Analogical knowledge in Reformed theology is not to be confused with the Roman Catholic idea of *analogia entis* ("analogy of being"), which Barth scathed polemically as an "invention of the antichrist." See *CD* I/1, 238–239. Whereas Barth opposed *analogia entis* mainly on philosophical and soteriological grounds, Van Til opposed it on metaphysical and epistemological grounds relative to the Creator-creature distinction. See Van Til, *An Introduction to Systematic Theology*, 16.

35 "Christians believe in two levels of existence as derived from the level of God's existence as self-contained and the level of man's existence as derived from the level of God's existence. For this reason, Christians must also believe in two levels of knowledge, the level of God's knowledge which is absolutely comprehensive and self-contained, and the level of man's knowledge which is not comprehensive but is derivative and re-interpretive." Van Til, *An Introduction to Systematic Theology*, 12.

36 *DKG*, 23.

37 H. Bavinck, *Reformed Dogmatics*, vol. 2, ed. J. Bolt. (Grand Rapids, MI: Baker Academic, 2004), 47.

38 Ibid., 95. For an extended examination on the place of archetypal and ectypal theology in historical theology, see John Barber, *The Road from Eden* (Palo Alto, CA: Academica Press, 2008), 469–473.

39 On the fact that accommodated knowledge is nonetheless true knowledge, see also Cornelius Van Til, *In Defense of the Faith* (Phillipsburg, NJ: P&R Publishing (1967), 57.

40 H. Bavinck, *Reformed Dogmatics*, vol. 2, ed. J. Bolt. (Grand Rapids, MI: Baker Academic, 2004), 95.

41 G. Clark, *An Introduction to Christian Philosophy*, 2nd ed. (Jefferson, MD: Trinity Foundation, 1993), 67.

42 Ibid. A favorite retort of Clark's focused on the consequences of the analogical position that verified coherence but not content. So he asked whether God has a different arithmetic, in which 2 + 2 = 5? See ibid., 76. Van Til replied that to know 2 + 2 = 4 clearly, as Clark suggests, is to know it exhaustively, which violates the incomprehensibility of God. But we can know that 2 + 2 = 4 on the basis of an "identity of reference point." Van Til, ibid., 167.

43 Ibid., 77.

44Similarly, Augustine gave expression, "We are speaking of God. It is any wonder if you do not comprehend? For if you comprehend, it is not God you comprehend. Let it be a pious confession of ignorance rather than a rash profession of knowledge. To attain some slight knowledge of God is a great blessing; to comprehend him, however, is totally impossible." Augustine, *Lectures on the Gospel of John*, tract 38, NPNF (1), VII, 217–221.

45 C. Van Til, *An Introduction to Systematic Theology* (Phillipsburg, NJ: P&R Publishing, 1974), 167. Turretin had said that even in the state of glory, human beings remain human beings there, raised above "their natural position" but never "above their own kind and "that which is analogous to that." F. Turretin, *Institutes of Elenctic Theology*, XX, qu. 8, 12.

46 Zanchi develops the analogical point of reference in theology according to two types of analogy: first, the relations numerous things bear to a common reference point; and second, the relationship between two things, namely, God and creature, in which the creature is always the subject. For this excurses, see Jerome Zanchi, *De natura Dei*, 18–22. A developed explanation of Zanchi's analogical system is provided by Dolf te Velde, *Paths beyond Tracing Out: The Connection between Method and Content in the Doctrine of God, Examined in Reformed Orthodoxy, Karl Barth and the Utrecht School* (Delft: Eburon Academic Publishers, 2010), 99–105, esp. 102.

47 G. Clark, *An Introduction to Christian Philosophy*, 2nd ed. (Jefferson, MD: Trinity Foundation, 1993), 64.
48 Ibid., 76.
49 N. Pitchford, "Van Til: His Logic, Epistemology, and Apologetic," 2006, http://www.reformationtheology.com/2006/06/van_til_his_logic_epistemology.php; date of access: December 12, 2012.
50 In a personal email to the author dated Dec. 12, 2012. In a separate interview, Frame also clarified the possibility of the seeming oxymoronic presence of analogical-literal language in epistemology. "The problem is that Clark had a different definition of analogical, namely 'nonliteral.' I'm inclined to agree with Clark's proposition that we do have some literal knowledge of God, which can serve as a means of interpreting the nonliteral knowledge. I asked Van Til once if he thought we had some literal knowledge of God, and he was not willing to say yes or no. At any rate, it is clear that he did not think that analogical is nonliteral. An example of analogical, literal language would be 'God created the heaven and earth.' This is literal, not figurative. But it is analogous in Van Til's sense, because God's idea of it is not identical to ours. God's knowledge of this proposition is original, ours derivative. The same is true of any item of ordinary propositional knowledge, like 'the sky is blue,' 'whales are mammals,' etc. Clark did not call these analogical, but Van Til did." Email to the author, dated Dec. 12, 2012.

Chapter 8

Lordship and the Apologetic Encounter

With a ready apprehension of what the believer does and can know, we are in position to interface with obdurate self-styled agnostics and atheists on the ground of Christian theistic principles.

This brings us to the third category earlier summated from Frame's apologetic frontline. "The apologist should press upon the non-Christian the evidence that God is clearly revealed in nature. But he should present it in the context of a biblical worldview, with an epistemology reflecting what the Bible says about knowledge. And he should present the Gospel in God's own authoritative voice, using Scripture's own arguments (as 1 Cor. 15:1–11) and other arguments that follow scriptural leads."[1]

Frame's call is for a rigorous presentation to the unbelieving interlocutor of *both* the testimony of nature *and* of Scripture. The united voice of natural and special revelation is complementary, inasmuch as people repress saving knowledge of God until God's grace renews their minds by the Holy Spirit.

Appropriate at this point is a brief analysis of Frame on these twin means of revelation as they relate to the practice of apologetics.

Natural and Special Revelation

Due to his perspectivalism, such a slim line exists in Frame's mind between *theologia naturalis* and *theologia revelata* it behooves us to treat them in sync.[2] The lack of hard and fast distinction between natural and special revelation is governed to a large extent by biblical concerns. In the most replete sense, apologetics is emphatically theocentric. The Lord is his own apologist.

In the Old Testament, the sovereign origin of apologetics finds richest expression, in that it is God who is actively communicating his will in history. From Adam (Genesis 1) to the introduction of prophets, to keeping the people from idols (Deuteronomy 19:9–15), to the revelation of Jesus Christ (Hebrews 1), the very nature of revelation is a sovereign disclosure of God to people as an act of *apologia*. Even before, redemption became a necessity with Adam's fall, and after that, God has been in dialogue with man. This is to suggest that the terms *natural* or *general revelation*, as well as *supernatural* or *special revelation* do not connote two different origins of revelation, the one general, the other special. In origin, all revelation is supernatural in a biblically theistic sense. Natural revelation, as Frame understands it, is hence a designate for divine revelation *through the medium of natural phenomena*. God as the immediate source of revelation uses two mediate agencies in his non-redemptive speaking to man: the non-rational creation and the nature of man himself.

Since the fall of man and the resultant curse of him and the creation, supernatural evidence through natural phenomena is noetically imprecise to us. That imprecision cannot be laid fully at the feet of fallen reason. God did not intend for reason, both natural and redeemed, to interpret nature, apart from the descriptive content of the word of God. The import of revelation for apologetics is perspectival. "Therefore, in a sense, natural and special revelation must never be separated in an evangelistic encounter. . . . The perspectival account of revelation is such that "Viewing 'creation in the light of Scripture' and 'applying Scripture to creation' are the same activity, seen from different perspectives."[3] We must therefore always look at evidence supplied by nature not in an intellectual vacuum, but through the "spectacles of Scripture"—a favorite term of both Van Til and Frame.

The two related forms of revelation are decisive and determinative for three apologetic tactics, all perspectivally related. Much earlier, I said that Frame's apologetic weds norm, subject, and situation. These angles are inherent to the shape of three intra-related divisions. (1) Apologetics as *proof:* presenting a rational basis for faith or proving Christianity to be true. (2) Apologetics as *defense:* answering the objections of unbelief. (3) Apologetics as *offense*: attacking the foolishness of unbelieving thought.[4] The apologetic types represent God's lordship attributes: control, authority, and presence, respectively. By extension, then, apologetics as proof is *normative*. Apologetics as defense is *existential*. And apologetics as offense is *situational*.[5] Also, it is helpful to know that the normative perspective focuses more on the role of Scripture and law (imperative), while the situational perspective relies more on natural revelation or the facts of our experience (indicative), though there is crossover.[6]

Regarding the three interrelated spheres of apologetics, a point that Frame has *not* made in his writings but that is apparent, is that apologetics as *defense* is really a broadened treatment of the first step in TAG, or apologetics as proof. As well, apologetics as *offensive* is actually an expansion of the second step of TAG—the exposing of non-Christian thought as foolish. Irrespective of which perspective is being employed, most important to the apologist is to uphold the holistic import of lordship in evangelism. That is to say that apologetics "is never complete without a presentation of Christ as Lord and as Lord of all."[7]

Apologetics as Proof

By now, we know that in addition to Scripture, Frame is open to auxiliary use of evidences in apologetics, as long as the transcendental goal is upheld. So I will not rehearse this point. For the purpose of deepened awareness, I will press on to ask, "What is the exact significance of proving the truth of Christianity in Frame's perspectivally charged apologetic?" I will look into this question in colloquia with Alvin Plantinga and Nicolas Wolterstorff.[8]

Both of these Reformed epistemologists have broadsided the evidentialist's claim that it is not rational to adopt religious belief unless that belief adheres to some form of internalism regarding justification, as well as strong access requirements—for example, infallibility, indubitability, or incorrigibility to basic beliefs. Plantinga has argued that Classical Foundationalism (CF) is self-refuting.[9] Plantinga's account of epistemology claims that argument or proof is not required for the "epistemic respectability" of belief in the existence of God.[10] Rather, belief in God is "properly basic," in the sense that the believer is within his *epistemic rights* to believe that God exists without inferential evidence such as those stemming from natural theology. In the language of Hans Rookmacher, who wrote that *Art Needs No Justification*, Plantinga maintains that belief in God is defensible and indefeasible, independent of circumferential propositions. The literature on the subject is extensive and well formulated, so I will move on to examine in general terms how the idea of warranted Christian belief matches up to Frame's perspectivalism.

At the forefront of the new Reformed epistemology's devaluation of CF is the ardent claim to our epistemic *rights* to believe in God. Frame, however, is far more interested in our epistemic *obligations* to believe. For as much as this is the case, the requisition of natural and special revelation finds the highest priority in the professor's apologetic. By limiting the criterion of knowledge to what is a priori and incorrigible (evident to the senses), and devaluing proofs relative to our noetic structure, in Frame's mind, Plantinga and Wolterstorff's approach "warrants one's right to believe in Christianity without being able to offer any reasons for so believing."[11] Wolterstorff, in fact, holds to a "noninnocent belief dispositions" criterion. That is, the Christian need not prove the reality of God at all, but the skeptic must prove the Christian wrong.[12]

Plantinga does not reject positive grounds for accepting those propositions he takes to be basic. He speaks of experience, beliefs in other minds, beliefs formed from memory, and the modal version of the ontological argument.[13] By showing interest in relevant argument, he therefore does not oppose faith to reason and manages to avoid Fideism. The problem, according to Frame, is that although Plantinga does not pit faith against reason, ultimately "he means to put belief in God's existence among the class of beliefs which are traditionally described as 'deliverances of reason.'. . . In Plantinga's brand of Calvinism, belief in God is by reason, not by faith!"[14] More succinctly, Wolterstorff declares, "Reason must be our last judge and guide in everything."[15]

Although Frame concurs with Plantinga and Wolterstorff that we can know God apart from evidence and argument without noetic impropriety, that, in his mind, is only a very small part of an apologetic directed to unbelievers. In demonstration of the *normative* perspective of apologetics, proofs are valuable as long as the Christian theistic starting point and goal are sustained. Considered thusly, apologetic discourse cannot progress on the ground that propositions about God are believable because it is rational to believe in them. The basis of the authority and efficaciousness of presenting a rational basis for faith is not something that exists first in the well-constructed domain of reasoned argument. Rather, reasoned argument resides in natural law as it is read through the spectacles of the perspicuity and sufficiency of Scripture. Contra Plantinga and Wolterstorff, we need not approach the bar of impartial and universal reason, "Because God has revealed himself clearly in Scripture and in creation, we can speak confidently about the justification of our knowledge of Him."[16]

What more can be said is that, versus Frame, the grounding of theistic belief in Plantinga and Wolterstorff is internalistic. Encouragingly, describes Frame, the "proper function" of epistemic propriety of theistic belief as developed by Plantinga in *Warranted Christian Belief* follows the Aquinas/Calvin model and its designation of the *divinitatis sensum*, in conjunction with the internal illumination of the Holy Spirit. But neither Plantinga nor Wolterstorff offer scriptural support for their positions.[17] The whole of the deontological/normative element of the Plantinga/Wolterstorff syllabus is missing. Wolterstorff seems clear on the point. "The so-called *subjective* concept of obligation is the only concept of obligation there is."[18]

Frame's most profound example of rationally demonstrated faith is his incisive explanation of 1 Corinthians 15:1–8.[19] He observes that Paul's proof of the resurrection of Jesus is not restricted to the five hundred people who saw him alive from the dead. The locus of proof lay in fact that the testimonies form part of the apostolic preaching. The physical proof, extraordinary as it is, is secondary to the supreme proof that God has spoken through the mouths of his servants. In contradistinction to the trend to isolate proof *in abstractio* from the content of the Bible—for example the trend from Warfield to Schaeffer—Frame epitomizes the New Testament structure of *apologia* that proof of the gospel is the gospel itself. By this sort of reasoning, Frame makes explicit with gratifying frequency the biblical principles on which he relies.

We can draw out Frame's insight even more sharply. In Acts, Paul does not defend the gospel. The gospel *is* his defense. In response to Agrippa, Paul's defense is more the prophetic disclosure of the gospel than Paul's ministry or person.[20] So in Philippians 1:16, the phrase "defense of the gospel" may be a close equivalent of the phrase in verse 15, "they preach Christ," and the expression in verse 17, "proclaim Christ." In this sense, the genitive "of the gospel" may better be understood as a definitive genitive than even an objective genitive. Expressly, the best defense of the gospel is the defense *that is* the gospel. Defense in its New Testament context has a strongly confessional element, which is missing from the pre-evangelism of Schaeffer and Clark Pinnock.[21]

Apologetics as Defense

The second type of Framian apologetics is "Apologetics as *defense:* answering the objections of unbelief."[22] This is apologetics from the existential perspective. Why existential and not normative or situational? Clearly these other perspectives are included. Frame legitimizes the classification on the grounds that knowledge requires a "knower." Beyond the obvious is a far more personal note. By relating "defense" to "existential," Frame wants our defense of the gospel to be carried out with great sensitivity to the *individual* with whom we are speaking. If we are not careful, equanimity in apologetics can quickly degenerate into a state of agitation. But Scripture tells us to offer up a defense "in gentleness correcting" (2 Timothy 2:25). If someone is offended by our defense, then let it be the gospel that offends and not us.

The existential criteria must also consider the *capacity* of the unbelieving self to organize data. A plethora of emotional, psychological, and physical elements exist and help orient an individual's processing of information, including information about the gospel. In this case, Frame is interested in "what works" for the unbeliever, given all that has shaped his noetic makeup. This is analogous to the "person variability" of apologetics mentioned earlier.

This also puts a new face on "point of contact." In *Apologetics to the Glory of God*, Frame treats this apologetic concept under the normative perspective: apologetics as proof.[23] However, in *Doctrine of the Knowledge of God* he is much more inclined to see point of contact under the existential perspective. This is because the functionality of point of contact implies identification, or, as he expresses, "The important thing is to present the message as clearly as possible. That implies that we must 'identify' as closely as possible with those whom we seek to win."[24] The downtrodden of Jesus' day structured their pain psychologically and emotionally in such a way that this informed his words. "Come to Me, all who are weary and heavy-laden, and I will give you rest" (Matthew 11:28). Physical and emotional fatigue is real, and Jesus does not hesitate to exploit that fatigue as a point of contact.

Frame also counsels the apologist to consider carefully his own character "existentially." He must be mature in the faith. Interaction with doubters also assumes a meeting of lives, each with his or her own stories, struggles, hurts, joys, and outcomes. The apologist is not a robot with a set of presuppositions. His presuppositions are shaped to some extent by his own individual reason, perhaps experiences with an emotionally absentee father, even struggles with ADHD, and so on. Frame thus allows for all of life to contribute to one's presuppositions and for the anthropological embodiment of those presuppositions to inform theology in general and the practice of apologetics in particular.[25] Yet our backgrounds and language must remain deferential to God's supreme yardstick of truth.

The existential perspective of the lordship principle also calls to account the *heart motive* of the apologist. In Frame, persuasion and proof do not ask us to second-guess the ability of data to persuade.[26] This does not mean that we do not wish to be persuasive. Lordship requires concern for the future of human existence *ex animo*. We say with Paul, "We are therefore Christ's ambassadors, as though God were making his appeal through us. We implore you on Christ's behalf: Be reconciled to God" (2 Corinthians 5:20). This signifies, once more, Frame's preeminent contribution to apologetics, such that he is eager to say, "Apologetics, therefore can never be far removed from evangelism, and vice versa. The two are perspectivally related: apologetics focusing on the means (godly reasoning based on Scripture) and evangelism focusing on the goal (the conversion of sinners)."[27]

This raises yet another related issue, that of *love and validity*. According to the appropriate function of lordship, for a proof to be persuasive it must be valid in the normal sense of logical entailment.[28] Equally so, in Frame, love of others *is* the most persuasive and valid argument one can offer.[29] The loving demonstration of the gospel, in conjunction with the work of the Holy Spirit, produces "cognitive rest"—which, in Frame, is the existential nature of knowledge as personally satisfactory.[30] Before the Samaritan woman, Jesus defended his ability to produce living water by telling her of the gift of God that never runs dry, thus satisfying her thirst for more than mere water (John 4:1–42). Would a talk about water have given Zaccheus cognitive rest? Really, a number of points come together here: perspectivalism, the person variability of the gospel, point of contact, broad argumentation, and a love for souls that is willing to be adaptable to where people are in life.

It is clear, then, that we are touching on a pragmatic theory of truth, yet not without normative guidelines. Unlike the radical subjectivism of the Sophists, Francis Bacon who stressed *ipsa scientia potestas est* (knowledge itself is power), or William James who defined belief by that which is simply useful to the believer, the existential justification of knowledge is understood as a subdivision of Scripture-based, Christian ethics. Thus, in reuniting what secularism can only abscind, the knower is ethically responsible to react rightly to the evidence (situational) as God has ordered it in his world and to the norms of knowledge (normative) God has availed to us. As well, to reiterate the priority of ethics in Framian thought, knowing is always the activity of what we "ought" to believe and "ought not" to believe."

Apologetics as Offense

Apologetics as *offense* represents a direct attack at the foolishness of unbelieving thought Offensive, or constructive, apologetics is in accord with the situational perspective. As the world around us is our outward environment, it has a bit more interest in the testimony of natural revelation. However, all facts that come to us from the outside world remain God's norms, and all norms are facts. Because the Bible is both a norm (imperative) and a fact, it is also an element in the situational perspective (indicative). Frame is not suggesting that the Bible is a *product* of our shared environment. Scripture is rather "our supreme criterion of reality."[31] Yet the import of empirical data remains important. Under the normative perspective, we learned that the real proof of the resurrection is not the numbers of witnesses to it (the situation) but is centered in the apostolic *kerygma* (the norm). This does not mean we discount the witnesses. The presentation of the empirical data broadens the argument. Of course, how can we know the empirical evidence of the witnesses to the resurrection, were if not for the fact that Scripture records the evidence?

Wolterstorff speaks in broadly similar terms of "situated rationality."[32] By this, he means that rationality can be determined only according to a person's *specific context*, not by externalized, abstract duties to believe.[33] So when the Yale professor speaks of "obligation," he does not mean it in the imperative sense, as does Frame. Rather, and as I have already shown, obligation in Wolterstorff always circles back to a subjective concept of obligation. The situation specificity of knowledge in Frame is not balanced by one's personal interpretation of what is a justifiable impression. For him, our "normative noetic criterion" is always in service to Scripture. Even our "noetic criterion," our capacity to know, is revealed by the word of God as an equal-opportunity suppressor: (Romans 1:18–32). Frame would never say that one should act from raw duty in the Kantian sense. He does, however, broaden the offensive argument appealing to the "facts" of God's historical judgments, the fulfillment of Old Testament prophecy, miracles, correspondence, and self-attesting Scriptures as basis enough to say, "[T]he evidence, then, is of such a high quality that it rightly obliges consent."[34]

Also on apologetics as offense, Frame says that our interlocutor is guilty of either atheism and/or idolatry, and this is where our offense must concentrate. Really, both always coexist, for atheism is never practiced without a replacement god. Together, atheism-idolatry is "essentially an escape from responsibility"—a consideration that again highlights the moral, rather than the epistemological, nature of unbelief in lordship theology.[35]

Hoping not to torture the point, according to Van Til, TAG has defensive and offensive elements. By way of defense, the believer asks the unbeliever to assume, "for the sake of argument," the veracity of the Christian stance and argues from there. By way of offense, the believer argues from the position of unbelief, "for the sake of argument," in order to show the gaping inconsistencies in the unbeliever's thought-system, as well as to demonstrate that even the non-believer's ability to say anything constructive about the world is "borrowed capital." This latter tact is, for Van Til, the essence of "offensive" apologetics." But as stated, Frame questions the falsity of atheism to prove the coherence of God's world. It is for this reason that Frame's offense relies less on *reductio* and more on positive points of argumentation.

Our offensive weapons? Frame's writings on apologetics indicate his advancement of three main emphases in constructive apologetics. (1) The state of the fallen creation.[36] (2) Deliberate dependence on Scripture. (3) Prayer. But, of course, the crux of the offensive is Frame's favorite argument for God—the moral argument—or, as he deduces, "Moral values, therefore God."[37] The moral argument is his preferred argument because he believes it forces the inquirer to consider the foundation of ethical *norms*, which he thinks are generally ignored today.

A helpful summation of the significance of lordship relative to Framian apologetics might look like this: the normative perspective of apologetics presents the knower with belief consistent with God's laws of thought revealed in Scripture. The existential perspective is concerned with meeting the knower "where he is at" and with the apologist's own maturity in Christ. The situational perspective presents the knower with Christianity consistent with tangible reality.

Reflection on the Decline of Apologetics

It remains consistent that many an informed reader of theology remains committed to the discipline of apologetics. However, with rare exception, such as Alister McGrath, the field of study and practice is in decline in schools of theology in Western Europe, if not altogether absent. The same is happening in Canada, America, and South Africa. Why, might we ask, is this so? Could it be that because the uniqueness of Christianity has so declined in many of today's established schools and churches, they no longer see a need to defend it? With the emphasis now on Muslim studies and all of the emerging applied theories and techniques of sociology, psychology, anthropology, theosophy, spiritualism, and critical theory, the clear bell that once rang with clarity through the halls of the older academic institutions and ecclesial bodies for the crown rights of King Jesus over all the earth appears to grow evermore dim.[38]

More so, university programs of the academic study of religion are evermore shy to treat Christianity on a par with, much less superior to, world religions. But if the claim "I am the way, and the truth, and the life; no one comes to the Father but through Me" (John 14:6) is not our imperative, it is no wonder, then, that although the language of transcendence still finds a place in theological education and life, it is really more the evolutionary world-spirit that in various ways accounts for this conception of *geist leben.*[39]

So, in one sense, these sections on Frame's apologetic are instructive not only for those looking to engage humanity's self-proclaimed act of deicide, but they also speak volumes to those who have abdicated their apologetic responsibility.

Evangelistic apologetics maintains a close attachment with Frame's great awareness of, and commitment to, the centric role of the gospel in the transformation of culture(s). The next pages demonstrate the germaneness of the trispectival method to Framian cultural theory. No area of Frame's practical theology is more self-consciously aware of the fastidious role of lordship than are his thoughts on culture.

Endnotes

---

1 See "Apologetics," retrieved at http://www.frame-poythress.org/apologetics/; date of access: June 9, 2014.

2 Three points on the shared relationship of natural and special revelation in Frame. First, there is no understanding, even on the part of redeemed man, of the universe gained by reflective observation of natural things. "God never intended man to attend to natural revelation while ignoring His spoken word." *DKG*, 144, Second, God's works revealed in nature *insist* on belief. "Those who view the mighty works of God are obligated, on the basis of that experience, to believe in Him. . . . Thus both the mighty work itself and the official testimony to God's mighty acts compel belief." *DKG*, 148. Third, general revelation does not provide us details of redemption. "One thing is lacking in God's revelation through nature: it does not reach teach people the way of salvation. That knowledge comes from the gospel, and the gospel comes through preaching (Rom. 10:13–17)." *DCL*, 136.

3 J. M. Frame, *Apologetics to the Glory of God* (Phillipsburg, NJ: P&R Publishing, 199), 25.

4 For Frame's developed account of these three types of apologetics, see *AGG*, 3–4, 92–168.

5 This is a restatement of Frame's own correlation in ibid., 3, n. 5.

6 See *DKG*, 141.

7 Ibid.

8 Though not readily recognized as "apologists," Plantinga and Wolterstorff are nevertheless Reformed epistemologists with apologetic interest.

9 Plantinga has made this case against CF in a number of his writings on epistemology. See "Reason and Belief in God," reprinted in *The Analytic Theist*, ed. James Sennett (Grand Rapids, MI: Eerdmans, 1998), especially 135–138; *Warrant: The Current Debate* (Oxford: Oxford University Press, 1993), 84–86; *Warrant and Proper Function* (Oxford: Oxford University Press, 1993), 182–183; and *Warranted Christian Belief* (Oxford: Oxford University Press, 2000), 82–85, 94–97. The differences between Plantinga's and Wolterstorff's presentation of the argument are very slight, as the same idea seems to be present in each of their work. I note only those differences Wolterstorff brings to the table that are of import for our present discussion.

10 A. Plantinga, "The Reformed Objection to Natural Theology," *Christian Scholar's Review* 11, no. 19 (1982): 19.

11 *DKG*, 387.

12 "A person is rationally justified in believing a certain proposition that he does believe unless he has adequate reason to cease from believing it. Our beliefs are rational unless we have reason for refraining. . . . They are innocent until proved guilty, not guilty until proved innocent." Alvin Plantinga and Nicolas Wolterstorff, eds., *Faith and Rationality* (Notre Dame, IN: University of Notre Dame Press, 1991), 163.

13 In *God and Other Minds: A Study of the Rational Justification of Belief in God* (New York: Cornell University Press, 1967), Plantinga's principle point is that the belief in God is like the belief in other minds. "There may be other reasons for supposing that although rational belief in other minds does not require an answer to the epistemological question, rational belief in the existence of God does. But it is certainly hard to see what these reasons might be. Hence my tentative conclusion: if my belief in other minds is rational, so is my belief in God. But obviously the former is rational; so, therefore, is the latter." (271).
14 *DKG*, 389. Cf. Alvin Plantinga, *Reason and Belief in God*, 89, and for a general review of this thought, Patrick Roche, "Knowledge of God and Alvin Plantinga's Reformed Epistemology," *Quodlibet Journal* 4, no. 4 (November 2002), http://www.quodlibet.net/articles/roche-plantinga.shtml.
15 Alvin Plantinga and Nicolas Wolterstorff, eds., *Faith and Rationality*, 182, n. 3.
16 *DKG*, 124.
17 Ibid., 384.
18 Alvin Plantinga and Nicolas Wolterstorff, eds., *Faith and Rationality*, 179.
19 *AGG*, 146.
20 See Acts 26:27–28.
21 In 2 Timothy 4:16, Paul speaks of his first apologia in Rome, a likely reference to his first Roman trial and imprisonment. Here the word has a very formal, judicial sense. But in verse 17, he amplifies his behavior at this first *apologia*. He describes it also as a *kerygma*, a "proclamation," or that the "the message might be fully proclaimed" (NESV). So, then, Paul's *apologia* was also a *kerygma*.
22 It appears to me that Frame's *defense* is Van Til's and Bahnsen's *offense*: the germinal point of the last two is the transcendental method as defense that attacks the foolishness of unbelieving thought.
23 *DKG*, 365–367.
24 Ibid., 367. Ibid., 365–367, present a vigorous case for point of contact under the existential perspective.
25 This "hermeneutical circle" was developed in conversation with Hays in the previous chapter on ethics. One place Frame elaborates on the concept is in *DKG*, 320.
26 The twin concepts of persuasion and proof are treated by Frame in *AGG*, 62–64. See again n. 62 as well.
27 *DKG*, 355.
28 In deductive arguments, validity is highly important. Such arguments are generally considered valid if the conclusion is entailed by the premises. A valid argument, then, would be: *Some Italians play the accordion; therefore, some accordionists are Italians.* An invalid deductive argument would be: *Some Italians are accordionists and some accordionists play poorly; therefore, some Italians are bad accordionists.* This is an invalid argument: the bad accordionists might all be Argentineans, for example.
29 *DKG*, 357, explains this simple idea further.
30 That is, belief that is personally meaningful and satisfying. For more on this idea, see ibid., 152–153.
31 *DKG*, 141.

32 Further quotations of Wolterstorff regarding "situated rationality" are in *DKG*, 390.
33 Wolterstorff therefore favors a "noetic criterion" and a "normative noetic criterion." The former is a person's belief-regulating capacity; the latter focuses on the fact that the belief in view *seems* justifiable to the person holding the belief." See Plantinga and Wolterstorff, eds., *Faith and Rationality*, 170.
34 *DKG*, 142.
35 *AGG*, 194–196. In the sections, Frame credits Francis Schaeffer with doing the most to challenge the irrationalism of atheism and Dooyeweed and Vollenhoven with advancing argumentation against the rationalism of idolatry. While it is tempting to triangulate Frame with the main representatives of the Dutch "Philosophy of Idea of Law" at this point, I will save my comments on Dooyeweed and Vollenhoven for my treatment of lordship and culture. This postponement is largely due to Frame's advice to me.
36 I.e., the use of natural revelation. In *Apologetics to the Glory of God*, Frame writes a play act. The characters are Al, an agnostic, and John, a preacher. At one point, Al demands evidence from John for the existence of God. John replies that every fact in the world testifies to God. But Al, quick on his feet, cites the cockroaches that infest his home and asks John whether they, too, indicate the existence of God. John's retort is crucial. "Hmmm . . . Isn't that just the sort of thing you'd expect if the Bible is true? Scripture says that because man fell into sin, the earth produces thorns and thistles to make our work difficult and our existence wearisome. Cockroaches are part of that." *AGG*, 207.
37 Ibid., 91. Frame raises the moral argument under apologetics as proof, but in the give and take of real-life apologetics, the proof can surface anywhere, including apologetics as offense.
38 P. Clayton, *Transforming Christian Theology: For Church and Society* (Minneapolis: Fortress Press, 2009).
39 B. Seifer, *When the Soul Awakens: The Path to Spiritual Evolution and a New World Era* (Chicago, IL: Gathering Wave Press, 2009), 51.

Chapter 9

Lordship and Culture

In the year 389, Ambrose thought he had defeated the need for answers to life's questions when, in defending the prisoner in Plato's cave who refused to turn his head, he stated that "To discuss the nature and position of the earth does not help us in our hope of the life to come. It is enough to know what Scripture states."[1] Ambrose meant that Christians have no need to grapple with questions about the world around us. Spiritual truth is sufficient. The absolute antithesis of Ambrose is seen in the thought of John M. Frame. Frame's many articles, and the whole of his dogmatics, resound with ubiquitous attention to the idea that Christ is the transformer of culture. It is nonetheless, with the publication of Frame's *The Escondido Theology*, that his deep ardor for the fact that "theology is application" *urbi et orbi* ("to the city and to the world"), and of especially the need to protect that worldview against efforts designed to tone it down, comes through with resounding clarity.[2]

With that before us, these subsequent sections will be oriented toward answering what lordship means in Frame's lordship theology, with an eye on culture. Of first concern is to identify Frame's unique contribution to the question of Christ and culture. This detection will include an analysis of Frame's methodology—that is, I want to ask *how* Frame arrives at his Reformed one kingdom position (hereafter, R1K) on Christ and culture.[3]

This added step is not mere reevaluation of Frame but is essential for understanding how his theorizing differs from others whom have arrived at the same general consensus.[4] Second, I will survey, to some extent, in what manner Frame's views are germane to leading areas of culture. Third, I will evaluate Frame's polemical discourse with those whom he finds in error on the "enduring problem" as Niebuhr has called it. Finally, a few concluding and clarifying thoughts will be presented to this discussion. Obviously, some oversimplification of the whole of this study will undoubtedly occur, due to the impossibility to provide a complete analysis of all of the issues.

One Kingdom Starting Point

Chief within Frame's intellectual context is his explicit recognition that "Scripture teaches a 'one kingdom' view."[5] The wider context he presents of the lordship of God creates two equally significant levels to this R1K texture that complement each other synergistically. On one hand, the lordship principle holds out the prospect of many perspectives upon norms, facts, situations, and experiences of the world around us, and untrammeled creativity within God's world. On the other hand, Frame's thorough perspectivalism comes with an accompanying suspicion of anything that claims, though even mildly, the detachment of the concrete world of things from God's sovereign rule. There is always a unity in God's sovereignty, never a two kingdoms interpretation of Christ and culture (hereafter, R2K).

The meaning, then, of lordship in Frame's theology of culture is (a point that has been made already) is this. "*There is one kingdom, ruled over by one Lord, who governs the affairs of all people by a single rule of faith and practice, and everything is related perspectivally.*"[6]

Missing from Frame is even the slightest hint of Platonic idealism with its own particular form of "over-against."[7] The fully compatibilist doctrine of Frame is, as Brian Walsh and J. Richard Middleton argue in a different context, "a vision that illuminates all of life, and empowers us to walk obediently before the Lord."[8]

Frame's theology of culture is a fully ciphered system of Niebuhr's fifth category of Christ and culture: Christ, the transformer of culture. By "transformation" of culture, Frame is not advocating theocracy. Rather, "transformationalism . . . is simply 'bringing every thought captive to obey Christ' (2 Cor. 10:5), or doing 'all to the glory of God' (1 Cor. 10:31), on the assumption that what brings glory to God is also best for the world."[9] Frame can therefore define culture this way. "Culture is the human response, in obedience or disobedience, to the Cultural Mandate, God's command to Adam and Eve to replenish the earth and subdue it. As such, culture expresses our religion, our service to God or to an idol."[10] In fewer words, "Creation is what God makes; culture is what we make."[11]

Frame's investiture on methodology leading to RIK thought is accomplished in three related categories: systematic theology; symbiotic relationships, which include the institutions of family, Church, and state; and finally, biblical theology.[12]

Systematics

Frame's systematic theology develops the notion that the very name "Lord" is enough for all creatures great and small to recognize their obligations before him. CAP, as I have discussed, are covenantal attributes of God with significant meaning not only for the titular *sacred sphere*, but also for all people and cultures. "There is no doubt that the covenant is redemptive in its thrust . . . [but] Scripture does not teach any general distinction between sacred and the secular."[13] This *solum* leads Frame to attenuate traditionally well-defined discriminations in dogmatics between law and gospel, law and grace, creation and redemption, and natural and special revelation. So when Frame presents us with an affirmation of all people's responsibility before the Lord, he is ready to rekindle Paul's thought in Romans 1:18–20 that people's practical turning away from God is inherent in the very understanding of him. Perspectivalism also provides Frame with multiple ways to articulate a R1K discernment of the cosmos. Because God controls all, his kingdom is supreme over all. God's absolute authority means that it covers every particle of human life. And because the Lord is in all, all things are for him.

This line of thought in Frame allows us to connect with certain theological sensitivities at play in the work of Abraham Kuyper. The father of the neo-Calvinist movement, Kuyper brought the idea of a *gratia communis* (common grace) of God—previously stated in more general terms by Calvin—to maturation.[14] Kuyper's definition is based on a distinction between God's common, or non-saving, grace and his special or redemptive grace. In a nutshell, common grace is said to be that gracious operation of God, after the fall, that permits man and civilizations to develop, when, according to his justice, he had every reason to end the world.[15]

Though dimensions of Kuyper's interest in common grace are compatible with Frame's lordship principle—that is, both disallow human autonomy—there are two points of distinction between Kuyper and Frame. For one, while Frame speaks of "common grace," the texture of his discussion in *The Doctrine of God* especially presents common grace more as a consequence of God's universal kingship with immense eschatological meaning.[16] Common grace is really God's patience or "God's common goodness or common love" by which he brings his redemptive plan to complete fulfillment.[17] Kuyper's main interest in the doctrine is mainly philosophical: it stems from the same awareness that motivated Calvin to ask how it is that the unregenerate can evidence virtue when, morally speaking, their natures are awash in sin. This does not suggest that Kuyper's cultural theory disallows for the linear possibilities of history. Kuyper makes a critical distinction between the *constant* and the *progressive* operations of common grace. This distinction draws attention to the fact that God not merely *allows* human history after the fall, but is actively *working in* its achievements. He says,

> Yet common grace could not stop at this first and constant operation. Mere maintenance and control affords no answer to the question as to what end the world is to be preserved and why it has passed throughout a history of ages. If things remain the same what should life be continues at all. . . . Accordingly there is added to this first constant operation of common grace . . . another, wholly different, operation . . . calculated to make human life and the life of the whole world pass through a process and develop itself more fully and richly.[18]

Still, this "progressive" component to common grace serves mainly to provide a theocentric basis for the advancement of civilizations, yet comes up short of a thoroughly worked-out eschatology. This is what Nicolas Ansell contemplated when, with great discernment into current neo-Calvinist developments, he stated that "Kuyperian thinking to date has typically ignored or minimized the eschatological dimension of the biblical narrative(s) even though this neglected horizon has also made its presence felt in our tradition (most notably in the theology of Herman Bavinck)."[19]

A second difference between Frame and Kuyper is that whereas Frame's perspectivalism attenuates divisions between natural and special revelation, much as did Calvin, Kuyper's theory of common grace relies more heavily on *souvereiniteit in eigen kring* (sphere sovereignty), whereby Kuyper can speak of God's sphere of the state.[20] Though formal treatment of natural law is absent from Kuyper, such as we find in Thomas and Grotius, his language of "the ordinances which must govern human existence in Society and State" means that the church and the state have separate sovereignty, and magistrates, though they rule according to God's ordinances, are at liberty to render decisions "apart from the direct influence of the church and vice versa."[21] Kuyper is thus somewhat at variance with Calvin, who "demanded intervention of the government in the matter of religion" and who gave the sphere of government power to guard against idolatry in its various forms.[22] He also presents a different paradigm from what we find in Frame, who calls the institutional church to preach to the state and to always show concern for all matters of public policy, for "many political issues are straightforwardly questions of morality. If the church is to preach the whole council of God, it must preach against abortion, homosexuality, relativism, and so on."[23]

However, it is to violate Kuyper's thought to propose, as David VanDrunen has done, that Kuyper's language of common and special grace and of ordinances "displays considerable similarity to the use of the natural law and the two kingdoms doctrines in earlier Reformed theology."[24] There will be a more appropriate place to speak of the viability of VanDrunen's comment. But for now, it behooves us to see that VanDrunen is eager to paint Kuyper as one who laid the control of government under natural law without direct appeal to the voice of Scripture. In fact, Kuyper believed that the state is responsible before both general and special revelation. He was quite clear on the Christian nature of the state. "The sphere of the state is not profane. But both Church and State must, each in their own sphere, obey God and serve his honor. . . . The first thing of course is, and remains, that all nations shall be governed in a Christian way; that is to say, in accordance with the principle which, for all statecraft, flows from the Christ."[25]

These differentiations between Frame and Kuyper surface an important detail. Although Frame is at home with neo-Calvinism and has called himself a "Kuyperian," this is true only to a point. Frame is Kuyperian, in that he believes the church has a transformative task in culture. He also stands with the Dutch thinker in affirming a universal love and goodness of God to all people. That said, while Kuyper is a monumental inspiration for Frame, looking closely, one sees that important aspects of the structure of Frame's cultural theology are more analogous to that of another Dutchman, Klass Schilder.[26]

Frame follows Schilder mainly in two ways. First, the centerpiece of Schilder's theology of culture is that with man's office comes a Cultural Mandate from God.[27] The expression was born out of Schilder's dispute with Abraham Kuyper over common grace. Schilder argued that to erect the believer's cultural activity on the ground of God's *permitting* of culture after the fall is to ground it via *negativa* only and inadequately. Alternatively, he insisted that Scripture also bases our response to the world in a positive affirmation of dominion, specifically the command of Genesis 1:28. Kuyper justifies Christian cultural accomplishment in God's universal grace. Schilder grounds it in a specific law of God that all believers are required to obey. Schilder's position is Frame's, as readily seen in Frame's very definition of culture: "Culture is the human response, in obedience or disobedience, to the Cultural Mandate, God's command to Adam and Eve to replenish the earth and subdue it."[28] To describe culture in terms of a reply to a Divine ultimatum demonstrates significantly the lordship principle on a global scale.

Second, the specter of Schilder is also seen in Frame's expansion that culture is not just a fact but also a "norm"—a point I will revisit further ahead. On the ethical nature of culture, Frame explains, "Adam was not to rule merely for himself, but for God, glorifying God in all he did." Thus, "Culture is for God's sake . . . subject to his commands, his desires, his norms, his values."[29] Schilder's steadfastly focused on calling the church to an obedient faith—a call that finds rich expression in his public theology. Subject to this end, Schilder's enduring work *Christ and Culture*, as the name implies, is protective of a thoroughgoing Christocentric focus. The point of this focus is to draw a correlation between Christ's obedience and our own. God endowed the original man with an "office" wherein he is a "prophet, priest, and king."[30] The ethical standard for man's created office is Christ's Divine office.[31] Common grace authorizes Christians to *participate* with non-Christians in cultural pursuits. But Kuyper's *permission to participate* is not the same as Schilder's and Frame's *mandate to cultivate*, which comprises its own means of ethical assessment. So I think that more than Kuyper, Schilder and Frame place more stress on the end of culture—the glory of God. And both go further than Kuyper to accentuate the antithesis between believing and non-believing thought.[32]

Symbiotic Relationships

Frame's systematic formulations on CAP give rise to a unity or symbiotic relativity between three institutions. I have already addressed some of this under the chapter on ethics. However, the significance for lordship and culture is that family, church, and state are not partitioned but are organically related, therefore created in such a way as to be formally submitted to God.[33] This reciprocity of institutions becomes of great import for Frame's reading of the relationship of states and/or nations to God. Although he can speak in terms of Christians being members of "two nations"—language somewhat familiar to R2K alliteration—he speaks this way only for practical discussion. [34] Frame sees church and state united under God, with the result that "The church and the earthly nations are related, then, like two different families with overlapping members, occupying the same territory. They serve the kingdom of God, but it is misleading, in my view, to describe them as two institutional forms of the kingdom coordinate with one another, as is often done in Reformed literature."[35]

In framing institutions this way, the theologian again reveals yet another point of departure with Kuyper, thus another way he has advanced argumentation. In Kuyper, society is understood as a group of other spheres of life that include the family, business, art, science, and more, which "do not owe their existence to the state."[36] In reaction, Frame says, "But I do not agree with Kuyper that the family, church, and state are radically distinct spheres. The state is the family of Adam; the church is the family of Christ. Both are trying to accomplish the same things for their members, but in the end only the family of Christ will prevail."[37]

Kuyper's political theology seeks to explain how God exhibits sovereignty in the state, society, and the church. Frame assumes an organic bond between family, church, and state with God as Head. Frame can also agree with Kuyper, however. Kuyper's outline of duty is no assurance that the institutions of which he speaks will not cross over into the others' spheres, whereby the sphere of society attempts to "shake off" the authority of the state, while the sphere of the state tries to assert itself over the sphere of society.[38] Likewise, Frame warns, borrowing from Kuyper's own language, "We expect conflict between these families, as each tries to claim for its own lord 'the whole domain of human existence.'"[39]

In a significant paper, Jason Lief argues contra David VanDrunen's R2K position that "Calvin . . . also believed that the kingdom of God is a present reality and that the restoration of 'all things' is 'in the course,' which is the basis for the neo-Calvinist emphasis upon transformation."[40] Lief's defense of the continuity in Calvin between the spiritual and the temporal realms takes shape in his investigative process, which focuses on a symbiotic connection among Calvin's equivalent understanding of the inherent unity of the human person, the person of Christ, and soteriology.[41] The similarity between Calvin and Frame is that both see all datum involved in a single history and under the express sovereignty of the Lord. One difference is that Frame derives the state from the narrative of creation, thus incorporating it under a R1K doctrine, while (following the scholarship of Lief) Calvin's R1K view is at one with his theological understanding of Christology, soteriology, and anthropology.[42]

However, it is worth noting that Calvin's Christology alone opposes the partitioning of spiritual and temporal powers. For instance, Hans-Joackim Kraus observes that like Luther, Calvin warned against confusing the "two regiments"—"the political regiment of this world and the spiritual regiment of Christ."[43]

Yet due largely to the persecution of the Huguenots, Calvin's commentary on Daniel reveals a change in tone, one that identifies the first advent of Christ with a new order. "In Daniel 2 . . . Calvin identifies 'kingdom of God' with Christ and explains 'that by his advent Christ has taken away whatever was splendid and wonderful and magnificent in the world.'"[44] So Kraus can characterize Calvin's newer, modified view of the two regiments this way. "The kingship of God that came down with Christ is crisis and judgment over all earthly kingdoms. Christ alone is Lord and King."[45] Here, Calvin gives credence to the same R1K framework as we find in Frame.

Calvin is nevertheless content with the *language* of duality between sacred and secular administrations, as long as church and civil government are co-equal branches under the authority of God. When Frame says that it is confusing to describe church and state as "two institutional forms of the kingdom coordinate with one another," he is asking for language that conveys something stronger than the image of the proverbial "flip sides of the same coin." He is looking for an articulation that reflects the church and the state as different metals *within* the same coin.[46] So although Frame shares a theological point of departure with Calvin regarding the duty of church and state before God, Frame seems to press for the uniformity of that duty more stringently than perhaps did even Calvin.

Biblical Theology

Above all, it is a biblical-theological point of reference that provides the special *locus* for Frame's fundamental values on culture. Let it be understood that my own careful search through Frame's corpus reveals this to be the epicenter from which his R1K position finds its most fertile expression. The specific point is this: the gospel of Jesus Christ is that *the kingdom of God has come.* "It is the reign of God that is good news, news that ensures peace and salvation."[47] The striking parallel between the Pauline "gospel which I preached to you" (1 Cor. 15:1) and the coming of the kingdom with its moral vision of a new cosmos lay in the situational specificity Frame stresses of the redemptive-historical development of the gospel of the kingdom. Not only is the kingdom the new beginning, in which Jews and gentiles find unity in Christ—an important theme in Romans. It embodies the tangible coming of God's cosmic design to extend his reconciling power *into* the world through the growth of the body of Christ toward full maturity.

Directly associated with this vision of the earthly meaning of the kingdom of heaven is its cosmic span. Frame often exploits the great biblical theologian Geerhardus Vos, who, in contradicting restricted notions that land the kingdom of God exclusively within the visible church, explains that for "[Jesus] the kingdom exists there, where not merely God is supreme, for that is true at all times and under all circumstances, but where God supernaturally carries through his supremacy against all opposing powers and brings men to the willing recognition of the same."[48]

Agreeing with Vos, Frame can say that "Here, 'kingdom of God' is an ongoing historical project—a divine war-drama. The church is more static—an institution that continues through the historical drama. I often refer to the church as the 'headquarters' of the Kingdom."[49] Hence, Frame rejects out of hand R2K proponents who portray the institutional church as the only present form of the kingdom.

Even so, Vos sounds very Kuyperian when speaking of the kingdom transforming *spheres*.

> Undoubtedly the kingship of God, as his recognized and applied supremacy, is intended to pervade and control the whole of human life in all its forms of existence. This the parable of the leaven plainly teaches. These various forms of human life have each their own sphere in which they work and embody themselves. There is a sphere of science, a sphere of art, a sphere of the family and of the state, a sphere of commerce and industry. Whenever one of these spheres comes under the controlling influence of the principle of the divine supremacy and glory, and this outwardly reveals itself, there we can truly say that the Kingdom of God has become manifest.[50]

Placed as conversation partners, Frame dislikes Vos's sphere-structured arrangement of culture. Rather than repeat language in the mold of Kuyper and his followers, wherein the church is only one of many spheres on the same level with state, school, labor union, newspaper, political party, and so on, Frame sees the church as central and its ministry as comprehensive.

Ipso facto, the visible church rules and motivates believers to carry out the kingdom project—to bring transformative change to all of the aspects of human life. Frame can thus agree with Vos that church and kingdom are not identical. But for Frame, the church as an outward expression of the

Kingdom is always superior to all cultural institutions in authority, centrality, and significance.

This focuses us in a bit more on Frame's contribution. From Kuyper's time and now to the first decades of the twenty-first century, neo-Calvinism continues to be characterized by a *fractured* measurement between kingdom of God and sectors of culture. Frame is working toward a *fractal* concept (to borrow a term from modern mathematics) of kingdom and culture. Culture is not distributed "forms of existence," citing Vos, each with its own sphere. As much as life on earth in all its rich variety reflects God's norms and values, it displays self-similarity with the Creator. What does not exhibit those standards, the kingdom of God has come to transform. Cultural life will not exhibit *exactly* all that constitutes the fullness of the kingdom in the here and now. But the same *nature* of life must appear on all planes.

A corrective that might be brought to Frame's attention is how little lordship, as a cultural motif, is expressed as the lordship of the Risen One. The eschatological promise of 1 Corinthians 15:24 ("then *comes* the end, when He hands over the kingdom to the God and Father, when He has abolished all rule and all authority and power") foresees the guarantee and significance of the end of the current pattern of the cosmos, and all cultures in it, according to the dominant act of history: the resurrection.[51] It is not that Frame fails to champion the resurrection. It is "The greatest miracle."[52] Nevertheless, Easter Day does not come into sight as *elementum* in the lordship theology. The resurrection is a warrant for belief, an example of God's covenant presence, a sign we are in the last days, a basis for confidence our cultural labors will succeed, the main motivation for Sabbatical worship, the historical axis for the continuity of the Cultural

Mandate and the Great Commission, and more.[53] He forthrightly decrees the all-inclusive rule of Jesus according to the post-resurrection and chief confession of the New Testament church: "Jesus is Lord."[54] Yet the declaration seems to take on secondary status, as it is employed in a polemic against the insufficiency of natural law to administer culture and not as the final "yes" for his lordship theology.

Applications for a Contemporary Context

Culture and Values

Thoughts and suspicions immediately follow Frame's endorsement of God's kingdom pervading all areas of life, including public. So attention to some important ways Frame envisions the lordship of Christ functioning in a practical manner is now explored. In much earlier sections of this book, I undertook a comparative analysis of Frame and van de Beek. I have noted that in its philosophical and mundane manifestations, the modern West is home to an overall culture of melancholy, despair, and self-criticism. This dominant attitude, the child of the extreme self-introspection of nineteenth-century Romanticism is, in a postmodern period, joined ironically to the earlier theme of the Enlightenment: its academic skepticism of metaphysics. The road from modernism to postmodernism has not solved anything but has only ended in a dead end. Recalling Robert B. Pippen's incisive remark on European culture, "Everywhere the images have been and are the images of death and loss and failure, and the language is the language of anxiety, unease, and mourning."[55]

In defining for us the nature of culture, Frame provides a very worthwhile aspect that speaks powerfully to our human aspiration for meaning. He first speaks of the *normative* understanding of culture: that it simply *is*. Or, stated another way, that culture is a given among humans, as no one can live apart from it. But then he adds to this a *descriptive* aspect—what culture "ought to be, both real and ideal."[56] "Ought" is an ethically charged word that suggests that no one comes to the table of culture minus a moral motivation. So, by way of definition, Frame says that "Culture is what a society has made of God's creation, together with its ideals of what it ought to make of it."[57]

He does not mean that everyone lives culturally according to God's ideal for culture, but according to his or her own. We all have some ideal in mind of how our respective cultures "ought" to look and behave. It may take someone to question us to bring to our consciousness the values we hold subconsciously, but they are there. Even nihilism has its own peculiar "ought." Frame thinks that the description of culture we see with our mind's eye is somehow related to our hearts. In other words, "When we talk about values and ideals, we are talking about religion."[58] Try hard though we may, we can never divorce our choice of dress, food, music, and entertainment from whom we think governs our existence—whether it be us or God. "So now we can see how culture is related to religion. When we talk about values and ideals, we are talking about religion."[59]

It was this very idea that Schleiermacher phrased in a question intended to provoke the cultural elite of Europe over a century ago to rethink the religious ground of their cultural ideals. He asked, "What can man accomplish that is worth speaking of, either in life or it art, that does not arise in his own self from the influence of the sense for the Infinite?"[60]

The secularist pays little attention to the need for religion and even less so the more a religion speaks of a personal God. There is a problem with a personal God. He wants to control things. He is, the secularist thinks, totalitarian. But Frame wonders whether it is possible to be human without an inner ideal and whether that worldview is not a controlling, authoritative voice of our thoughts and actions. Michel Foucault thought he had dispensed with innate ideals and perceptions focusing on the "discourse" that make up cultures.[61] This resulted in the concept of "myth" and its social construction of reality and the rejection of truth as objective norm. Yet are not our ideals revealed when we say it is true that there is no *real* truth? When Roland Barthes called for the "emptying out of interiority to the benefit of its exterior signs," was he correct that cultures are mere signs, words, and objects that are only ever arbitrary, made, and contingent?[62] If so, then what was the political and philosophic justification for the European Union? Did no one hear Barthes say that this would be impossible?

The West is the snake eating its tail. The prophetic elements of Nietzsche and the "death of man" anti-humanism inspired by Foucault, along with the "end of modernity" rhetoric of Lyotard and Vattimo, are choking us. And we wonder if it is not high time to ask if the culture-bound strategy of postmodern thought has not put the final nail in the coffin of anthropological dissatisfaction in the West. Can anyone reading this truly say that people are devoid of psychology and that central to it is the desire for comprehensive meaning? We are not left with the denial of systematic meaning but with the choice of who will help us understand and live it. Listen to Frame: "Every worldview, every philosophy, even if it professes to be nonreligious, has this totalitarian influence on human life and, followed consistently, will dictate a certain kind of culture. Culture, therefore, is never religiously neutral. Everything in culture expresses and communicates a religious conviction: either faith in the true God or denial of him."

Evaluating Culture

A good bit has been said in this volume about the dark cloud of skepticism and hopelessness that hangs over many Western societies. The caluminatory nature of modern life did not arrive quickly, however. Neoclassicism was a second vaulting back, after the Renaissance, to the ideals and goals of the Roman Republic. With that move came the mounting discontent among the French *prolétariat* with that frolicsome contemporary life, which the French courts had come to epitomize. Neoclassicism was the language of turmoil, of anticipation, and of revolution. Finding early expression in the Paris salons among the literary scholars and philosophers, Romantics believed they could actually achieve what the French Revolution had proved the Age of Reason could not do—reconstruct society.

With this new movement came a form of religious introspection so open-ended that Fichte could equate God with the "moral order of the universe."[63] The mechanism articulating the new set of values was neither historicism nor positivism but aesthetics—all culminating in the radicalization and deification of art *fin de siècle* ("end of century"). The cultural crash of Romanticism's climb is a story in itself. But Proust's withdrawal from European high culture spoke for many, proving perhaps a fitting analogy of the deadening effect and dissolution of Romantic self-introspection. With him went the old ways of envisioning the novel and also the crumbling of high culture that even the poet could not rescue. A new tone could now be heard among the educated in their unpleasant rejoinder to European high culture. Distaste with bourgeois smugness, doubt about modern optimism and mass culture, and consumer mentalities of art were reactions to presumptive hubris.

It was Nietzsche who galvanized this vacuous view of reality into an "honest atheism." According to him, life itself is inherently devoid of sense and meaning. Life's meaning is only that which we give it. For Nietzsche, the catalyst for such meaning came through art. For meaning, he thought, is imparted to life through artistic creativity. It is through art that man may find the path to self-aggrandizement, to the Übermensch. Thus, his own poetic muse assumes that "Nothing is beautiful, except for man alone: all aesthetics rests upon this naïveté."[64]

Heidegger, however, could see the irony. His critique of modernism culminated with Nietzsche. He claimed that for all of his exposure of nihilistic fate, Nietzsche was also a prisoner of the nihilism of modernity. Rejecting metaphysics and turning to ontology, "[Heidegger] criticized the tradition of Western philosophy, which he regarded as nihilistic, for, as he claimed, the question of being as such was obliterated in it."[65] The problem Heidegger placed his finger on was the problem of modern (and we can now add postmodern) society and the high culture it produces. Less elliptically is his view that Nietzsche's view of value was conditioned by the same metaphysical view of truth that philosophy had taken for granted.

Heidegger's new view of value is most detectable in his own specific ideas on art. Perceiving that Nietzsche was still working within an aesthetic vision that presupposed traditional coherence of values, Heidegger moves the value of art from the realm of Being to "becoming," from the realm of transcendence to "transfiguration." In this way, then, "Transfiguration creates possibilities for the self-surpassing of life at any given point of limitation."[66]

To Nietzsche's critique of high culture, Heidegger was right to say that, after all, Nietzsche could only affirm what is true in the "holding-to-be-true." Problematically, however, Heidegger's evaluation of high art left us with chaos. In the words of Lesley Chamberlain, "And so Heidegger can say aesthetics was another set of beliefs left with no ground to stand on. Beauty did not relate to an impulse of delight the Creator wished to share with mankind."[67] So we are still left looking for a solution to the problem of nihilistic high culture.

In Framian perspectivalism, there is a way to both reorient and clarify art and life in their being and, on this basis, to transcend the limits of nihilistic culture. Beyond the obvious difference that Nietzsche and Heidegger both sought the end of the Christian stimulus in culture, Frame establishes coherence between *experience* and what *is* in the fixated absolutes of *God's word*. The italicized words may correspond to the existential, ontological, and metaphysical realms.

By now, we know that Frame's theological outline places Christian ethics as determinative of metaphysics. So for Frame there is nothing "traditional" in Nietzsche's view of harmony between ideal and value in culture, as Heidegger saw it. In fact, since the existential focus of both men lacks *a priori* essences, values, and norms, as seen in Scripture, it is safe to say that Frame would see both men as lacking any real basis to know anything truly; therefore neither can act as a reliable judge of philosophy, art, and culture.

This leads to a very different *evaluation* of culture. To expound on Frame's ethical precedents, "modernity" is not a philosophical problem or, for that matter, any other sort of problem with novels, poetry, music, or painting. This is obviously the way bourgeois society saw it. But we are far too close to complex phenomenon to understand why so much of culture is so vacuous and reactive, and why self-loathing is not beyond us all. The absolute of God's word replaces failed diagnostic self-determination. It enables us to see that we do not have a problem. We are the problem. Sin is our worst enemy. So we need more than a philosopher. We need a Savior.

At the same time, though, our paradise of culture is not totally lost for the reason that, as Frame says, "Our world is fallen, but it is also the object of God's common and special grace. Therefore, both good and bad are to be found in all people and social institutions."[68] Yet again, it is Frame's ethics that is decisive. The question then becomes how can one discern "good" from "bad" in culture? Frame answers the question by distinguishing sharply between the *world* and *culture*. Or, as he puts it negatively, "it is wrong to identify the 'world' as 'culture.' The world is the negative side of culture."[69] The deep dichotomy, then, in Frame, is not between metaphysics and culture (Nietzsche) or ontology and culture (Heidegger), but between sin and culture.

To transform our existing world and its cultures requires, if I am reading Frame correctly, less pretension of the modern assertion of human power or, on the other end, critiques of phenomenological data and language of power, and more attention to the problem of human finitude. Indeed, it was modernity's self-confidence that precipitated the advent of nihilism that took shape in the high culture of European art, philosophy, literature, and more. That Frame engages the subject of art, but only within the context of sin and redemption (not to be confused with Christian moralisms) is therefore quite useful.

Specifically advantageous is Frame's reorganization of what constitutes "high" and "low" art. As during the neoclassical period, when prejudice ran high for the myth of the sophistication of high art, many people continue to confuse style with substance. Ipso facto, they prefer the elegance of urbanity over what they think is the aesthetically inane and culturally parochial nature of pop culture. But Frame cautions that "The problem is not with one [art] genre or another, but, as Van Til emphasized, that sin corrupts everything."[70] Thus "*higher* must not be borrowed from fallen culture, but must recognize the dimensions of worldview and communications" (italics added).[71]

The "dimensions of worldview" would have been of great help to the European bourgeois social class. Their traditionalism evaluated high art over low art and people of position over those who had little, when in fact *sola scriptura* reveals the equalitarian effect of sin that inexorably enervates all of God's good creation.

Frame uses the "dimension of communication" to counter the way cultural traditionalism tends to hinder contextualization of the greatest story ever told. So his themes are not a repetitive anecdote, whereby the language of anxiety is exchanged for the language of the apocalyptic "end of modernity." He communicates the end of hopelessness and alienation in the redemptive plan of the kingdom of God. This thorough lordship paradigm has as its goal the transformation of human lives and of culture.

Norm and Freedom in Culture

Art

During the Enlightenment, cultural thought was locked into the established ideas of scientific order and regularity that were the mark of philosophy and mathematics. This resulted in an objective evaluation of beauty. So the father of modern aesthetics, Alexander Baumgarten, could still assert that God is simultaneously legislator and author of all natural obligations because he is the author of the world.[72] We see then that an ordered conceptual analysis of culture is implicit in conceptual order. Kant, however, rejected Baumgarten's constructivist theory that the outward appearance of beauty could be judged according to a priori laws to which our judgment of taste must conform.[73]

Reacting also to the Enlightenment project, *Sturm und Drang* took cultural theory in a new direction. Hamann's *Aesthetica in nuce: Eine Rhapsodie in Kabbalistischer* provides special treatment for the new means of critical discourse between artists and patrons. Hamann does not consider art in terms of a priori rules over the cosmos but as windows to a hidden aesthetic relationship between art and patron.[74] Eighteenth-century art critics asked, "What does this art piece mean?" Now the question was, "What does this work of art mean to me?" Reflective analysis based on the mystical unknown was at one with the overall irrationalism of the age, which, in turn, helped guide intellectual Europe to skepticism and insidious despair. Accordingly, practical chaos is the child of conceptual chaos.

The Russian philosopher Nikolai Berdyaev made an attempt to bridge the autonomous reason of Kant and the mystical aesthetic of Hamann. His goal:

to introduce a broader narrative of freedom within which God played a prominent role. His prototype was the writings of Jakob Boehme. Berdyaev finds Boehme's mystical theory persuasive because he does not believe that freedom originates with God but, like God, existed before all creation.[75] Boehme's *Ungrund* (Groundlessness) thus becomes Nothingness in Berdyaev: a primal freedom that precedes all Being and through which God brought all Being into existence.[76] James McLachlan can thus say that Berdyaev expresses "a fundamental truth about existence that is incapable of being expressed in an objective conceptual arrangement."[77]

In Berdyaev's theory of culture, people, like God, have creative freedom. It is through the creative act that our creative*ness* complements God's creative*ness*.[78] By using freedom *within* the created order of God to create, we bring the freedom lying *outside* of existence, and of God, into play. Berdyaev's famous quote is "God awaits from us a creative act which is the response to the creative act of God."[79]

On one hand, Berdyaev joins Kant to say that freedom is beyond the limits of reason. On the other hand, his was not a revolt against reason as such. In Hamann, irrationality normally indicates opposition to enlightened reason. Berdyaev did not think he was arguing for irrationality as an epistemological given but for freedom as the spring of cultural potentiality and which always remains beyond rational inquiry.[80]

Berdyaev is an example of a thinker who has seen that the problem of modernity is largely the result of an inability to marry norm and freedom. Thinkers who accept independent absolute norms lean toward rationality, while those who accept nebulous freedom tend toward irrationality. Political history, according to Frame, records the excesses of each direction, of either totalitarianism or anarchy, a subject that will play more prominently in a moment.[81] Balancing authority and freedom therefore becomes a compelling subject for Frame. So let us ask two questions. What are some notable differences between Frame and Berdyaev? And in what sense is Frame's solution to the norm/freedom dichotomy compelling?

For one, Frame locates the impetus in people to craft culture in a biblical/theological point of reference, specifically, the Cultural Mandate and the Great Commission of Scripture. Tracing the Cultural Mandate from Genesis 1:28 to the new covenant, he presents the Great Commission "as a 'republication' of the Cultural Mandate for the semieschatolgical age."[82] The congruence of these twin mandates is a logical entailment in Frame of the binding nature of the kingdom in all ages and on all people. Therefore, "Just as Adam was to take care of the garden (Gen. 2:15), so Adam's family was to take care of the earth."[83] As such, the Great Commission occasions a holistic message, such that "the preaching of the church presents to the world a way of life that transforms everything, including politics."[84] The fall does not therefore negate the Cultural Mandate, not even for unregenerate people, for we are all Adam's family.

Furthermore, Berdyaev speaks in Christian tones, but his thought is dependent on the existential tradition of which Sartre is the apex. With both Berdyaev and Sartre, existence precedes essence; in Berdyaev's case, the existence of freedom is prior to Being and God. From a Framian perspective, that makes freedom an impersonal force and God a contingent being like the rest of us. We may well find here an example of what Frame calls the "rational/irrational" tension. Berdyaev, like Kant, makes God an extension of thought and is therefore guilty of rationalism. But because freedom in Berdyaev is beyond rational inquiry, he is guilty of the irrationalism of Hamann, though Berdyaev would deny the claim.

Finally, there is Berdyaev's distinction between the *individual* and the *person*. His existentialism operates on the idea that people are only individuals, parts of nature, until the time their inherent value is actualized and developed through the free action of creativity. What actualizes personhood is *personality*, through which we reflect God and his creativeness.[85] In Frame's system, people's impetus to create lay externally in the norm of the Cultural Mandate and internally in their inherent design in the *imago Dei* as co-creators. Their personhood is not a holding pattern until they create. They are created as fully formed persons with personality *to be* stewards of the non-rational creation. So, in contrast to Berdyaev, Frame's response to Kantian rationalism is based in his acceptance of the limits of reason, yet he also recognizes God as ultimate norm. He answers the irrationalism of Hamann by accepting the realm of mystery, yet he also recognizes that God has provided sufficient means to real truth.

Medical Ethics

To explore something of the meaning of this discussion for cultural ethics, I segue to a point Frame makes in the context of medical ethics. In a review of the book *Christian Faith, Health, and Medical Practice*, Frame counters the authors' notion that because "Human freedom presupposes an established self," this "implies that we should never give medical treatment without a person's 'informed consent.'"[86] Although Scripture does not give "divine warrant" to doctors to force care, says Frame, "That fact, however, is not based on the patient's metaphysical freedom."[87] That is not to say that government and/or parental authorities cannot override a patient's choice.

The point is "rather that God has not authorized the medical community to overrule it."[88]

Frame's position on "informed consent" is consistent with a broader outline in his writings on the historic difficulty of balancing norm and freedom in cultural activity. This point is especially salient in reading Frame on political freedom. On the fifth commandment, he has much to say about the propensity of secular, rationalist thinkers to argue for a law-based society, in which only the very smart, such as themselves, are fit to rule. Conversely, irrationalist thinkers disdain all authority, leading to anarchy, but, of course, on their authority![89] One side violates freedom; the other violates order. Both eventually violate life and true prosperity.

Frame's answer to the historic dilemma is based in the implications of lordship. The state, for example, has a role in our lives, "But this authority is not absolute; it is limited by God's higher authority. . . . In this respect, [rulers] are to reflect God's own covenant presence, his covenant solidarity with his people. . . . So Scripture gives us a charter for limited government and personal liberty."[90] These thoughts can be distilled into a single phrase: *The norm of God and his word do not negate freedom but protect it.* Every social and cultural institution is under the lordship of God and is to function only so far as, but no less than, God has authorized it. We are free to create, build, and do all things cultural, but within the established lines of divine authority.

It is in this context that Frame's transformative vision of culture, especially his controversial call for a "Christian government," finds expression. Again, he is no theocrat but asks, "Should the state be governed by Scripture?"[91] The answer is "Certainly. All of life should be governed by God's word."

He further asks, "Should the state recognize Jesus Christ as king? Yes, for that is who he is—the King of Kings and the Lord of Lords."[92] These specific thoughts are germane to Frame's views on norm and freedom; otherwise, they can be taken as a platform for the forcible imposition of non-Christians to live as Christians. But as I have demonstrated, his cultural theory means to provide a bulwark against the hegemony of self-autonomy and outside forces and to enhance people's experience of human freedom in all areas of life. I said that during the Enlightenment, ordered conceptual analysis of culture was contained in its concept of an ordered universe. And that practical chaos was the inevitable result of Romanticism's conceptual chaos. Frame's commitments in social ethics seek to balance practical order and freedom in the revealed will of the God of norm and freedom.

Attention now turns to an evaluation of Frame's polemical discourse with those whom he finds seriously mistaken on the question of Christianity and culture. This consideration keeps in mind the central question that first inspired this book, "What does lordship mean in the theology of John M. Frame?"

Endnotes

1 Ambrose, *Hexaemeron*, i. cap 6.
2 *TET*.
3 There are many ways that Frame goes about justifying his R1K view. Perhaps the more beneficial list of reasons is given in his article "Is Natural Revelation Sufficient to Govern Culture," reprinted in *DCL*, 951–956. Some may bristle at the inclusion of the "R" in R1K, but the abbreviation follows conventional nomenclature in Reformed circles.
4 Frame does not organize in systematic form all data that he thinks leads to the one kingdom finding. Rather, that finding arises in varied didactic discourses, all arranged around particular issues of practical importance.
5 *DCL*, 611.
6 Although earlier this general summary was made with regard to the whole of Frame's theology, it seems most apparent in his theology of culture.
7 To this, I can add in-compatibilist schemas of nature against grace (Thomas), *res corporea* against and *res cogitans* (Descartes), and individualism and multiculturalism (Lyotard).
8 B. Walsh and J. Middleton, *The Transforming Vision: Shaping a Christian World View* (Downers Grove, IL: InterVarsity Press, 1984), 93.
9 *TET*, 79.
10 *DCL*, 863.
11 *TET*, 854.
12 These are my terms for what I see as the three main branches of Frame's method, all leading to "how" he arrives at the R1K position, as opposed to two divided kingdoms, represented by the spiritual and material worlds.
13 *DWG*, 157. Of God's control, it is his prerogative to tell his creatures [and cultures] what to do (see *DCL*, 22). And "God's very being is ethically normative" for all cultural aspects of the world." *DCL*, 133.
14 It is worth noting that Frame does not refer to himself as a "neo-Calvinist," although others identify him as such, but as a Calvinist. The word *neo-Calvinism* was used by Barthians in the 1930s in a derogatory way. Nowadays, the term is used in a less pejorative sense. Frame does not distance himself from this epitaph due to the Barthian attack. He is simply more at home with the older nomenclature and sees no reason to change. On Calvin's commitment to the idea of a work of God that provides a reason for the positive contributions of unsaved men to society, he writes, "The most certain and easy solution of this question, however, is, that those virtues are not the common properties of nature, but the peculiar graces of God, which he dispenses in great variety, and in a certain degree to men that are otherwise profane." *Institutes* 2.3.4. Cf., 2.2.16. For Kuyper on common grace, see Abraham Kuyper, *De Gemeene Gratie*, vols. 1–3 (Leiden: 1902–05). (The latest edition is through Nabu Press, 2011.)
15 More fully, Kuyper defines common grace as "that act of God by which negatively He curbs the operations of Satan, death, and sin, and by which positively He creates an intermediate state for this cosmos, as well as for our human race, which is and continues

to be deeply and radically sinful, but in which sin cannot work out its end." Quoted in C. H. Spurgeon, *Free Will—A Slave* (Allentown, PA: Sword and Trowel, 1973), 17–18.
16 *DG*, 429.
17 In light of God's common grace, "[God] has chosen to write a drama and spread it out in temporal sequence. . . . So he tolerates evil for a time . . . waiting until later to judge it fully." *DG*, 432.
18 A. Kuyper, *De Gemeene Gratie*, vols. 1–3 (1902–1905), 05:2:601. Now, to be true to Frame's own view of the matter, he sees his views as consistent with those of Kuyper, whom he sees stressing common grace in the larger context of God's redemptive schema, but different from Charles Hodge—one among many "Reformed writers . . . who restrict common grace to the beneficial effects of the gospel upon society." *DG*, 430; also important is n. 43 of *DG*. But as I have said, we see an even deeper difference between Frame and Kuyper within the common grace as it relates to redemption.
19 N. Ansell, "It's about Time: Opening Our Reformational Paradigm to the Eschaton," *Calvin Theological Journal* 47, no. 1 (April 2012): 1–2. Paper first presented at the Institute for Christian Studies, September 26, 2003.
20 According to Calvin, "It is a fact that the law of God which we call the moral law is nothing else than a testimony of the natural law and of that conscience which God has engraved upon the minds of men. Consequently, the entire scheme of this equity of which we are now speaking has been proscribed in it. Hence, this equity alone must be the goal and rule and limit of all laws." *Institutes* 4.20.15. Readers may consult Gregory Johnson, who explains Calvin's observation, saying, "The law of God, the moral law, the natural law, the conscience engraved by God on the human mind, equity—all are here equated as having essentially the same content. And this natural law is the same as what Calvin calls the "perpetual rule of love," summarized in the Decalogue, and is seen manifest in the "common laws of the nations." Gregory Johnson, "Natural Law and Positive Law in Calvin's Thought" (1996), http://gregscouch.homestead.com/files/calvinlaw.html#_ftn1; date of access: Jan. 16, 2013.
21 Kuyper speaks to this point in *Lectures on Calvinism* (Grand Rapids, MI: Eerdmans, 1931; first published in 1898), vi. However, magistrates are never to rule apart from God, as documented in Kuyper, *Lectures on Calvinism*, 79. That this was Kuyper's view is supported by V. Bacote, *The Spirit in Public Theology: Appropriating the Legacy of Abraham Kuyper* (Eugene, OR: Wipf and Stock Publishers, 2010), 81.
22 A. Kuyper, *Lectures on Calvinism*, 99.
23 *DCL*, 617.
24 D. VanDrunen, "Abraham Kuyper and the Reformed Natural Law and Two Kingdoms Traditions," *Calvin Theological Journal* 42, no. 2 (2007): 284. A potent reply to VanDrunen's reading of Kuyper is Timothy P. Palmer, "The Two-Kingdom Doctrine: A Comparative of Martin Luther and Abraham Kuyper," *Pro Rege* 37, no. 3 (March 2009): 13–23. Palmer's copious reply is also electronically recorded at http://www.dordt.edu/publications/pro_rege/crcpi/Pro_Rege_Mar_2009.pdf. Along these same lines and instructive is Ryan C. McIlhenny, "Presentism and the Two Kingdoms

Perspective," *Pro Rege* 42, no. 3: 16–22. Electronically filed at http://www.dordt.edu/publications/pro_rege/crcpi/Pro_Rege_Mar_2014.pdf.
25 A. Kuyper, *Lectures on Calvinism*, 104. In "A Pamphlet on the Reformation of the Churches" (1883), Kuyper shows concern for the original language of Article 36 of the Belgic Confession on "The Civil Government." That article gives civil government the responsibility over the protection of true religion. It states in part, "And the government's task is not limited to caring for and watching over the public domain but extends also to upholding the sacred ministry, with a view to removing and destroying all idolatry and false worship of the Antichrist; to promoting the kingdom of Jesus Christ; and to furthering the preaching of the gospel everywhere; to the end that God may be honored and served by everyone, as he requires in his Word." What Kuyper opposed, however, was reading into the article the necessity to kill heretics and not, as some have suggested, the general idea that the state has a God-given mandate to assist the church. So he wrote in the pamphlet, "We would rather be considered not Reformed and insist that men ought not to kill heretics, than that we are left with the Reformed name as the prize for assisting in the shedding of the blood of heretics." The pamphlet is electronically filed at http://standardbearer.rfpa.org/series/Pamphlet-Concerning-the-Reformation-of-the-Church.
26 Because Scripture does not use the language of "grace" as a benefit to the unregenerate, Frame goes as far as to question Kuyper's language of a "common grace," preferring instead God's "common goodness, or common love" to explain the delay of God's judgment, the basis for God's blessings to all, and the general knowledge of God and of things appurtenant to all people. For this, see *DG*, 429. That would align Frame with Kuyper more on aspects relative to soteriology than on cultural philosophy, though the two are not inseparable.
27 In Schilder's enduring work *Christ and Culture*, trans. G. van Rongen and W. Helder (Winnipeg: Premier Publishing, 1977), the author refers to Genesis 1:28 as the "creation mandate" and later as the Cultural Mandate. Schilder often alludes to the Cultural Mandate as "the ABCs" of the first days of the world and, at other times, as the "first principles of the world" (13, 16).
28 Again, this quote is found in *DCL*, 863.
29 J. M. Frame, "Responding to Some Articles." 856.
30 K. Schilder, *Christ and Culture*, trans. G. van Rongen and W. Helder (Winnipeg: Premier Publishing, 1977), 54.
31 So strong is that ethical standard that Schilder went as far as to say that cultural escapism is sin. "First of all, we must emphasize that, since there is a Cultural Mandate that existed even prior to sin, abstention from cultural labour is always sin: those who abstain from it are on strike." Schilder, *Christ and Culture*, 68.
32 That is not to say that Kuyper was anything less than clear on the antithesis. He says, "[W]e, of course, have to acknowledge two kinds of human consciousness: that of the regenerate and the unregenerate; and these two cannot be identical. . . . If, therefore, it be true that man's own consciousness is his *primum verum*, and hence must be also the starting-point for every scientist, then the logical conclusion is that it is an impossibility

that both should agree, and that every endeavor to make them agree must be doomed to failure." Kuyper, *Lectures on Calvinism*, 137. Despite this, he still wants to say that God is in some way delighted with the cultural work of the unregenerate. Both Kuyper and Herman Bavinck used Revelation 21:24–26 to say that God is so pleased with the excellencies of unregenerate culture that he will gladly receive them into the New Jerusalem. Referenced in Richard J. Mouw, *He Shines in All That's Fair: Culture and Common Grace* (Grand Rapids, MI: Eerdmans, 2001), 50. Kuyper speaks to this idea in "Uniformity: The Curse of Modern Life" (lecture given in Amsterdam, April 22, 1869). An English translation of the exact quote is published in James D. Bratt, ed., *Abraham Kuyper: A Centennial Reader* (Grand Rapids, MI: Eerdmans/Carlisle: Paternoster Press, 1998), 199. Bavinck makes this point in *Reformed Dogmatics*, vol. 4, *Holy Spirit, Church, and New Creation* (Grand Rapids, MI: Baker, 2008), 720. Berkhof agrees that "the cultural treasures of the nations" will be brought into the New Jerusalem. See *Christian Faith* (Grand Rapids, MI: Eerdmans, revised 1991), 543.

33 In *DCL*, 600–660, Frame uses the word *state* in its narrow sense of a nation's government, but at times he can also use it in the broader meaning of "nation." Compare the use of these words in pages 600–601 of *DCL*.

34 He can speak of "both kingdoms," *DCL*, 258, or even "two kingdoms," *DCL*, 601.

35 Ibid., 610.

36 A. Kuyper, *Lectures on Calvinism*, 90.

37 *DCL*, 616.

38 See J. Budziszewski, *Evangelicals in the Public Square: Four Formative Voices on Political Thought and Action* (Grand Rapids, MI: Baker Academic, 2006), 59.

39 *DCL*, 616.

40 J. Lief, "Is Neo-Calvinism Calvinist? A Neo-Calvinist Engagement of Calvin's 'Two Kingdoms' Doctrine," *Pro Rege* 37, no. 3 (March 2009): 7.

41 Ibid., 4.

42 Leif reveals Calvin's connection between the unity of the two natures of Christ and the unification of the body and soul relationship in people. Reference *Institutes*, 2.15.1. From here, Leif traces the analogy to Calvin's soteriology, in which the inseparable link between justification and sanctification has rich meaning for culture. Calvin writes, "The whole may be thus summed up: Christ given to us by the kindness of God is apprehended and possessed by faith, by means of which we obtain in particular a twofold benefit: first, being reconciled by the righteousness of Christ, God becomes, instead of a judge, an indulgent Father; and secondly, being sanctified by his Spirit, we aspire to integrity and purity of life." *Institutes* 3.11.16–23. The spiritual benefit of Christ restores us to love of God, while the temporal benefit of Christ restores us to our love of our fellow man. "Rooted within this soteriological unity of justification and sanctification we discover Calvin's basis for a Christian engagement of culture life. Vocation specifically becomes the means by which believers fully engage the cultural life, using their gifts to 'cultivate the particular department that has been assigned to [them]' for the benefit of their neighbor." Leif quoting Calvin's "Commentary on Matthew 22:39," which is electronically filed at http://www.ccel.org/ccel/calvin/calcom31.html.

43 H. Kraus, "The Contemporary Relevance of Calvin's Theology," in *Toward the Future of Reformed Theology: Tasks, Topics, Traditions*, ed. D. Willis-Watkins, M. Welker, and M. Gockel (Grand Rapids, MI: Eerdmans, 1999), 324.
44 Ibid., 324.
45 Ibid.
46 So, then, rather than two "institutional forms," Frame prefers to maintain the language of the seminal family and to categorize church and state as "two families: the family of Adam and the family of Christ." *DCL*, 601. This means that "What we call 'states,' then, are governmental structures of the family of Adam. 'Church government' is the ruling body of the family of Christ." *DCL*, 601. Calvin does not believe that church government and civil government are antithetical, but he is still willing to speak of "two kingdoms" or "a two-fold government"—or as other scholars have coined it—"two regiments." Calvin takes up the role of civil government most effectively in *Institutes*, 4.20.2. And for his differentiation between "two kingdoms," which is really a discussion based in the context of freedom of individual conscience, see *Institutes*, 3.19.15. Also helpful in defining these matters in Calvin's thought is Sheldon Wolin, "Calvin and the Reformation: The Political Education of Protestantism," *American Political Science Review* 51, no. 2 (1957): 428–453, especially 433.
47 *DCL*, 186.
48 G. Vos, *The Teaching of Jesus Concerning the Kingdom of God and the Church* (New York: American Tract Society, 1903), 85–86.
49 In an email to the author, dated, Jan. 17, 2012.
50 G. Vos, *The Teaching of Jesus Concerning the Kingdom of God and the Church* (New York: American Tract Society, 1903), 162–163. In the same way, Vos notes, "While it is proper to separate between the visible church and such things as the Christian state, Christian art, Christian science, etc., these things, if they truly belong to the kingdom of God, grow up out of the regenerated life of the invisible church." Vos, ibid., 165.
51 Earlier, I evinced differences between van de Beek's somber *theologia crucis* and Frame's regnant "theology from above." But even there, the covenant lordship of God, not the risen Christ, is the starting point for Frame.
52 *DG*, 272.
53 These select examples are easily found by referencing the indexes in Frame's dogmatics. A section that strongly ties lordship together with dominion is *DCL*, 225, where the resurrection has exalted Jesus and whereby he has fulfilled Adam's lost dominion. All the same, I cannot help but note that the immediate context of this point is not the lordship of Christ over culture, but the relationship of angels to the situational perspective in ethics.
54 *DCL*, 954–955.
55 R. Pippin, *Modernism as a Philosophical Problem*, 2nd ed. (Oxford: Blackwell Publishers, 1999), xii.
56 *DCL*, 857.
57 Ibid.
58 Ibid., 858.
59 Ibid.

60 Though written before Foucault, a good treatment on the attempt to eliminate the innate ideal of God is Friedrich Schleiermacher, *On Religion: Speeches to Its Cultured Despisers* (London: Trubner and Co., 1893), 39. The tempting thing about "the Infinite" is that it is impersonal and thus broad enough to mentally consolidate into one's own view of reality (or the Infinite). And this is largely how Schleiermacher treated it. So Schleiermacher's question became more of an apologetic within his own circles and less of a force for religious reformation. Cornelius Van Til stated in a far more biblical context than did Schleiermacher that in every area of life "There is no alternative but that of theonomy and autonomy." Cornelius Van Til, *Christian Theistic Ethics* (Ripon, CA: Den Dulk Foundation, 1971), 134.

61 Above all, see Michel Foucault, *The Order of Things: An Archaeology of the Human Sciences* (New York: Vintage Books, 1970).

62 Roland Barthes, *Mythologies*, trans. Annette Lavers (New York: Hill and Wang, 1972), 16.

63 Fichte's pronouncement caused him to lose his chair at Jena. Despite this, his new views influenced Schleiermacher and the Schlegel brothers.

64 F. Nietzsche, *The Portable Nietzsche*, ed. and trans. W. Kaufman (New York: Penguin Books, 1982), 20.

65 Source: A. Grafton, G. Most, and S. Settis, eds., *The Classical Tradition* (Cambridge, MA: Harvard University Press, 2010), 421. Mark Blitz further explains, "The place of Nietzsche in Heidegger's analysis is simple: Nietzsche's work is the end of philosophy, end in the sense that with him the basic possibilities of metaphysics are completed, and, indeed, exhausted. This is especially clear for the modern metaphysics of subjectivity, with its evident emphasis on 'will,' but as Heidegger sees it, the possibilities that Nietzsche unfolds ultimately are contained in metaphysics as Plato originated it." Mark Blitz, "Heidegger's *Nietzsche* (Part II), *Political Science Reviewer* (1993): 57. See also Martin Heidegger, *Nietzsche*, vol. 4: *Nihilism*, trans. David Farrell Krell (New York: Harper & Row Publishers, 1982), 63. Of further significance for this study, see Gregory B. Smith, *Nietzsche, Heidegger, and the Transition to Postmodernity* (Chicago: University of Chicago Press, 1996).

66 Mark Blitz, "Heidegger's *Nietzsche*, Part II," *Political Science Reviewer* (1993), http://www.scribd.com/doc/131706077/Blitz-Mark-Heidegger-s-Nietzsche; date of access: January 22, 2013.

67 L. Chamberlain, "Back to Origins: Heidegger through Post-Darwinian Eyes," *TLS* 5578 (February 2010): 18.

68 Retrieved at Frame, http://www.frame-poythress.org/frame_articles/1999Traditionalism.htm#_edn12; date of access: Jan. 24, 2013. "Van Til even spoke of antithesis between Christianity and secular learning. He did not mean to say that everything in secular philosophy and science was false, but that it was deeply flawed by an anti-Christian epistemology and could never be taken for granted." *DCL*, 890. This idea circles back to Frame's reflection on secular ethics, viz. there is truth in all secular ethics, but that truth is not complete, and even the truth assumed is curtailed by autonomous assumptions.

69 *DCL*, 888. By "world," Frame is referring to John's use of the *kosmos* in the heightened ethical sense of any obstacle to the cause of Christ.
70 Ibid., 892.
71 Ibid., 893.
72 See A. G. Baumgarten, *Initia philosophiae practicae primae* (1760; reprinted in [KGS] XIX), §100. This section of my book is greatly indebted to Josef Schmucker's important *Die Ursprünge der Ethik Kants* (Meisenheim: Verlag Anton Hain, 1961), esp. 278ff.
73 Kant's critique of Baumgarten is thus tied to his conception of legislation. Kant said, "Thus no one, including God, is the author of the moral laws, since they do not spring from the will [choice], but are practically necessary." In Paul Menzer, *Eine Vorlesung Kants Über Ethik* (Berlin: Pan Verlag Rolf Heise, 1924), 61–63. For an extended discussion on Kant's theory of self-legislation, see *Patrick Paul Kain*, "Kant's Moral Constructivism and his Conception of Legislation," *Archiv für Geschichte der Philosophie* 86 (2004): 257–306.
74 See Erich Loewenthal, ed., *Sturm und Drang: Kritische Schriften* (Heidelberg: Verlag Lambert Schneider, 1963), p. 148.
75 Berdyaev: "I am thinking of Boehme, who is not only a great German mystic, but also one of the greatest mystics of all time; and particularly of his *The Dark Nature of God* . . . Somewhere, in immeasurably greater depths, there exists a state which may be called *Ungrund* or groundlessness to which neither human words nor the categories of good and evil nor those of being or non-being are applicable." Nikolai Berdyaev, *The Meaning of History*, 2nd ed., trans. George Reavey (London: Centenary Press, 1936), 54–55.
76 McLachlan writes, "Boehme's dialectical voluntarism is based on the image of groundlessness which is the beginning of the development of Being. The *Ungrund* contains within it all of the antimonies, but they are unrealized and only potential: Boehme calls the *Ungrund* the eternal silence." James Morse McLachlan, *The Desire to Be God: Freedom and the Other in Sartre and Berdyaev* (New York: Peter Lang Publishing, 1992), 124.
77 J. McLachlan, *The Desire to Be God: Freedom and the Other in Sartre and Berdyaev* (New York: Peter Lang Publishing, 1992), 122. Definitive as well is McLachlan's important paper "Nicolas Berdyaev's Existentialist Personalism." *Personalist Forum* 8, no. 1 (1992): 57–65.
78 His seminal and most enduring work is *The Meaning of the Creative Act*, trans. Donald A. Lowrie (London: Victor Gollancz, Ltd., 1955).
79 Nikolai Berdyaev, *Dream and Reality* (New York; Collier Books, 1962), 208–209.
80 This point is made well by Isaiah Berlin, *The Magus of the North: J. G. Hamann and the Origins of Modern Irrationalism*, ed. Henry Hardy (London: Fontana Press, 1993), 39 ff.
81 See *DCL*, 49, for an able dissection of these twin problems in cultural history.
82 *DCL*, 310.
83 Ibid., 856.
84 Ibid., 616.

85 He says, "Man is a person only if he is a free spirit reflecting the supreme Being." N. Berdyaev, *Towards a New Epoch*, trans. Oliver Fielding Clarke (London: Geoffrey Bles, 1949), 23.

86 *DCL*, 987–988. See Hessel Bouma III, Douglas Diekema, Edward Langerak, Theodore Rottman, and Allen Verhey, *Christian Faith, Health, and Medical Practice* (Grand Rapids, MI: Eerdmans, 1989). Frame's article originally appeared in *Christian Renewal* (June 18, 1990): 16–17.

87 *DCL*, 988.

88 Ibid.

89 See ibid., 602–604. "Arguments for law and order, carried out consistently, lead to totalitarianism. Arguments for freedom lead to anarchy." Ibid., 602.

90 Ibid., 48.

91 Frame rejects "the view that modern governments should follow the Mosaic civil law in exhaustive detail." *DCL*, 60. But he finds some merit in theonomic teaching without embracing theonomy. For examples, "Penultimate Thoughts on Theonomy," at http://www.frame-poythress.org/penultimate-thoughts-on-theonomy/; "Review of Bahnsen's Theonomy in Christian Ethics," at http://www.frame-poythress.org/review-of-bahnsens-theonomy-in-christian-ethics/; and "Review of R. J. Rushdooney, *The Institutes of Biblical Law*, in *DCL*, 957–978. Elsewhere, Frame chides theonomists for overestimating the simplicity of their position, without distinguishing adequately between ceremonial and cultural laws. E.g., John M. Frame (1990), "The One, the Many, and Theonomy," in William S. Barker and W. Robert Godfrey, eds., *Theonomy: A Reformed Critique* (Grand Rapids, MI: Zondervan, 1991), chapter 4.

92 *DCL*, 602.

Chapter 10

Lordship and the Question of One Kingdom or Two

Polemics on R1K vs. R2K

Within Reformed circles, there is mounting dismissal of transformationist, public theologies as neo-Calvinist, New School, semi-liberal, and less than true to sola-fideism. "One Kingdom" and "neo-Calvinist"—ideals once held in honor among Reformed thinkers—are increasingly viewed as pejoratives. Men on the other side of the fissure, mainly in America, identify themselves as R2K, Klinean, non-transformationist, natural law advocates, and classical, Old School Calvinists. Most vocal among the budding movement are, in Frame's view, most of the theologians at Westminster Theological Seminary (Escondido, California).

Frame is absolutely firm that the Escondido theologians believe that cultural transformation is exclusively eschatological: "that the blessings of salvation are all 'spiritual,' that God promises to believers no 'temporal' blessings until the return of Christ."[1] Society is governed by Providence, and the only standard we can bring to bear on culture is natural law, not the Bible. Darryl Hart's *A Secular Faith*, the natural law theology of David VanDrunen, the Lutheran two kingdoms view, and the republication of the covenant of works in the Mosaic Law idea are important sources of their thinking.

Regarding their seminal inspiration, "The Escondido theologians, under the influence of Meredith Kline . . . sharpened Luther's sacred/secular dichotomy into a broad distinction between church and culture."[2] I will return to this point. However, if Frame is right, then the preponderance of teachers at Escondido are following Kline's premise that the Sabbath is intrinsic to the whole of Israelite life under God's theocratic rule, whereby all is holy, not common. Kline reads into the theocratic life of Israel a strict segregation of cult and culture, whereby, "In the new covenant, culture reverts to the common grace status it had from Adam to Moses, and in the nations outside Israel. It is no longer holy, but common. God gives no covenant promise to the common culture today."[3]

In the conviction that these theologians represent "a distinctive school of thought," Frame has reacted, rather uncharacteristically, with stinging force. *The Escondido Theology* is the result.[4] The main areas of disagreement between Frame and Escondido on R2K center on the law/gospel distinction and natural law theory.

Law and Gospel

Frame's most unsympathetic appraisal of what he deems to be an extreme division between law and gospel at Escondido is reserved for Michael Horton's *Christless Christianity* and *Covenant and Eschatology*. Here the focus will be only on Frame's evaluation of *Christless Christianity.*[5] Horton sets himself up as an easy target for censure when he says of law and gospel, "It is important to point out that law and gospel do not simply refer to the Ten Commandments and John 3:16, respectively. Everything in the Bible that reveals God's moral expectations is *law* and everything in the Bible that reveals God's saving purposes and acts is *gospel*."[6] Horton's law/gospel delineation occurs within the context of his scathing evaluation of Joel Osteen, whom he charges with preaching vapid moralisms that lack the condemnation of the Law. From here, Frame is able to present a valid judgment of Horton: "But for [Horton] the law must always bring condemnation, so that he doesn't think one is really preaching the law unless he preaches it as condemnation."[7] Frame is quite correct that Horton is out of accord with classic Reformed theology, in that he is only willing to preach the Law to reveal one's need for justification but not unto sanctification.[8] Relating all of this back to the context with Osteen, "[Horton] cannot seem to reconcile himself to the fact that redemption involves sanctification as well as justification. . . . so when Osteen presents a message that almost entirely lacks a focus on justification, Horton replies with an emphasis entirely lacking in sanctification."[9]

Significantly, the law/gospel contrast that undergirds Horton's dichotomy between justification and morality has repercussions for culture. The same gospel that does not stress personal change, as its stress lies on what has been accomplished for us, does not infer a worldview and has no relevance for "societal change."[10] At stake for Frame is the fact that Christianity presents a distinct ethic, metaphysic, and epistemology. Consequently, its worldview is unmistakable and hence unavoidable. Because believers are called to do all to the glory of God, all sorts of injustices in the world must therefore be objects of our worldview. Stated in terms of lordship, without a lived-out faith the gospel is an abstraction.

To add to Frame's evaluation of Horton is my conclusion that one of the negative motivations for the bifurcation of law and gospel among most of the Escondido theologians is their correct and vehement rejection of Theonomy and Federal Vision. However, there is a temptation to swing to the opposite extreme when one's theological polemic is governed by negative factors. This very tendency can be seen in a critique of Rick Lusk and James Jordan by John V. Fesko, professor of systematic theology and historical theology at Escondido. Fesko claims that Lusk and Jordan reject the covenant of works in their adherence to Federal Vision. Fesko sees the heart of Lusk/Jordon problem in this remark by Lusk, who traces the history of theological dualisms to the likes of Peter Ramus: "Ramus developed an alternative to Aristotelian logic, based on a dichotomizing method that arranged ideas in two's, e.g., law vs. gospel, nature vs. grace, faith vs. works, reason vs. revelation, wrathful God vs. merciful Christ, covenant of works vs. covenant of grace, etc. The Ramist system rapidly became master rather than servant of the biblical revelation, fragmenting the unity of the Scriptural narrative."[11] Fesko blames Lusk (and Jordan) for dismantling the apartheid of law and gospel, based on what they see as the erroneous theory and influence of Ramus, in order to make room for "works" in redemption.

What Lusk and Jordan have missed, as well as Fesko's retort, is that Ramus's primary argument was against Quintilian (and, by extension, Aristotle and Cicero), whom he felt had given far too much epistemic propriety to rhetoric. The rest is an unwarranted extrapolation by Lusk and Jordan. Despite that, it is Fesko's reply to Lusk that ties to this discussion. He quotes the Westminster Shorter Catechism, followed by a brief commentary: "'Faith in Jesus Christ is a saving grace, whereby we receive and rest upon him alone for salvation, as he is offered to us in the gospel' (SC, q. 86). Notice the divines make no mention of obedience in their definition of faith."[12] For the sake of space, this one statement is typical of the problem Frame sees at Escondido: a hard and fast junction between law (obedience) and gospel.

The catechism is correct in its definition of faith. What Fesko overlooks is that it is only that, and not a definition of Christian living *coram Deo*. In other words, the gospel cannot be reduced to justification by faith. Instead, "[T]he gospel in the New Testament is the good news that the kingdom of God has come in Jesus."[13] Or he can say, "It is the reign of God that is good news, news that ensures peace and salvation."[14] Frame's consistent conclusion on the relationship of law and gospel is perspectival. "As gospel includes law, so does law include gospel. . . . so the definitions that sharply separate law and gospel break down on careful analysis. In both law and gospel, God proclaims his saving work and demands that his people respond by obeying his commands. . . . Each concept is meaningless apart from the other. Each implies the other."[15]

Although virtually any effort to speak of law and gospel, law and obedience, and grace and obedience in the same breath almost always triggers the rash propensity of our epistemological faculties to opt for one over the other, Frame is clear that we are not dealing here with mere theological categories. Scripture confronts us with the living God who wants all of us: heart, soul, and mind. And as was made abundantly clear by now, the meaning of lordship in Frame's theology of culture always sees kingship as no less than a universal prerogative. Only from this elevated biblical revelation of the lordship of God over his creatures are the whole of God's demands on us consistently expressed and appropriated.

Natural Law and the Bible

The R1K systematization is most often justified on the grounds of its selection of natural law as the sole, preferred moral compass for a public theology. Accordingly, natural law is thought to provide an ethically normative account of how life is to be lived in the civil kingdom that is rationally discernible by all. Escondido theologian David VanDrunen provides helpful argumentation in defense of this concept. He defines natural law as "the moral order inscribed in the world and especially in human nature, an order that is known to all people through their natural faculties (especially reason and/or conscience) even apart from supernatural divine revelation that binds morally the whole human race."[16] The definition is positioned in such a way as to justify a distinct and functional revelation of God that operates "even apart from supernatural divine revelation."[17] This is not a mere heuristic division but a fragmentizing of natural law and special revelation that in the end leaves them essentially incompatible.[18]

Beginning with the creation narrative, VanDrunen argues that God gave Adam a command to rule over the earth but only as "the image of God carried with it a natural law, a law inherent to human nature and directing human beings to fulfill their royal commission."[19] Tracing this ostensible work of natural law from Adam to Noah, he asserts an administration of a "civil" order under Noah, in contradistinction to the covenant with Abraham, which dealt only with "religious, redemptive affairs."[20]

Contra VanDrunen, Frame's lordship theology insists on a civil code of conduct grounded in nature but made manifestly plain by special revelation. Frame impeaches VanDrunen for using natural law to fabricate a bifurcated reality, in which God mediates "civil" issues by natural law and "spiritual" issues by supernatural revelation. Interacting directly with VanDrunen's exegesis of Genesis 1–3, Frame objects to an all-sufficient natural law to Adam's native and moral conscience, pointing out in addition that "Adam received direction from supernatural divine words directed to him."[21]

Contradicting VanDrunen's assessment of a "civil order" only under Noah, Frame retorts, "God's promise to Noah is an encouragement to believers that the apparent delay of Jesus' return is part of God's redemptive plan (2 Peter 3:4)." Frame is saying that the Noahic covenant prepares for the working out of other redemptive covenants (Jer. 33:20–21) and is a covenant instituted in connection with a sacrifice of atonement. It thus cannot be relegated to God's post-flood economic provision for a "common, cultural realm."[22]

A further example of Frame's contestation is with VanDrunen's finding in Job and other passages of Scripture the basis for a prototypical, non-religious, civil kingdom that unites "a common humanity."[23] Castigating the idea, Frame retorts that VanDrunen pays too little attention to the seminal passage, Romans 1, which specifies that although the fall has not eradicated mankind's sense of the Law, it has so distorted it that competing gods and moral systems are now more attractive.[24] This paradoxical situation is further exacerbated by the prevailing religious pluralism, in which there are real competing value systems at work in societies worldwide. Only the voice of special revelation is a full corrective to secularists and/or pluralists who are not inclined to concede to the God of creation.

In his review of VanDrunen's book, Nelson D. Kloosterman underscores the epistemological and ethical challenges facing fallen men to respond to a civil ethic predicated in natural law only.

> Natural revelation communicates truth about God, about right and wrong, and about oneself; nevertheless, special revelation is absolutely required (positively) to apprehend these truths, and (negatively) to correct inevitable misapprehensions drawn by fallen creatures from natural

> revelation. Second, as to the ethical objection, the will of the unregenerate person is incapable of conforming to a true code of morality derived from creation, since the natural man cannot, does not, and will not do what he in some measure senses to be good and right, since he actively suppresses all truth in unrighteousness.[25]

To clarify Frame's dispute with VanDrunen on natural law, I return ever so briefly to Frame's disagreement with Van Til on "antithesis." Frame critiques Van Til for being inconsistent and even wrong at times in characterizing the unbeliever as unable to utter so much as a true proposition, while failing to provide an adequate explanation for how the unbeliever can simultaneously do and know many things that seem good and true. Frame replies that for Van Til to say that unregenerate people *always* misinterpret revelation is to read too much into the doctrine of total depravity. And for Van Til to say that general revelation is an objective disclosure with no restraining power over sin is to read too little into the doctrine of common grace. On total depravity, Frame believes that the effects of the fall are not *absolute* on man's psychical faculties, but they are *complete* as grounds for condemnation. Regarding common grace, although fallen men cannot discern good and evil on an autonomous basis correctly, they can, for example, rescue a drowning child. Nonetheless, such good things are done in a *restricted* sense, viz., not in accordance with God's higher criteria of goal, standard, and motive. The affiliation of this discussion with VanDrunen is this. Frame agrees with VanDrunen that natural law can be *known* by non-Christians apart from Scripture, but apart from VanDrunen it cannot be "*rightly used*" in the context of a theistic worldview.[26]

What are Frame's various rationales for rejecting natural law as wholly determinative for public life? His reasons are multitudinous. However, in my view, three ideas are crucial and illustrative of how lordship settles the natural law issue for Frame.

First, Frame agrees with the presuppositionalism of Cornelius Van Til that "the idea that there is some impersonal mechanism called 'nature' or 'natural law' that governs the universe is absent from the Bible."[27] Frame understands that nature is not a "brute fact"—autonomous from its Maker. His propensity is to react to the presentation of natural forces acting on the intellect as improper when, according to Scripture, non-rational objects or forces like gravity and weather are only ever secondary causes of God. Frame is not adjusting Thomas Aquinas, who thought of natural law (*lex naturalis*) in the Platonic sense of "nothing else than the rational creature's participation of the eternal law."[28] Rather, with reference to the lordship principle of CAP, behind all natural data, whether external or internal to man, "even behind the apparent randomness of events, stands the personal God who *controls* all things by his powerful word" (italics added).[29]

Second, it is my view that Frame's negative response to natural law as foundational for cultural science is one with his logic that the secular advance in philosophy and theology has damaged the biblical metaphysic. It has been said that the legacy of a modern age is the Enlightenment project that created an anti-metaphysical spirit in Europe. Frame is of this very opinion. Out of his polemic against metaphysical skepticism—for example, Barth's "wholly other," the existential theology of Bultmann, and Moltmann and Pannenberg's linear theories history—comes an association in his mind of these errors with the substitution of natural law for divine law. Incidentally, when Frame cites Kant as a mouthpiece for metaphysical skepticism, I do not think that Frame gives enough credit to Kant for attempting to rescue metaphysics from the Age of Reason.[30] Just the same, CAP forms the basis of his retort to the aforementioned substitution. Thus, on the metaphysical plane,

> He deserves the role of Lord, because he is different in nature from all his creatures. Not everyone can *control* all the events of nature and history—only one with unique nature. Not everyone can speak with absolute *authority*—only one who is such a being that he has the right to be obeyed. Not everyone can be *covenantally present* to the whole universe, remaining distinct from it. To perform these functions, one must be different from all other beings, possessing a distinct nature" (italics added).[31]

Third, Frame's position on miracles illustrates his thought process on lordship relative to natural law. The typical idea of a miracle is that of God *disrupting* the normal flow of nature. Hume defined a miracle as a "violation of the laws of nature."[32] In a review of Colin Brown's *Miracles and the Critical Mind*, Frame applauds Brown for denying natural events as brute facts, but, negatively, he does not agree with Brown's dichotomy between faith and evidence. Brown's conclusion is that "miracles cannot be the object of scientific investigation, for science can only deal with nature as it is left to itself."[33] Knowledge of God comes only through faith. Without conflating faith and evidence, Frame argues that all facts are faith laden, both in science and in theology. The Brown thesis draws too hard a line between faith and proof. Guiding Frame's issue with Brown is his theological understanding that a miracle is not a *breaking in* to history. It is not as though nature is self-sustaining, but then God decides to interrupt it by way of miracle. In Frame, God upholds nature every second by his providential control, authority, and presence. There is therefore no "sharp distinction between providence and miracle."[34] The difference between the Lord's providential care of nature and a miracle is not, therefore, one of *kind* but of *degree*. A miracle is merely an acceleration or a permutation of data by way of that same divine control, authority, and presence. This intersection of ideas sheds more light on why Frame cannot endorse Brown's chasm between faith and evidentialism regarding miracles. More to the point of this study, it shows why Frame cannot accept Escondido's sharp line between natural law and divine revelation in any area of life, including a social ethic.

The Dutch Philosophy of Law Idea

This is essentially the basis of Frame's critique of Herman Dooyeweerd.[35] The transition to the culturally oriented Dooyeweerdian philosophy may at once seem to be a bridge too far. But in Frame's thought, modern-day Kuyperians and Klinens share a mutual failing: both consign the role of Scripture to private spirituality, leaving social issues, politics, art, and so on, to the direction of natural law. Theology can indeed sometimes make for strange bedfellows.[36]

Frame rejects the sharp line in Dooyeweerd's philosophy between two forms of thought: "naive experience" and "theoretical thought," or "pre-theoretical" and "theoretical thought." These appositive distinctions suggest essentially that there can be no theoretical knowledge of God or of self. Precisely in keeping with our purposes here, Scripture does not speak directly to any sphere of culture. Rather, such guidance must look to natural law ("creation word") as it is mediated through the voice of philosophy, science, and more. Couched in the traditional language of the Reformed worldview, Dooyeweerd's dualism "furnishes the reason why there can be no theoretical study of the central biblical themes of creation, fall and redemption. . . . It shows us why theology studies only the 'result' of a 'theoretical abstraction' and never 'the full or integral reality' of God."[37] While Kuyper taught that Scripture was relevant to all areas of life, Dooyeweerd emphasized that Scripture deals only with the "realm of faith."

Properly speaking, the "sharp line" in Dooyeweerd's thought is defensible. His interest was to combat dualism in Christian thought. He believed that the history of Christian theology was rife with the bequest of Greek form/matter dualism that drove a wedge between being and meaning. The Greeks' ground motive assumed a thing can exist in itself—apart from its meaning. So when Dooyeweerd speaks against theoretical thought, he has in view this older problem, which he traces to the nature-grace scheme of High Scholasticism and then to the problem of modernity. Against the Greek model, he endorsed the Hebrew thought-world (or ground motive) that accepted life under God as an integrated whole, as God created it. His Cosmonomic philosophy thus seeks a Christian, philosophical framework that abates this age-old split, whereby science, technology, business, and more are accounted for, according to a Christian worldview. Dooyeweerd allocated as many areas of culture under no less than fifteen "modal aspects" of reality.

The similarity with perspectivalism is seen in the Cosmonic idea of *inter-aspect analogy*: each modal aspect is capable of echoing something of the others.[38] For instance, feeling is from the sensitive aspect, but one can have a feeling for justice, or love, or logical correctness, and so on and so forth. Conceptualization is indicative of the analytical aspect, yet we find echoes of it in other aspects, such as economic, for we are able to conceive roughly how much of a tip we think our waiter ought to receive. The modes, however, are irreducible.[39] That is, the nucleus and laws of one modality cannot be fully explained in terms of those of another. Dooyeweerd calls this "sphere sovereignty."

Now Frame would not argue that all of the spheres of life are reducible. A French horn player, for example, must follow the rules of music, which are different from the rules a doctor must follow. Where Frame differs is on the role of Scripture in all phases of reality. The Bible is not a handbook on science, statecraft, or music, but Scripture is *sufficient* for what we *need* to know on any subject. Dooyeweerd, in reacting against the unwillingness of fundamentalism to invest Scripture into any area of culture, on one hand, and the problem of modernity, which he thought had attempted to define essences apart from their meaning, on the other hand, tried a *middle way* of sorts. He retrieved the Hebrew ground motive but made each of his fifteen modal aspects answerable to independent rules known only through natural law.[40] In so doing, though he defended the general Hebrew narrative of creation, fall, and redemption, he placed that narrative outside the reach of Scripture. He also minimized the work and competence of theology amid the vast universe of philosophical interest. This gives the multi-aspectual approach a completely different flavor from perspectivalism, even though both camps agree on the sweeping demands of God's sovereignty over all allegiances.

Luther's Two Kingdoms Worldview

Earlier we gathered from Frame that the point of origination in Escondido's gapping distinction between church and culture is Luther's sacred/secular dichotomy (via Kline). Synoptic attention is therefore given in what follows to the magisterial Reformer's doctrine, in order to test the cogency of Frame's idea.

Deciphering Luther's two kingdoms concept is made difficult by the fact that Luther scholarship is not agreed on the issue.[41] In fact, according to William J. Wright, much of it is spurious. Wright holds that Troeltsch falsely identified Luther's distinction between law and gospel with a narrow effort to do away with the *corpus christianum* ("Christian society") of medieval Europe, in favor of *Eigengesetzlichkeit*—autonomous laws operating over each sphere of earthly life.[42] He furthermore claims that the Niebuhr brothers did the most to foster Troeltsch's errant interpretation of Luther. Complicating matters further is the effort by many Lutheran scholars to resuscitate Luther's two kingdoms doctrine, which was perverted by the Nazis and collaborating German churches.[43] Wright believes that through these and other stimuli, Luther's two kingdoms idea came to be seen as a mere philosophy of state that assumed a dual moral code for private and public life.

We do know that the two kingdoms idea presses for far more than a mere political conception. Luther elicited the idea for the whole of life, distinguishing the invisible church from the world; human arrangements in church, state, and vocational roles; the new man and the old man; heavenly and earthly righteousness; and God and the devil. We also know that within the political sphere, the attribution to Luther of anything close to *Eigengesetzlichkeit* is certainly spurious. Early in *On Secular Authority*, Luther appeals to Romans 13:1 and 1 Peter 2:13 to show that the exercise of governmental power is founded on the ordinance of God.[44] However, God rules in two ways: the earthly or "left-hand" kingdom through secular government, and the heavenly or "right-hand" kingdom through the gospel or grace.

A most important purpose of secular authority is to preserve the creation in light of the age-old battle between good and evil. "We are obliged here to divide Adam's children and all men into two classes," stated Luther, "the first belonging to the kingdom of God (*reych Gottis*) and the second to the kingdom of the world (*reych der welt*)."[45] It is within God's providential restraint of the *reych der welt*, indeed the *civitas diaboli*, that his doctrine of two kingdoms, or regiments, must be seen. It is not that Luther denied *corpus christianum* or that he was a pietist. But looking for a way to provide a hedge of protection for God's spiritual work in the world, he limited the jurisdiction of government, separating it from the church. As John R. Stephenson points out, "It is essential to grasp that Luther regards secular government within this framework as an integral part of the good divine work of preservation, for—especially when it conscientiously respects its appointed limits—civil authority acts as a curb against the kingdom of the devil."[46]

Despite these qualifications, the dualism inherent in his system remains glaring. Luther drew a sharp line between the sacred and the secular. Commenting on the Sermon on the Mount, he noted how people make mistakes in applying its teaching because they "fail to distinguish properly between the secular and the spiritual, between the kingdom of Christ and the kingdom of the world."[47] For those who expected a great advance of the kingdom on earth, Luther maintained that Jesus taught people how to live *spiritually* in contrast to the earthly kingdom. All Christians lived in two kingdoms: one spiritual, the other temporal. Within the spiritual kingdom was the man of God living by faith and fulfilling his discipleship duties, while within the earthly kingdom, the Christian had an *Amt* ("office") that was carried out by reason and natural law. In fact, Luther viewed reason as corrosive to faith. Reacting largely out of the milieu in which contentions between scholastics and nominalists over the capability of reason had prompted doubt and confusion, Luther's council for overcoming *morbum dubitationes* ("the disease of doubt") is that "Therefore, faith must wrestle with doubt and against reason."[48]

An enunciated characterization of Luther's extreme dualism is seen in his reading of Ecclesiastes. Luther describes life "under the sun" that is ruled by God *indirectly* and life "above the sun" that is ruled by God *directly*. God's indirect rule encompassed all earthly affairs, while God's direct rule was over spiritual things. Luther was not promoting asceticism. His doctrine of vocation looked to Genesis 1:28 and the fact that all things physical are subservient to God but are to be governed by creation law, reason, and the senses, that is, "indirectly" through people. Ecclesiastes therefore did not present a spiritualized set of rules for education or statecraft but depicted a world whose suitable goal was the glory of God in all occupational and material areas. The creation was God's good gift where man fulfilled his earthly call.[49]

Luther did not believe, however, that fulfilling our earthly call could bring marked transformation to the world. Such change is an eschatological expectation only. Toward the close of his commentary on Psalms 82, he regrets that "Worldly governments will make no progress." We must therefore "pray for another government and the kingdom in which thing will be better."[50] In his lectures on 1 Corinthians in 1532, he sets out the Christian's expectations for this life. "Christ's kingdom on earth is a kingdom of faith."[51] At a later time, this invisible kingdom will become visible but only in heaven. He was especially noncompliant to the idea of Christian government. Not only were Christians outnumbered, which in itself relegated Christians to the minority, but, more to the point of the two kingdoms doctrine, government was subject to reason, not faith, and existed for the common good of both believer and non-believer. "For this reason nothing is taught in the Gospel about how [government] is to be maintained and regulated, except that the Gospel bids people honor it and not oppose it."[52] In the interim, Christians can only await the *Parousia*.[53]

The Escondido theologians' cultural paradigm is indicative of Luther's approach. The "left hand" and "right hand" quotient of civil and spiritual realms is upheld by VanDrunen, who calls for a "distinction between the spiritual kingdom (finding institutional expression in the present age only in the church) and the civil kingdom (encompassing the various non-ecclesiastical cultural endeavors, particularly the work of the state)."[54] He reiterates the same idea in the context of Luther's suspension of social and cultural change until the Second Coming: "The civil kingdom pertains to temporal, earthly, provisional matters not matters of ultimate and spiritual importance." By contrast, the spiritual kingdom "pertains to things that are of ultimate and spiritual importance, the things of Christ's heavenly, eschatological kingdom."[55] More tersely, Darryl Hart, in trying to dispel the biblical basis for a Christian vision of transformative social change, chides, "I want those advocates of Christianity's public role and political responsibility to take seriously Jesus Christ's words when he said, 'My kingdom is not of this world.'"[56]

Important to spot, however, is that compared with Hart, Luther presents a nuanced understanding of the church and politics. Perhaps the most excessive point in Luther's dualistic syllabus is that the visible church is part of the physical kingdom. Because daily church life deals with externals—paying the pastor's salary, fixing the church edifice, and so forth—these activities were little different from the sacraments and preaching, for they, too, were worked out on the terrestrial plane and required input by finite people. In this way, Luther considered the visible church a human institution.[57] It was an object of God's *indirect* rule, placed with the order of daily life and politics. It would thus be a mistake to assume a strict one-to-one correspondence between Hart and Luther on Christians in public life as Hart sees the church as fully spiritual.

If we invite Frame back into this discussion, recall that he joins Vos, who believed that the kingdom encompasses more than the church. Among many things, this denotes that although Frame denies the possibility of any nation fulfilling the theocratic position of ancient Israel, such is not because God's physical rule has *lessened* under the new economy. Rather, now, "the whole world is the promised land."[58] As a result of this amplification, "God's kingdom power includes all his mighty acts in history, especially the resurrection of Christ."[59] Hart, following Luther, believes that "The kingdom of Christ [is] a spiritual entity, not a political one."[60] Frame accedes that the kingdom is not limited to electoral politics. However, lordship broadens the acts of God beyond church life, making all history a realistic narrative of the kingdom of God and all data, including political, answerable to the kingdom standard.

Toward a Resolution

Important evidentiary data can help us assess the debate between Frame and Escondido. Let us begin with the first issue, 1RK vs. 2RK, then move to methodology—or the open question of whether natural law or Scripture offers the best course to treat the ills of the world.

1RK vs. 2RK

Herman Bavinck's now famous quote is worth repeating here. "Grace does not remain outside or above or beside nature but rather permeates and wholly renews it. And thus, nature, reborn by grace, will be brought to its highest revelation."[61] James Eglinton is altogether right to see Bavinck's metanarrative of "grace restoring nature" as part of a fully developing eschatological movement of God throughout history, which takes its direction from God's providence. Providence is not, however, without meaning for the present. "This teleological development cannot be understood apart from Bavinck's doctrine of revelation, through which grace works to transform nature."[62] That "grace transforms nature" is to think with an intensely R1K focus and is the heartbeat of the transformationist view of culture. As well, Bavinck gives indication of the deficiency of natural law when he makes the media of revelation primary in the transformation of nature to its God-designed goal.[63]

As important as is the voice of Bavinck in substantiating the full-orbed meaning of the kingdom (and I could add more voices), it seems only right to follow Frame's own approach in settling theological questions. So we shall hear from Scripture. Albeit the ethical schema of Richard B. Hays was found wanting on certain levels in an earlier section of this book, it is to his interpretive skills to which I now turn. In my view, since Hays does not have a "dog in this fight," his standpoint may in fact provide the kind of legitimacy that both sides can listen to.

Hays's point is that to hear the Apostle Paul in the light of Isaiah's ardent prophetic hope for a new order in the earth leads to the clear conclusion that the church has already entered the eschatological age.[64]

> When we hear 2 Corinthians 5 in the context of Isaiah's fervent prophetic hope for the renewal of the world, we understand that Paul is proclaiming that the church has already entered the sphere of the eschatological age. The apocalyptic scope of 2 Corinthians 5 was obscured by older translations that rendered the crucial phrase in verse 17 as "*he is* a new creation" (RSV) or—worse yet—*he is* a new creature (KJV). Such translations seriously distort Paul's meaning by making it appear that he is describing only the personal transformation of the individual through conversion experience. The sentence in Greek, however, lacks both subject and verb; a very literal translation might treat the words "new creation" as an exclamatory interjection: "If anyone is in Christ—new creation!" The NRSV has rectified matters by rendering the passage, "If anyone is in Christ *there is* a new creation." Paul is not merely talking about an individual's subjective experience of renewal; rather, for Paul, *ktisis* ("creation") refers to the whole created order (cf. Romans 8:18–25). He is proclaiming the apocalyptic message that through the cross God has nullified the *kosmos* of sin and death and brought a new *kosmos* into being.[65]

On Hays's reading, redemption involves *both* insular salvation *and* the wider creation, such that even now God's kingdom has invalidated the fallen order and is reconstituting the earth. The "natural" and "spiritual" rupture of R2K, with its radicalized eschatology that postdates the effects of the cross on the creation only after the *Parousia*, is negated. The presence of the Holy Spirit in the church is an eschatological sign of which Paul can speak of in metaphorical terms in 2 Corinthians 1:22 and 5:5 as an *arrhabōn*, or "earnest money," in anticipation of the final payment. Yet the Spirit-filled Church is more than a semieschatolgical prefigurement. It stands as witness to a change of order in the world.[66]

Frame makes fundamentally the same point as Hays when he sums Christ's redemptive work from Scripture according to a one kingdom standpoint.

> New creation is not only a symbolic way of talking about human ethical transformation, though it is that. Our new creation is the beginning of a cosmic renewal, a renewal as comprehensive as was the original creation. Our transformation by the grace of God is only the beginning of a new heavens and new earth (Isa. 65:17–18; 66:22; 2 Peter 3:10–13; Rev. 21:1–4) in which dwells God's righteousness. Believers are the beginning of a work of Christ, by which he will eventually reconcile "all things" to himself (Col. 1:15–20).[67]

Methodology

As to methodology (natural law vs. Scripture for a healthy public sphere), it seems clear that in a pluralistic age, the human community is splintered politically, culturally, and economically. But by and large, it shares a wide margin of commonly held interests in justice, peace, family life, prohibitions against murder and theft, and more. The natural theologian looks beneath the surface of our differences and agreements and sees a common human reason and intuition, which, if appealed to, might well fashion a common moral vision on important cultural issues. Norman Geisler supports the use of both natural and special revelation in ethics but says that because a Bible is not available to everyone, God inscribed the

Law on human hearts as a means for people to agree and live together in human community.[68] So Geisler presents a circumstantial argument for natural law in a cultural apologetic. Frame thinks that to argue only from the nature of things, the "is" of life to what "ought" to be, is to invite the naturalistic fallacy. To avoid this, we need the supplementation of Scripture. Perhaps by soliciting a particular social issue, we can come closer to shaping an answer to this part of the debate. The issue is abortion. Is a fetus a person by natural law? Following Aquinas's view that natural law alone should determine civil law, the contemporary Roman Catholic Church has adopted the "argument from purpose."[69] It teaches that an embryo should be treated as a human being from the moment of conception because it is the purpose of an embryo to be a fully functional human. This response is not entirely based on the assumption of the value of an embryo from conception but presents a way of informed solution via natural law by asking what the purpose is of something is. In that an embryo is designed to grow into a person, it would be wrong to abort it. At first, the argument from purpose seems reasonable and avoids the "is-ought" problem.

There is also the "argument from substance." In disputation with the pro-choice position, Francis Beckwith appeals to a philosophical anthropology that grounds the protection of the unborn fetus in the thought that "The human being is a particular type of substance—a rational moral agent—that remains identical to itself as long as it exists, even if it is not presently exhibiting the functions, behaving in ways, or currently able to immediately exercise these activities that we typically attribute to active and mature rational moral agents."[70] To employ a simple illustration, the substance John Frame is a *human* substance, different from Lassie, a *canine* substance.[71] Beckwith continues, "Thus if you are an intrinsically valuable human being now, then you were an intrinsically valuable human being at *every moment in your past* including when you were in your mother's womb."[72]

Both the arguments from purpose and from substance could strengthen substantially the pro-life position in the abortion debate, without running aground on the naturalistic fallacy. But would it not be fair to say that the Christian who depends on these forms of argumentation from natural law is interpreting them through the lens of a preconditioned Christian worldview? Take that away, and, according to Darwinian science, the metaphysical realism of Aquinas and Aristotle that posits human worth in "being" or "purpose" is a fiction. Humans simply arise from the vast eons of natural selection in cooperation with random genetic mutations and other possible forces.

To avoid misguided readings of metaphysics, we can link the core of natural law to a firm theory of ethics. But whose ethics shall we employ? We could conceivably unite a theory of natural law to a theory of immorality. Hitler read the rule of nature, concluding that it called for the extermination of the Jews. Jeremy Bentham once wrote that "[N]ature has placed mankind under the governance of two sovereign masters, pain and pleasure. It is for them alone to point out what we ought to do, as well as to determine what we shall do."[73] If pain and pleasure are our guides, then abortion on demand remains permissible. G. E. Moore expressed a robust moral realism that models choice after some supra-sensible way that can be known only through a special faculty of intuition. Though couched in meta-ethical jargon, Moore's basis for ethics is an abstraction that denies the intrinsic value of the unborn child and that would permit a woman's "intuition" to decide its future, regardless of the circumstances. So we have gained nothing.[74]

The uphill challenge in trying to persuade against a pro-choice position is therefore not one of philosophical starting point only. It is not as if we could just get the evolutionist, utilitarian, or moral realist to agree intellectually to our first proposition—for example, ontological or moral proofs broadly defined—and she will follow the train of our logic to a scripturally based, pro-life position. Ultimately, the gridlock is the result of trying to read a law of nature without the Lawgiver. So, to read natural law, as Blackstone said—"being co-eval with mankind and dictated by God himself"—is to read it in the light of the authority of the Lawgiver. Nowhere is that authority made more manifestly clear than in Scripture.[75] In the words of Daniel Strange,

> We need natural revelation to apply the "divine words" of Scripture to any given situation. Natural-law arguments may have their place in certain cultural situations and can be deployed. They may be persuasive on occasion. What I question, however, especially in our current cultural context, is the stability and prescriptive power of natural law as a basis for public theology and moral consensus and the apologetic appeal and persuasive power of a "naked" natural law apart from the ultimate supplementation of Scripture.[76]

Realistic Expectations in the Culture War

Yet all of this raises the practicability of the plan. A critical section in Frame on lordship and civil life occurs in *DCL*, under the situational perspective. There he says unabashedly, "The ultimate goal of political apologetics is nothing less than to present Christ as King of kings and Lord of Lords. The political goal of biblical Christianity is a civil state that acknowledges him for who he is. Every institution of human culture, as well as every individual human being, is called to pay homage to King Jesus."[77]

Previously, Frame's call for a "Christian government" was interpreted in the context of liberty from outside constraint on conscience—a position that follows Luther. But it seems he has more in view. He also would have the church head toward the formation of a civil state that concedes the lordship of Christ. That point raises serious questions. For one, is Frame advocating for the civil takeover by the institutional Church?

It does appear so. Rather, he encourages us to be active in the world through informed and prayerful evangelism and discipleship.[78] As a consequence, Frame envisages a kingdom covering the earth, as people, *changed by the Spirit*, love their neighbors. That process "will inevitably change institutions as well," for "When people are converted to Christ, they bring their new faith and love into their daily work."[79] I do not, therefore, find in Frame a triumphalist call for Christian militancy. The general purport of his political pronouncement is summed in the Pauline injunction: "Whether you eat or drink, or whatever you do, so all to the glory of God" (1 Cor. 10:31). That "God's lordship, therefore, is totalitarian" is to proceed solely on the basis of honoring God in all we do, in the hope of affecting the whole of human existence.[80]

Many, however, such as Carl Trueman, are extremely cynical about the transformationist vision for progress in culture.

> The best way to prove me wrong, of course, is . . . to transform society. I would indeed love to be not only proved wrong but to be proved so wrong that I am shamed into never writing another word of cultural commentary (and I am sure

> many readers will join me in saying "Amen!" to that). Living in a world where the worst that happens is that I receive critical pushback on a blog post is one thing; living in a world where Christians cannot rent space in order to worship on a Sunday, where millions of abortions take place every year, and where every ethical value I hold dear is routinely mocked or ignored or characterized as "hate" is quite another. I know in which world I would rather live; thus, I look forward to the transformation of the latter into the former by my critics and truly wish them well in their endeavour.[81]

In recent years, what some consider to be the insolvency of the Christian mandate to transform the marketplace of ideas and to foster social progress has led many Christians, such as Trueman, to view the rhetoric of transformative cultural theology as a pipe dream. Frame answers that setbacks for Christian cultural engagement are only ever God's "apparent defeats" in history.[82] In other words, as stated pages ago in the dialogue between Frame and van de Beek, what we think of as a "defeat" is really God's different way of working toward his ultimate victory over the world. That God has sovereign control over the historical setbacks of the semi-eschatological age ought therefore to reorient our attitude toward historical development. God is using even our failures at social and cultural reform to reconstitute the earth.

In this context, the meaning of lordship is found in the fact that a life of obedience to the kingdom mission of Christ (Gen. 1:28; 2:15; Matt. 28:18–20) must recognize that the Spirit's work in the world is never linear and progressively upward, as humans define *linear progress*. Frame's transformationist view does not depend on, or expect, flourishing cultures and upward trends in society as the norm. He does not view God as a CEO of a company who must always produce profits, in order for shareholders to see progress or in order for there to be progress. Lordship over culture(s) simply recognizes that God is having his way in the world. That includes both our successes and our failures in our work in culture. Not only does this fact change our definition of *success* in the culture war, but it also tells us that we must remain vigilant in the struggle, for how else will God work in and through our failures unless we are there to fail?

As I have stated elsewhere, "The quiet attitude of many is that unless massive, wholesale change occurs across the board in American culture and the world, the Christian agenda is failing. Not only is this untrue, it is not even close to the truth. . . . we are not charged with erecting a Christian utopia, but with representing the transcendent kingdom of God on earth that has the power to affect all of life."[83]

Frame says something very similar.

> Some theologians present the semi-eschatological age as a time of suffering, pain and defeat. Others present it as a time of victory for the gospel. In fact both positions are correct. The history of the church has been full of suffering and persecution. But the blood of the martyrs has been the seed of the church, and often the worst persecutions have given rise to the strongest churches. And through history, Christian people have brought profound change to society, in the treatment of widows and orphans, the growth of learning, the development of democracy, to mention only a few areas.[84]

Yet there is a further problem. If Scripture, not natural law, is primary in the church's public discourse with non-Christians, what are we to make of the fact that Christians are not in complete agreement on the meaning of

Scripture, for example, baptism, eschatology, and election? Does this not constitute another setback for Frame's cultural vision? The resolution to this particular predicament is that

> Sin affects our biblical exegesis as well as our apprehension of natural law. So we never in this life reach a perfect, inerrant reading of natural law. That's the same issue we face when we talk about sanctification. Sin remains in the believer, so, how are believers any different from unbelievers? The answer is, I think, that despite the continuing effects of sin, something new has happened: the *dominion* of sin has been broken (Rom. 8:14); there has been a *new creation* (1 Cor. 5:17). What redemption brings is not perfection, but a decisive step in the right direction.[85]

Frame means that the quandary of using Scripture as a guide for public life suffers from the same debility we face in using it in private life: sin muddies everything. But the "decisive step" of renewal has happened. Frame is thus optimistic that levels of consensus can develop among Christians on some issues: abortion, marriage, just war, and more. We will not arrive at unqualified consensus, but neither will we arrive at unqualified sinlessness in this life. Yet the likelihood of moving in the right direction is more feasible with the light of Scripture than with natural law. (Not that Scripture exclude God's laws in nature/creation.)

Finally, the meaning of lordship for cultural thought does more than censer the city of man, and with its lack of a priori essences, established values, and norms. Added to Frame's diagnosis of the problem of culture is his call for a *constructive analysis* of what can be done to build a positive program of change. In this sense, Frame positions his thought on culture toward a direction that even Niebuhr did not fully anticipate under his fifth category of culture. The transformationist agenda tends to focus on recreating the distorted, man-made portraits of God's creation but lacks vision of how to create its own portrait. By orienting the debate toward the future with a challenge to the globe to "pay homage to King Jesus," Frame causes the church to reflect on the point that God did not tell Adam to transform bad culture, but to build a God-honoring one, although we will always do so amid thorns until the new heavens and the new earth. One may take umbrage with the specificities of Frame's future vision, but that only leaves one to do better.

Endnotes

1 *TET*, 6.
2 Ibid., 3.
3 *DCL*, 522. Frame's critical review of Kline's *Kingdom Prologue: Genesis Foundations for a Covenantal Worldview*, which sets cult and culture in contradistinction, is in *TET*, 151–198.
4A supporting review of the Escondido Theology is W. Gary Crampton, "The Escondido Theology: A Reformed Response to Two Kingdom Theology," at http://whitefieldmedia.com/wp-content/uploads/2012/02/Book-Review-for-John-Frames-Book-Final.pdf.
5 Even though I stand by my endorsement of *The Escondido Theology*, one thing Frame does not seem to acknowledge is any variance of views on the faculty regarding culture. Horton is not Hart. And W. Robert Godrey claims to be Kuyperian on culture. Despite what distinctions may exist among the faulty, I think that Frame's critiques of the writers he does address in the book are well founded. Because the scope of this work does not allow me to individuate each teacher at the Escondido campus, the subsequent sections will follow Frame in speaking of a homogeneous "Escondido theology."
6 M. Horton, *Christless Christianity* (Ada, MI: Baker Books, 2008), 109. Horton's quote is an untenable position, biblically. Still, it finds precedence in the Lutheran heritage that came to reject the third use of the law in the life of the Christian, for the law, according to the Lutherans, only ever brings condemnation, a very different position than that held by Calvin and his followers.
7 *TET*, 45.
8 John Calvin, for instance, sees the source of sanctification as union with Christ. Calvin writes, "[A]s long as Christ remains outside of us, and we are separated from him, all that he has suffered and done for the salvation of the human remains useless and of no value for us." *Institutes.*3.1.1. On this basis, he speaks of a "double grace" that includes both justification and sanctification. See *Institutes.* 3.11.1 Calvin also speaks of progressive sanctification that involves "the true turning of our life to God, a turning that arises from a pure and earnest fear of him, and it consists in the mortification of the flesh and of the old man, and in the vivification of the Spirit." *Institutes* 3.3.5. Thus, for Calvin, although sin has no dominion over us, mortification and vivification are Christian duties that must be continually exercised. The third use of the Law plays a vital role in this process. "For no man has heretofore attained to such wisdom as to be unable, from the daily instruction of the Law, to make fresh progress toward a purer knowledge of the divine will." *Institutes* 2.7.12. Supporting studies are David K. Winecoff, "Calvin's doctrine of mortification," *Presbyterian* 13, no. 2 (Fall 1987): 85–101; and Randall C. Gleason, *John Calvin and John Owen on Mortification: A Comparative Study in Reformed Spirituality* (New York: P. Lang, 1995).
9 *TET*, 46.
10 M. Horton, *Christless Christianity* (Ada, MI: Baker Books, 2008), 105.

11 J. V. Fesko, "The Federal Vision and the Covenant of Works," lecture for the Meeting of the Stated Clerks of the PCA, December 2004, 1.
12 Ibid., 17.
13 *DCL*, 185.
14 Ibid., 186.
15 Ibid., 187.
16 D. VanDrunen, *A Biblical Case for Natural Law: Studies in Christian Social Ethics and Economics*, no. 1 (Grand Rapids, MI: Acton Institute, 2006), 1.
17 Ibid.
18 Consistent with this is a point in his Christology, such "that the Son of God rules the temporal kingdom as an eternal member of the Divine Trinity but does not rule it in his capacity as the incarnate mediator/redeemer," VanDrunen, *Natural Law and the Two Kingdoms: A Study In the Development of Reformed Social Thought* (Grand Rapids, MI: Eerdmans, 2010), 181. Such language practically implies a duality of persons within the second person of the Trinity and places a sharp fissure between the ontological and economic Trinity. Frame has not reviewed *Natural Law and the Two Kingdoms* for the reason that if VanDrunen cannot make the biblical case for R2K, then he is not interested in interacting with a historical treatment of the subject.
19 D. VanDrunen, *A Biblical Case for Natural Law,* 14.
20 Ibid., 24.
21 *TET*, 129.
22 This is VanDrunen's term. See *A Biblical Case for Natural Law*, 26. VanDrunen consistently applies his sacred-secular hermeneutic to the Abrahamic, the Mosaic, and the New Covenant under Christ. Frame replies to this in *TET*, 137–140.
23 See VanDrunen, *A Biblical Case for Natural Law*; the argument extends from page 49 to 54.
24 See *TET*, 144.
25 Retrieved at Nelson D. Kloosterman, "A Biblical Case for Natural Law," Ordained Servant Online, http://opc.org/os.html?article_id=77; date of access: Dec. 12, 2013. Of the same view is Peter J. Leithart, "Natural Law: A Reformed Critique," *Premise* 3, no. 2 (1996).
26 *TET*, 128. The reader is referred to the chapter on apologetics that dealt with propositional truth in Van Til and Frame. There I tried to clarify Frame's position by making a distinction that preserves the metaphysical situation in the unbeliever, so he can say and think something that is "right," but because that data lay outside Christian theism, as a unit, is not entirely "true," i.e., "true truth."
27 *DG*, 64.
28 T. Aquinas, *Summa* I–II, Q. 91, a. 2, http://www.ccel.org/ccel/aquinas/summa.html; date of access: March 18, 2013. Frame also discusses the problem in philosophy of nature treated as an impersonal mechanism in *DG*, 111.
29 *DG*, 53. The concept of the moral autonomy of institutional life as grounded in reason is found as early as the sixteenth century in the writings of Jean Bodin, Niccolò Machiavelli, and René Descartes. Though taking different shape, it is also found in the

thought of Immanuel Kant, Adam Smith, and Karl Marx. The idea of autonomous and determining laws of nature was also an ideological catalyst in Social Darwinism.
30 See ibid., 214. I am not here insinuating that any R2K adherent rejects ontology as biblical science. Frame is not even addressing R2K in this area of *DG*. The only point I wish to make is that what he states in *DG* on metaphysics is part and parcel of his reservations on natural law and culture. That seems clear, as he can just as easily refer to metaphysics as "worldview." For this association, cf., ibid., 215 and 231.
31 *DG*, 215.
32 D. Hume, *An Enquiry Concerning Human Understanding,* ed. L. Bigge (Oxford: Clarendon Press, 1902), 114.
33 C. Brown, *Miracles and the Critical Mind* (Grand Rapids, MI: Eerdmans, 1984), 145.
34 *DG*, 261.
35 Dooyeweerd's main work is *De wijsbegeerte der wetsidee* (*The Philosophy of the Law-Idea*), 3 vols. (Amsterdam: H. J. Paris, 1935–1936). *A New Critique of Theoretical Thought* (Jordan Station, Ontario: Paideia Press, 1953–1958) is a revised and enlarged edition of this work in English translation. Of further import is Dooyeweerd's *Transcendental Problems of Philosophic Thought* (Grand Rapids, MI: Eerdmans, 1948). Other early influential spokesmen of the movement were D. H. Th. Vollenhoven, also of the Free University of Amsterdam, and Prof. H. G. Stoker, University of Potchefstroom, South Africa.
36 Frame amplifies this thought in *DCL*, 951, n. 1.
37 Retrieved at John M. Frame, *The Amsterdam Philosophy: A Preliminary Critique*, at: http://www.frame-poythress.org/wp-content/uploads/2012/08/FrameJohnAmsterdamPhilosophy1972.pdf; date of access: Nov. 19, 2013. Frame is quoting Dooyeweerd, *In the Twilight of Western Thought* (Nutley, NJ: Craig Press, 1960), 135. An important set of articles by Frame contra Dooyeweerd is now under the general title "Dooyeweerd and the Word of God," at http://www.frame-poythress.org/dooyeweerd-and-the-word-of-god/. This is a compilation of formerly published papers.
38 See Dooyeweerd, *A New Critique of Theoretical Thought* (1955), 2:118.
39 See ibid., 1:41–44.
40 Of course, that did not lead to consensus. In economics, for example, Hendrik Van Riessen was very conservative and "Bob" Goudzwaard was moderately liberal, though both claimed to be working from Dooyeweerdian premises.
41 William J. Wright provides an immensely useful historical overview on the debate and the development of Luther's idea of the two kingdoms among scholars dating to the mid-nineteenth century. See William J. Wright, *Martin Luther's Understanding of God's Two Kingdoms: A Response to the Challenge of Skepticism* (Grand Rapids, MI: Baker Academic, 2010), 17–43. On the variant views of Luther by those close to him, see David M. Whitford, "Cura Religionis or Two Kingdoms: The Late Luther on Religion and the State in the Lectures on Genesis. Church History," *Church History* 73, no. 1 (March 2004): 41–62. For example, in "Concerning the Invented Faith, Protestation, A Clear Disclosure of the False Faith of an Unfaithful World," and "A Highly Necessary Defense and Answer

against the Soft-Living Flesh of Wittenberg" (1524), Thomas Müntzer was but the first in a long line of those who accused Luther of releasing the sword of secular authority from all church control and thereby opening up centuries of authoritarian subjugation. Then again, Peter Frarin argued in "An Oration against the Unlawful Insurrections of the Protestants of Our Time, under Pretense to Reform Religion" (1566) that Luther's views encouraged insurrection to civil order.

42 See Ernst Troeltsch, *The Social Teaching of the Christian Churches*, trans. Olive Wyon (Louisville, KY: Westminster/John Knox Press, 1992; German, 1911): 547–548.

43 See Richard V. Pierard, "The Lutheran Two-Kingdoms Doctrine and Subservience to the State in Modern Germany," *JETS* 29, no. 2 (1986): 193–203.

44 See *WA* 11. 247, 21–30.

45 Ibid., 11. 249: 24–25

46 J. Stephenson, "The Two Governments and the Two Kingdoms in Luther's Thought," *Scottish Journal of Theology* 34, no. 4 (1981): 2. Luther writes, "God has therefore ordained two regiment(s): the spiritual which by the Holy Spirit produces Christians and pious folk under Christ, and the secular which restrains un-Christian and evil folk so that they are obliged to keep outward peace, albeit by no merit of their own." *WA* 11. 251, 15–18.

47 *WA* 32:387, 389; *LW* 21:107, 109.

48 *WA* 42:452; *LW* 2:266.

49 See *WA* 20:161, 6–24; *LW* 15:148; Eccles. 9:7.

50 *WA* 31:1:218; *LW* 13:72.

51 *WA* 36:569; *LW* 28:124.

52 *WA* 51:242; *LW* 13:198.

53 See *WA* 36:570–71; *LW* 28:124–125.

54 D. VanDrunen, "Abraham Kuyper and the Reformed Natural Law and Two Kingdoms Traditions," *Calvin Theological Journal* 42, no. 2 (2007): 283–307. An excellent book *contra* the two kingdoms view is *Kingdoms Apart: Engaging the Two Kingdoms Perspective*, ed. Ryan C. McIlhenny (Phillipsburg, NJ: P&R Publishing, 2012).

55 D. VanDrunen, *A Biblical Case for Natural Law,* 24.

56 D. G. Hart, *A Secular Faith: Why Christianity Favors the Separation of Church and State* (Lanham, MD: Ivan R. Dee, 2006), 12.

57 See *WA* 43:70; *LW* 3:272–73.

58 *DCL*, 600.

59 Ibid., 185.

60 D. G. Hart, *A Secular Faith: Why Christianity Favors the Separation of Church and State* (Lanham, MD: Ivan R. Dee, 2006), 230.

61 H. Bavinck, "Common Grace," trans. R. Van Leeuwen, *Calvin Theological Journal* 24, no. 59 (1989): 59–60, 61.

62 J. Eglinton, "To Be or to Become: That Is the Question. Locating the Actualistic in Bavinck's Ontology," in *The Kuyper Center Review*, vol. 2, *Revelation and Common Grace*, ed. J. Bowlin (Grand Rapids, MI: Eerdmans, 2011), 112.

63 Evidently, VanDrunen disagrees with Eglington. See David VanDrunen, "'The Kingship of Christ Is Twofold': Natural Law and the Two Kingdoms in the Thought of Herman Bavinck," *Calvin Theological Journal* 45, no. 1 (April 2010): 147–164. A vitally important corrective to VanDrunen is Nelson D. Kloosterman, "A Response to 'The Kingship of Christ Is Twofold': Natural Law and the Two Kingdoms in the Thought of Herman Bavinck by David VanDrunen," *Calvin Theological Journal* 45, no. 1 (April 2010): 165–176. Nelson Kloosterman's fine analysis of the issues is accessible at http://richardsibbes.com/_hermanbavinck/Kloosterman-2Kingdoms.pdf.
64 Isaiah 65:17–19 records, "For behold, I create new heavens and a new earth; And the former things will not be remembered or come to mind. But be glad and rejoice forever in what I create; For behold, I create Jerusalem for rejoicing And her people for gladness. I will also rejoice in Jerusalem and be glad in My people; And there will no longer be heard in her The voice of weeping and the sound of crying."
65 R. Hays, *The Moral Vision of the New Testament: Community, Cross, New Creation: A Contemporary Introduction to New Testament Ethics* (San Francisco: HarperSanFrancisico, 1996), 20.
66 Also germane is Paul's statement "For it was the Father's good pleasure for all the fullness to dwell in Him, and through Him to reconcile all things to Himself, having made peace through the blood of His cross; through Him, I say, whether things on earth or things in heaven" (Colossians 1:19–20). Paul does not say that God reconciled only the elect to Himself at the cross, but "all things" (see also Ephesians 1:22), including the lower creation that suffered unto vanity as a result of the original man's fall from grace (see Romans 8:19–22). The cross is the basis for the restoration of "all things," both personal and cultural. N. T. Wright shares Hays's view of the cosmic, kingdom scope of the gospel. On Colossians 1:19–20, he observes, "He [Paul] is emphasizing the universal scope of God's reconciling purposes; nothing less than a total new creation is envisage." N. T. Wright, *Colossians and Ephesians* (Grand Rapids, MI: Eerdmans, 1989, repr.), 77.
67 *ST*, 191.
68 Norman Geisler, *Introduction to Philosophy: A Christian Perspective* (Ada, MI: Baker Academic, 1987), 126. This is also the position held by Landon Rowland, whose rather fine student paper "A Comparative Analysis of the Question of Natural Law in Modern Reformed Conversation" is accessible at http://www.rts.edu/Site/Virtual/Resources/Student_Theses/Rowland%20-%20A%20Comparative%20Analysis%20of%20the%20Question%20of%20Natural%20Law%20in%20Modern%20Reformed%20Conversation.pdf.
69 See Thomas Aquinas, *Summa Theologiae*, I–II, 90–92, 95–97.
70 F. Beckwith, *Defending Life: A Moral and Legal Case against Abortion Choice* (Cambridge: Cambridge University Press, 2007), 132.
71 This example follows that the argument from substance by Francis Beckwith, in "Thomson's `Equal Reasonableness' Argument for Abortion Rights: A Critique," *American Journal of Jurisprudence* 49, no. 1 (2004): 188, available at https://bearspace.baylor.edu/Francis_Beckwith/www/Sites/AJJ2004.pdf; date of access:

Oct. 30, 2013. Beckwith is critiquing Judith Jarvis Thomson, "Abortion: Whose Right?" *Boston Review* 20, no. 3 (Summer 1995).
72 See Beckwith, *Defending Life*, 50.
73 J. Bentham, "An Introduction to the Principles of Morals and Legislation," 1789), I; http://www.econlib.org/library/Bentham/bnthPML1.html; date of access: August 21, 2013.
74 The *locus classicus* of non-natural realism is G. E. Moore, *Pricipia Ethica* (Cambridge: Cambridge University Press, 1903).
75 W. Blackstone, *Commentaries on the Laws of England*, vol. 1 (Philadelphia: Robert Bell, 1771), 41; http://oll.libertyfund.org/index.php?Itemid=269&id=320&option=com_content&task=view; date of access: August 21, 2013.
76 Retrieved at Daniel Strange, "Not Ashamed! The Sufficiency of Scripture for Public Theology," http://thegospelcoalition.org/themelios/article/not_ashamed_the_sufficiency_of_scripture_for_public_theology#a1; date of access: Oct. 31, 2013. Originally published in *Themelios* 36, no. 2 (August 2011): 238–260. Note, however, that in Frame, Scripture is never pure "supplement" to natural law. Scripture is always prior, if not sequentially, certainly presuppositionally. As demonstrated in the prior discussion on Framian apologetics, he prefers to begin with scriptural proofs but is adept enough to broaden the argument with the use of the traditional proofs, which often appeal to reason and other various perspectives on natural law. Yet those claims must always reflect biblical truth. Should I make a case by first appealing to data inherent in the universe, this procedure must also conform to the standard of scriptural authority. What must not happen is the rationalizing of beliefs thought inherent in human nature and discoverable by reason, rather than by revelation.
77 *DCL*, 294.
78 See Ibid., 894.
79 *DWG*, 218.
80 Ibid.
81 Retrieved at Carl Trueman, "I Hope to Be Proved Wrong (Really I Do)," *Reformation 21* (August 2013); http://www.reformation21.org/blog/2013/08/i-hope-to-be-proved-wrong-real.php; date of access: Aug. 28, 2013.
82 *ST*, 143. He makes the same point in *DCL*, 275.
83 J. Barber, *Earth Restored* (Geanies House, Scotland: Christian Focus Publications, 2002).
84 *ST*, 96.
85 In an email to the author, dated Nov. 6, 2012.

Chapter 11

Concluding Thoughts

The question that motivated this book is, "What does 'lordship' mean to John M. Frame?" and the importance thereof for our theological endeavors. Although I have given indicators to the answer throughout this book, it is now time to summate the answer in crystalline terms.

To Summarize

Frame's lordship theology stresses, above all, one thought. It is that covenantal lordship is a universal claim on the whole of creation, including all peoples of the earth. Although the following statement has appeared in this work, it presents the quintessential meaning of lordship in Frame. It thus bears repeating. Lordship means to Frame that "*There is one kingdom, ruled over by one Lord, who governs the affairs of all people by a single rule of faith and practice, and everything is related perspectivally.*"

Supporting Evidence

The summary is supported by a correlative study between important aspects of Frame's lordship theology and the *theologia crucis* of Abraham Van de Beek (chapter 2). This was followed by an analysis of Frame on ethics, apologetics, and culture (chapters 3 through 9).

Frame and Van de Beek

Frame's Christology is governed by his broader concern with God as Lord, while Van de Beek is preeminently interested in a Christology that bears especially the meaning of the cross of Jesus. This is evident in Frame's extensive treatment of the Doctrine of God, within which Jesus of Nazareth, although considered accurately within the biblical canon, takes his place among other theological strata in support of the lordship principle of control, authority, and presence. That Frame's *Systematic Theology* sets aside only twenty-two pages to discuss Christology proper supports the claim that for Frame, universalistic lordship is the most fundamental characteristic of God, which is verified by the historical Jesus.

Transpiring in the dialogue between Frame and Van de Beek is also the Creator/creature distinction. This distinction is extremely important for deciphering what lordship means to Frame. When taking up the issue of worldview, for example, Frame places the subject within the sphere of ontology. Thus, the Christian worldview affirms that the Lord is "personal" and "absolute"; one who maintains "a sharp distinction between Creator and creature, between the One who makes all things and the beings that he makes."[1] This definition is different from the motif of creation, fall, and redemption, commonly held by contemporary Reformed thinkers.[2] It is in contradiction with James Orr, who identified the biblical world and life view with "a very definite view of things."[3] In Frame's thoughts, worldview does not grow out of *our* view or even *our* theology, but presupposes the transcendental God, who governs the human task of theology and all creatures he has made.[4] Frame is insisting that before procuring God, the world, and the self in the internal structure *of* theology, we must first bow in fear before the ontic ground *for* theology.

Ethics

Frame emphasizes the importance of ethics when saying that "[E]verything can be boiled down to a matter of ethics." As stated earlier in Chapter 3, the implications for epistemology are unconventional. By making knowledge of God a heart-knowledge, "obedience is the criterion of knowledge."[5] Or, as I have also clarified earlier, we can say that because all thought is essentially an *activity* before God, epistemology is overtly ethical. Essentially, what is motivating Frame is his aversion to separate even thought about God from our servant status before the covenantal lordship of God. That the history of secular ethics has ventured into thought about God, the world, and the self, in disobedience to God, precipitated the main point on Framian ethics previously explored. This is that the normative, theological, and existential concerns of secular ethics all find a home in his ethics and do so in subservience to the Lord.

Apologetics

Frame on apologetics continues the lordship theme. This should not be taken to mean that Frame's posture on apologetics merely restates God's sovereignty. Rather, lordship creates the conditions for extending our obedience to the Great Commission: our obligation to defend our hope in the company of the nations. In his discussion of 1 Peter 3:15, Frame is crystal clear on this point: "Some theologians present apologetics as if it were almost an exception to this commitment."[6] Here, Lordship is its own validation for apologetics and thus a non-exceptional obligation for all Christians. Frame's presuppositional approach to apologetics is dictated by two ideas. (1) The Lord simply "is"—a fact that is axiomatic to all people

(Rom. 1:18). (2) Non-Christians practice suppression of the truth which necessitates "pulling the rug right out from under them."

Culture

The analysis of Frame's theology of culture shows once more the unavoidable implications of God's control, authority, and presence; this time, for our shared environment. Frame's commitment to the one kingdom position in Reformed thought is derived from three general areas in this analysis: systematic theology, symbiotic relationships, and lastly, biblical theology. Frame's transformationist position on culture places him squarely at odds with the two kingdom contexture of the Escondido theologians and with those of analogous views. A central stratagem to apply the R1K eschews any sort of Christian militancy. Instead, to repeat Frame's aim, "Our motive is not to try to make non-Christians live the Christian life, but simply to work out the implications of our faith in all areas of life."[7]

Theology Is Application

Closely tied to the meaning of lordship in Frame is that theology must be lived out for it to be theology. As attested earlier, Frame thinks that theology is application. To repeat his definition, "[T]heology is *the application of Scripture, by persons, to every area of life*."[8] Initially, one could take his definition to have meaning only for the Christian. Certainly, this would be true. Believers in Jesus Christ do apply Scripture to every area of life, or at least they should. And Frame's refining of the practical nature of theology, that it function "for the purpose of edification," underscores what he believes to be the practical and indeed pastoral nature of a decidedly Christian theology.[9]

However, when Frame says that theology is the application of Scripture "by persons," he does not intend to single out Christians but means that all people are in some sense applying Scripture. For if all theology is practical, and God has a universally binding covenant claim on all people, then that means that all people, Christian or not, whether they accept or reject Scripture as the word of God, are applying the word of God to every area of their lives. *Everyone is practicing theology*. Everyone's life is the result of a study of God, in the face of his word. The results may differ wildly, but the end product is always the same: people either embrace their covenant God or "Professing to be wise, they became fools" (Rom. 1:22). Frame's definition of theology thus serves his commitment to the more basic fact that lordship is a universal prerogative.

The Psalmist reveals the total lack of any nonconformist posture to God's lordship when he writes of how even the non-rational creation responds to its Creator in praise.

> Praise the LORD! Praise the LORD from the heavens; Praise Him in the heights! Praise Him, all His angels; Praise Him, all His hosts! Praise Him, sun and moon; Praise Him, all stars of light! Praise Him, highest heavens, and the waters that are above the heavens! Let them praise the name of the LORD, For He commanded and they were created. He has also established them forever and ever; He has made a decree which will not pass away." (Psalms 148:1–6)

On the contrary, Acts 17:26–31, with the support of Romans 1:23, has implications for a very different application of God's revelation, resulting in idolatry. Human history's a posteriori denial of innate knowledge of God represents nothing more than "the times of ignorance" (v. 30). Psalms 51:5,

"Behold, I was brought forth in iniquity, and in sin my mother conceived me," heightens the contrast.

Atheists will certainly argue with Frame that their response to the Lord has theological groundings. But as Van Til pointed out correctly, all decisions about God cannot escape the subject matter of which theology is the subject and of which God is its object. He said, "Arguing about God's existence, I hold, is like arguing about air. You may affirm that air exists, and I that it does not. But as we debate the point, we are both breathing air all the time."[10] Van Til stated in broad terms what Frame went on to specify, that the lordship principle of God's control, authority and presence terminates in God's "covenant headship" over all people, to which their lives are a response in real time and real space.[11] This must be so, or else God is not God. R.C. Sproul expressed this very idea, when he affirmed that "If there is one single molecule in this universe running around loose, totally free of God's sovereignty, then we have no guarantee that a single promise of God will ever be fulfilled."[12]

The Prospect for Perspectivalism

This book closes with thoughts on the future of perspectivalism. The event that gave rise to this book was my impression of the post-Christian condition of modern-day Europe while visiting there in 2008. The nineteenth-century "revolt against reason," in the hope that the world could be renewed by harnessing the "inner world" of the individual and society, has crashed on the rocks of disenchantment.[13] In thinking through a biblical answer to this problem, Frame's lordship principle, which balances the objective, the subjective, and situated daily life, appeared—in my view, at least—to be the theological model European thinkers (indeed, those around the world) can look to, to find fresh inspiration for how to bring head, heart, and life together. Since the Enlightenment, theology has labored to find a voice that can account for a complete way of life, one that does not sacrifice one life perspective to another. Frame's lordship theology just may well provide the answer to our long search.

Endnotes

---

1 *ST*, 38–39, 48.
2 E.g., Al Wolters, *Creation Regained*: *Biblical Basics for a Reformational Worldview* (Grand Rapids, MI: Wm. B. Eerdmans, 1985).
3 J. Orr, *The Christian View of God and the World* (New York: Charles Scribner's Sons, 1908), 16.
4 Even the language of the Lord's transcendence and immanence is inspirited in Frame. Rather than transcendence meaning that God is "up there" and immanence meaning he is "down here, "transcendence refers to God's rule as the Sovereign Lord, so immanence refers to his presence in the world he has made." *ST*, 42.
5 *DKG*, 44.
6 *AGG*, 4.
7 *DCL*, 973.
8 *ACT*, 18.
9 Ibid., 6.
10 Cornelius Van Til, *Why I Believe in God* (Philadelphia: Committee on Christian Education, Orthodox Presbyterian Church, 1966), 3.
11 *DKG*, 12.
12 R. C. Sproul, *Chosen by God* (Nashville: Thomas Nelson, 1986), 26–27.
13 S. Bastow and J. Martin, Third Way Discourse: European Ideologies in the 20th Century (Edinburgh, Scotland: Edinburgh University Press, 2003), 26–29.

Bibliography

Ambrose. *Hesaemeron.*

Ansell, N. "It's about Time: Opening Our Reformational Paradigm to the Eschaton." *Calvin Theological Journal* 47, no. 1 (April 2012): 98–121. Paper first presented at the Institute for Christian Studies, September 26, 2003.

Aquinas, T. *On Being and Essence*. Translated by A. Maurer. Toronto: Pontifical Institute of Medieval Studies, 1968.

Aquinas, T. *Summa.* http://www.ccel.org/ccel/aquinas/summa.html. Date of access: March 18, 2013.

Augustine, A. "Lectures on the Gospel of John." *Nicene and Post-Nicene Fathers*. Vol. 1, tractate 7, 217–221.

Augustine, A. *De Trinitate*. http://www.ccel.org/ccel/schaff/npnf103.iv.i.html?highlight=augustine,de, trinitate#highlight. Date of access: April 5, 2013.

Bacote, V. *The Spirit in Public Theology: Appropriating the Legacy of Abraham Kuyper.* Eugene, OR: Wipf and Stock Publishers, 2010.

Bahnsen, G. *The Crucial Concept of Self-Deception in Presuppositional Apologetics*. 1995. http://www.cmfnow.com/articles/PA207.htm. Date of access: March 13, 2012.

Bahnsen, G. *Presuppositional Apologetics: Stated and Defended*. Edited by Joel McDurmon. Powder Springs, GA: The American Vision, 2008.

Barber, J. *Earth Restored*. Geanies House, Scotland: Christian Focus Publications, 2002.

Barber, J. *My Almost for His Highest*. Eugene, OR: Wipf and Stock Publishers, 2010.

Barber, J. *The Road from Eden*. Lakeland, FL: Whitefield Media, 2013.

Barth, *CD* II/1, 121.

Barth, K. *Dogmatics in Outline*. Harper Perennial, 1959.

Barthes, Roland. *Mythologies*. Translated by Annette Lavers. New York: Hill and Wang, 1972.

Bastow, S., and J. Martin. *Third Way Discourse: European Ideologies in the 20th Century*. Edinburgh, Scotland: Edinburgh University Press, 2003.

Bavinck, H. *An Introduction to the Science of Missions*. Translated by D. Freeman. Phillipsburg: NJ: P&R Publishing Company, 1960.

Bavinck, H. *Philosophy of Revelation.* Eugene, OR: Wipf and Stock Publishers, 2003. First given for the Stone Lectures, 1908–1909.

Bavinck, H. *Reformed Dogmatics*. Vol. 2, edited by J. Bolt. Grand Rapids, MI: Baker Academic, 2004.

Bavinck, H. *Essays on Religion, Science, and Society*. Grand Rapids, MI: Baker Academic, 2008.

Bavinck, H. "Common Grace." Translated by R. Van Leeuwen. *Calvin Theological Journal* 24, no. 59 (1989): 60–61.

Beckwith, F. *Defending Life: A Moral and Legal Case against Abortion Choice*. Cambridge: Cambridge University Press, 2007.

Bentham, J. "An Introduction to the Principles of Morals and Legislation." 1789. http://www.econlib.org/library/Bentham/bnthPML1.html. Date of access: August 21, 2013.

Berdyaev, Nikolai. *Dream and Reality.* New York; Collier Books, 1962.

Berdyaev, N. *Towards a New Epoch.* Translated by Oliver Fielding Clarke. London: Geoffrey Bles, 1949.

Berkouwer, G. C. *General Revelation*. Grand Rapids, MI: Eerdmans, 1955.

Blackstone, W. *Commentaries on the Laws of England.* Vol. 1. Philadelphia:http://oll.libertyfund.org/index.php?Itemid=269&id=320&option=com_content&task=view. Date of access: August 21, 2013.

Blitz, M. "Heidegger's *Nietzsche*, Part II." *Political Science Reviewer* (1993). http://www.scribd.com/doc/131706077/Blitz-Mark-Heidegger-s-Nietzsche. Date of access: January 22, 2013.

Bratt, J. *Abraham Kuyper: A Centennial Reader*. Edited by J. Bratt. Grand Rapids, MI: Wm. B. Eerdmans, 1998.

Brown, C. *Miracles and the Critical Mind*. Grand Rapids, MI: Eerdmans, 1984.

Brown, S. "John Frame: The Closet Radical." In *Speaking the Truth in Love: The Theology of John M. Frame*, edited by J. Hughes. Phillipsburg, NJ: P&R Publishing, 2009.

Budziszewski, J. *Evangelicals in the Public Square: Four Formative Voices on Political Thought and Action.* Grand Rapids, MI: Baker Academic, 2006.

Bultmann, R. *pisteuô.* In *Theological Dictionary of the New Testament*, edited by G. Kittle, 6:211. Grand Rapids, MI: Eerdmans, 1959.

Buswell, J. "The Fountainhead of Presuppositionalism." *TBT* 42, no. 2 (1948): 48.

Calvin, J. *Institutes of the Christian Religion.* Translated by Ford Lewis Battles. Philadelphia: Westminster Press, 1960.

Camino, R. "Choosing My Religion." *American Demographics* 63 (1999).

Chamberlain, L. "Back to Origins: Heidegger through Post-Darwinian Eyes." *TLS* 5578 (February 2010): 18.

Clark, G. *An Introduction to Christian Philosophy*. 2nd ed. Jefferson, MD: Trinity Foundation, 1993.

Clark, S. "Peace (with Evangelicalism) in Our Time." 2009. http://heidelblog.net/2009/10/subjectivism-and-peace-with-evangelicalism-tim-keller/. Date of access: March 4, 2011.

Clayton, P. *Transforming Christian Theology: For Church and Society*. Minneapolis: Fortress Press, 2009.

Cooper, T. *Paul Tillich and Psychology: Historic and Contemporary Explorations in Theology, Psychotherapy, and Ethics*. Macon, GA: Mercer University Press, 1996.

Constable, T. "Notes on Romans." 1999. http://www.soniclight.com/constable/notes/pdf/romans.pdf. Date of access: February 25, 2012.

Cranfield, C. E. B. *A Critical and Exegetical Commentary on the Epistle to the Romans*. 6th ed. London: Bloomsbury T&T Clark, 2000. http://www.amazon.com/Critical-Exegetical-Commentary-Epistle-Romans/dp/0567050408.

Dabney, R. *Lectures in Systematic Theology*. Grand Rapids, MI: Zondervan, 1878; reprint 1972.

Dahl, N. A. *Jesus the Christ: The Historical Origins of Christological Doctrine*. Minneapolis: Fortress Press, 1991.

Douma, J. *Algemene Genade*. Goes: Oosterbaan & Le Cointre, 1996.

Edgar, W. "Two Christian Warriors: Cornelius Van Til and Francis A. Schaeffer Compared." *Westminster Theological Journal* 57, no. 1 (Spring 1995): 57–80.

Eglinton, J. "To Be or to Become: That Is The Question. Locating the Actualistic in Bavinck's Ontology." In *The Kuyper Center Review*. Vol. 2, *Revelation and Common Grace*, edited by J. Bowlin, 112. Grand Rapids, MI: Eerdmans, 2011.

Follis, B. *Truth with Love: The Apologetics of Francis A. Schaeffer*. Wheaton, IL: Crossway Books, 2006.

Fesko, J. V. *Last Things First: Unlocking Genesis 1–3 with the Christ of Eschatology*. Fern Tain, Scotland: Christian Focus Publications, 2007.

Fesko, J. V. "The Federal Vision and the Covenant of Works." Lecture for the Meeting of the Stated Clerks of the PCA, December 2004.

Frame, J. M. "Covenant and the Unity of Scripture." IIIM Magazine Online 1, no. 6 (April 5 to April 11, 1999). http://www.frame-poythress.org/covenant-and-the-unity-of-scripture/. Date of access: Aug. 12, 2012.

Frame, J. M. *The Regulative Principle: Scripture, Tradition, and Culture: An Email Debate between Darryl Hart and John Frame*. 1998. http://www.frame-poythress.org/frame_articles/1998HartDebate.htm.

Frame, J. M. *The Academic Captivity of Theology*. Lakeland, FL: Whitefield Media Productions, 2013.

Frame, J. M. *Apologetics to the Glory of God*. Phillipsburg, NJ: P&R Publishing, 1994.

Frame, J. M. *Cornelius Van Til: An Analysis of His Thought*. Phillipsburg, NJ: P&R Publishing, 1995.

Frame, J. M. *The Doctrine of the Christian Life*. Phillipsburg, NJ: P&R Publishing, 2008.

Frame, J. M. *The Doctrine of God*. Phillipsburg, NJ: P&R Publishing, 2002.

Frame, J. M. *The Doctrine of the Knowledge of God*. Phillipsburg, NJ: P&R Publishing, 1987.

Frame, J. M. *The Doctrine of the Word of God*. Phillipsburg, NJ: P&R Publishing, Publishing, 2010.

Frame, J. M. *No Other God: A Response to Open Theism*. Phillipsburg, NJ: P&R Publishing, 2001.

Frame, J. M. *Systematic Theology*. Phillipsburg, NJ: P&R Publishing, 2013.

Frame, J. M. *The Escondido Theology.* Phillipsburg, NJ: P&R Publishing, 2011.

Frame, J. M. "In Defense of Something Close to Biblicism: Reflections on Sola Scriptura and History in Theological Method." *Westminster Theological Journal* 59 (1997): 269–318. http://www.frame-poythress.org/in-defense-of-something-close-to-biblicism-reflections-on-sola-scriptura-and-history-in-theological-method/. Date of access: February 16, 2010.

Frame, J. M. *The Academic Captivity of Theology*. Lakeland, FL: Whitefield Publications, 2012.

Frame, J. M. *The Amsterdam Philosophy*. Phillipsburg, NJ: Harmony Press, 1972.

Frame, J. M. "Review of Bahnsen, *Presuppositional Apologetics: Stated and Defended.* In *John Frame's Selected Shorter Writings*. 1:174–186. Phillipsburg, NJ: P&R Publishing, 2014.

Frame, J. M. "Some Thoughts on Schaeffer's Apologetics." 2010. http://www.frame-poythress.org/frame_articles/2010ScrivenerInterview.htm. Date of access: September 11, 2011.

Frame, J. M. "Van Til and the Ligonier Apologetic." *Westminster Theological Journal* 47, no. 2 (Fall 1985).

Frame, J. M. "Reply to Collett on Transcendental Argument." 2003. http://www.frame-poythress.org/reply-to-don-collett-on-transcendental-argument/. Date of access: September 12, 2011.

Frame, J. M. "Responding to Some Articles." In *Speaking the Truth in Love: The Theology of John M. Frame*, edited by J. Hughes. Phillipsburg, NJ: P&R Publishing, 2009.

Frame, J. M. *Van Til: The Theologian.* Phillipsburg, NJ. Pilgrim Press, 1976.

Gallagher, D. "The Obedience of Faith: Barth, Bultmann, and Dei Verbum." *Journal for Christian Theological Research* 10 (2006): 55.

Geisler, N. *Christian Ethics*. 2nd ed. Grand Rapids, MI: Baker Academic, 2010.

Geisler, Norman. *Introduction to Philosophy: A Christian Perspective*. Ada, MI: Baker Academic, 1987.

Grafton, A., G. Most, and S. Settis, eds. *The Classical Tradition.* Cambridge, MA: Harvard University Press, 2010.

Habermas J. *The Structural Transformation of the Public Sphere.* Translated by T. Burger. Cambridge, MA: MIT Press, 1991.

Haldane, R. *An Exposition on the Epistle to the Romans*. Vol. 2. London: Hamilton, Adams, and Co., 1842.

Hart, D. G. *A Secular Faith: Why Christianity Favors the Separation of Church and State*. Lanham, MD: Ivan R. Dee, 2006.

Hart, T. "Redemption and Fall." In *The Cambridge Companion to Christian Doctrine*, edited by Colin E. Gunton. Cambridge: Cambridge University Press, 1997.

Hauerwas, S. "Love's Not All You Need." *Cross Currents* 172 (Summer–Fall 1972).

Hauerwas, S. "The Moral Authority of Scripture." In *From Christ to the Word: Introductory Readings in Christian Ethics*, edited by Wayne Bolton, Thomas D. Kennedy, and Allan Verhey, 33–50. Grand Rapids, MI: Eerdmans, 1994.

Hays, R. *The Moral Vision of the New Testament: Community, Cross, New Creation: A Contemporary Introduction to New Testament Ethics*. San Francisco: HarperSanFrancisico, 1996.

Heidegger, Martin. *Nietzsche*. Vol. 4: *Nihilism*, translated by David Farrell Krell. New York: Harper & Row Publishers, 1982.

Horton, M. *Christless Christianity*. Ada, MI: Baker Books, 2008.

Hughes, John J., ed. *Speaking the Truth in Love: The Theology of John M. Frame.* Phillipsburg, NJ: P&R Publishing, 2009.

Hume, D. *An Enquiry Concerning Human Understanding.* Edited by L. Bigge. Oxford: Clarendon Press, 1902.

Johnson, R. C. *Authority in Protestant Theology*. Philadelphia: Westminster Press, 1959.

Kant, I. *Grounding for the Metaphysics of Morals*. 3rd ed. Translated by J. Ellington. Indianapolis: Hackett Publishing Co., 1993.

Kelsey, D. *The Uses of Scripture in Recent Theology*. Philadelphia: Fortress Press, 1975.

Kline, M. *Images of the Spirit* with his later "Kingdom Prologue." Privately published, 1991.

Kline, M. *The Structure of Biblical Authority*. 2nd ed. Grand Rapids, MI: Eerdmans, 1972.

Kraus, H. "The Contemporary Relevance of Calvin's Theology." In *Toward the Future of Reformed Theology: Tasks, Topics, Traditions*, edited by D. Willis-Watkins, M. Welker, and M. Gockel, 323–338. Grand Rapids, MI: Eerdmans, 1999.

Kuyper, A. *De Gemeene Gratie*. Vols. 1–3. 1902–1905.

Kuyper, Abraham. *Lectures on Calvinism.* Grand Rapids, MI: Eerdmans, 1931; first published in 1898.

Lief, J. "Is Neo-Calvinism Calvinist? A Neo-Calvinist Engagement of Calvin's 'Two Kingdoms' Doctrine." *Pro Rege* 37, no. 3 (March 2009): 1–12.

Loewenich, W. *Luther's Theologia Crucis*. Translated by H. J. A. Bouman. Belfast: Christian Journals, 1976.

Luther, Martin. *D. Martin Luthers Werke*. CD-ROM: ISBN 0-85964-464-2.

MacArthur, J. *Ashamed of the Gospel: When the Church Becomes Like the World*. Wheaton, IL: Crossway Books, 1993.

McDermott, G. *The Great Theologians: A Brief Guide*. Downers Grove, IL: InterVarsity Press, 2010.

McDonagh, E. "Love." In *The New Dictionary of Theology*, edited by Joseph Komanchak. Wilmington: Glazier, 1987.

McGoldrick, J. "John Calvin, Practical Theologian: The Reformer's Spirituality." *The Outlook* 59, no. 6 (June 2009): 10–15. http://www.reformedfellowship.net/articles/mcgoldlrick-calvin-practical-june09v59-n6.htm. Date of access: January 1, 2013.

McGrath, A. *The Christian Theology Reader*. Oxford: Blackwell Publishing, 2007.

McGrath, A. *Mere Apologetics: How to Help Seekers and Skeptics Find Faith*. Ida, MI: Baker Books, 2012.

McLachlan, J. *The Desire to Be God: Freedom and the Other in Sartre and Berdyaev*. New York: Peter Lang Publishing, 1992.

Miller, D. *Principles of Social Justice*. Cambridge, MA: Harvard University Press, 1999.

Moltmann, J. *Theology of Hope: On the Ground and Implications of a Christian Eschatology*. New York: Harper, 1967.

Mounce, R. "Romans." In *The New American Commentary*. Nashville: Holman Reference, 1975.

Nietzsche, F. *The Portable Nietzsche*. Edited and translated by W. Kaufman. New York: Penguin Books, 1982.

Oliphint, S. *Covenantal Apologetics: Principles & Practice in Defense of Our Faith.* Wheaton, IL: Crossway, 2013.

Orr, J. *The Christian View of God and the World.* New York: Charles Scribner's Sons, 1908.

Pannenberg, W. *Christology from Below, in Jesus: God and Man.* Philadelphia: Westminster Press, 1968.

Pannenberg, W. *Revelation as History*. London: Sheed and Ward, 1969.

Pierard, R. "The Lutheran Two-Kingdoms Doctrine and Subservience to the State in Modern Germany." *JETS* 29, no. 2 (1986): 193–203.

Pinnock, C. *A Wideness in God's Mercy: The Finality of Jesus Christ in a World of Religions*. Grand Rapids, MI: Zondervan, 1992.

Pinnock, C. *The Openness of God: A Biblical Challenge to the Traditional Understanding of God*. Downers Grove, IL: Intervarsity Press Academic, 1994.

Pippin, R. *Modernism as a Philosophical Problem: On the Dissatisfaction of European High Culture*. Hoboken, NJ: Wiley-Blackwell, 1999.

Pippin, R. *Modernism as a Philosophical Problem*. 2nd ed. Oxford: Blackwell Publishers, 1999.

Pitchford, N. "Van Til: His Logic, Epistemology, and Apologetic." 2006. http://www.reformationtheology.com/2006/06/van_til_his_logic_epistemology.php. Date of access: December 12, 2012.

Plantinga, A. "The Reformed Objection to Natural Theology." *Christian Scholar's Review* 11, no. 19 (1982).

Plantinga, Alvin, and Nicolas Wolterstorff. *Faith and Rationality*. Notre Dame, IN: University of Notre Dame Press, 1991.

Rawls, J. *Justice as Fairness: A Restatement*. Edited by Erin Kelly. Cambridge, MA: Belknap Press of Harvard University Press, 1991.

Reimer, J. *Paul Tillich: Theologian of Nature, Culture and Politics*. Munster, Germany: Lit Verlag, 2004.

Reymond, R. *A New Systematic Theology of the Christian Faith.* Nashville: Thomas Nelson, 1998.

Ricoeur, P. *Oneself As Another.* Translated by K. Blamey. Chicago: University of Chicago Press, 1992.

Sanders, J. *What about Those Who Have Never Heard? Three Views of the Destiny of the Unevangelized.* Downers Grove, IL: InterVarsity Press, 1995.

Schaeffer, F., and C. Koop. *Whatever Happened to the Human Race?* Old Tappan, NJ: Fleming Revell, 1979.

Schaff, P. *The Creeds of Christendom.* Vol. 1. Grand Rapids, MI: Baker Book House, 1998.

Schilder, K. *Christ and Culture.* Translated by G. van Rongen and W. Helder. Winnipeg: Premier Publishing, 1977.

Seifer, B. *When the Soul Awakens: The Path to Spiritual Evolution and a New World Era.* Chicago, IL: Gathering Wave Press, 2009.

Selderhuis, H. J. *Marriage and Divorce in the Thought of Martin Bucer.* Kirksville, MO: Truman State University Press, 1999.

Sproul, R. C., L. Gerstner, and A. Lindsley. *Classical Apologetic.* Grand Rapids, MI: Zondervan, 1984.

Sproul, R. C. *Chosen by God.* Nashville: Thomas Nelson, 1986.

Stephen, F., and V. Kharlamov. *Theosis: Deification in Christian Theology*. Eugene, OR: Wipf and Stock, 2006.

Stephenson, J. "The Two Governments and the Two Kingdoms in Luther's Thought." *Scottish Journal of Theology* 34, no. 4 (1981): 321–337.

Stanley, J. "Restoration and Renewal: The Nature of Grace in the Theology of Herman Bavinck." In *The Kuyper Center Review*, edited by J. Bowlin, 2:81–104. Grand Rapids, MI: Eerdmans, 2011.

Strange, Daniel. "Not Ashamed! The Sufficiency of Scripture for Public Theology."http://thegospelcoalition.org/themelios/article/not_ashamed_the_sufficiency_of_scripture_for_public_theology#a1. Date of access: Oct. 31, 2013. Originally published in *Themelios* 36, no. 2 (August 2011): 238–260.

Strawson, P. *Introduction to Logical Theory*. London: Methuen & CO., 1952.

Sweet, L. *Quantum Spirituality: A Postmodern Apologetic*. Trotwood, OH: United Theological Seminary, 1991.

Taylor, H., ed. *The Mediæval Mind*. Vol. 1. Whitefish, MO: Kessinger Publishing, 2008.

Tillich, P. *Courage to Be*. 2nd ed. New Haven, CT: Yale University Press, 2000.

Troeltsch, E. *The Social Teaching of the Christian Churches*. Translated by Olive Wyon. Louisville, KY: Westminster/John Knox Press, 1992; German 1911.

Vacek, E. C. *Love, Human and Divine: The Heart of Christian Ethics*. Washington, DC: Georgetown University Press, 2004.

VanDrunen, D. "Abraham Kuyper and the Reformed Natural Law and Two Kingdoms Traditions." *Calvin Theological Journal* 42, no. 2 (2007): 283–307.

VanDrunen, D. *A Biblical Case for Natural Law: Studies in Christian Social Ethics and Economics*, no. 1. Grand Rapids, MI: Acton Institute, 2006.

Van Til, Cornelius. "Presuppositionalism." *The Bible Today* 4, no. 7 (April 1949): 218–228.

Van Til, C. *The Defense of the Faith*. Philipsburg, NJ: P&R Publishing, [1955] 1963.

Van Til, C. *An Introduction to Systematic Theology*. Phillipsburg, NJ: P&R Publishing, 1974.

Van Til, C. *Common Grace and the Gospel*. Phillipsburg: NJ: P&R Publishing, 1972; republished 1977.

Van Til, C. *Christian Theistic Evidences*. Vol. 6, in *In Defense of the Faith.* Phillipsburg, NJ: P&R Publishing, 1978.

Van Til, C. *Christian Theistic Ethics*. Vol. 3, in *In Defense of the Faith*. Phillipsburg: NJ: P&R Publishing, 1980.

Van Til, Cornelius. *Why I Believe in God.* Philadelphia: Committee on Christian Education, Orthodox Presbyterian Church, 1966.

Van de Beek, A. *Why? On Suffering, Guilt, and God*. Grand Rapids, MI: Eerdmans, 1990.

Van de Beek, A. *Jesus Kyrios: Christology as the Heart of Theology*. Studies in Reformed Theology, Supplement 1. Zoetermeer: Meinema, 2002.

Van de Beek, A. "Scriptural Authority and the Incomprehensibility of God." *Verbum et Ecclesia* 24 (2003): 205.

Vanhoozer, K. *The Drama of Doctrine: A Canonical Linguistic Approach to Christian Doctrine*. Louisville, KY: Westminster John Knox Press, 2005.

Vanhoozer, K. T*he Conversion of the Imagination: Paul as Interpreter of Israel's Scripture*. Grand Rapids, MI: Wm. B. Eerdmans, 2005.

Veenhof, J. *Revelatie en Inspiratie*. Amsterdam: Buijten & Schipperheijn, 1968.

Vos, G. *The Teaching of Jesus Concerning the Kingdom of God and the Church.* New York: American Tract Society, 1903.

Walsh, B., and J. Middleton. *The Transforming Vision: Shaping a Christian World View*. Downers Grove, IL: InterVarsity Press, 1984.

Warfield, B. B. "Apologetics." In *The New Schaff-Herzog Encyclopedia of Religious Knowledge*, edited by Samuel Macauley Jackson, 233. New York: Funk and Wagnalls Company, 1908.

Warfield, B. "John Calvin the Theologian." In *Calvin and Augustine,* edited by S. Craig, 485–486. Phillipsburg, NJ: P&R Publishing Company, 1971.

Wengert T. *The Pastoral Luther: Essays on Martin Luther's Practical Theology*. Grand Rapids, MI: Eerdmans, 2009.

Wiles, M. F. "Religious Authority and Divine Action." *Religious Studies* 7, no. (1971): 1–12.

Wittgenstein, L. *Tractatus Logico-Philosophicus*. New York: Harcourt, Brace, and Co., 1921.

Zwaanstra, H. "Louis Berkhof." In *Reformed Theology in America: A History of Its Modern Development*, edited by David F. Wells, 166–167. Grand Rapids, MI: Eerdmans,

Index

A

B

C

D

K

L

M

N

O

P

Q

R

S

T

U

V

W

www.ingramcontent.com/pod-product-compliance
Lightning Source LLC
LaVergne TN
LVHW061218100826
845148LV00004B/793

* 9 7 9 8 3 8 5 2 7 2 0 7 5 *